THE SOCIAL IDENTITY OF WOMEN

edited by
Suzanne Skevington and
Deborah Baker

SAGE Publications
London · Newbury Park · New Delhi

First published 1989

 SAGE Publications Ltd   SAGE Publications India Pvt Ltd
28 Banner Street   32, M–Block Market
London EC1Y 8QE   Greater Kailash – I
New Delhi 110 048

SAGE Publications Inc
2111 West Hillcrest Drive
Newbury Park, California 91320

British Library Cataloguing in Publication data

The social identity of women.
  1. Women. Psychotherapy
  I. Skevington, Suzanne II. Baker, Deborah, *1949–*
305.4'2

ISBN 0-8039-8205-4
ISBN 0-8039-8206-2 Pbk

Library of Congress catalog card number 89-62304

Typeset by AKM Associates (UK) Ltd, Southall, London
Printed in Great Britain by Billing and Sons Ltd, Worcester

Contents

Foreword

Barbara Lloyd

The aims of the editors, Suzanne Skevington and Deborah Baker, in planning this volume were to present research on gender inspired by Tajfel's social identity theory and to consider this body of work in a broader context. The open-ended and questioning nature of the ten chapters included in the book creates a context which stimulates thinking both about diverse issues in this rich and relevant domain and also about Tajfel's formal model of intergroup relations. Over and over again the reader is confronted by the question: can this theory, which evolved through the elegantly austere experiments of the minimal social situation, provide adequate conceptual tools to analyse the changing status of women in contemporary society?

There can be no doubt that gender is a relevant domain. To some extent it must engage each of us since membership in one of the social gender categories is obligatory if we are to participate in society. But it is a particularly seductive domain in which to locate such a discourse, as theorizing gender is replete with dangers. The most notorious trap is that of biological reductionism and the tendency to support the status quo with explanations of difference which appeal to hormones, genes, or reproductive strategies. Less often condemned, but perhaps equally treacherous, is the slippery slope of social determinism: the well-worn cry that the subjugation of women is all the result of conditioning. Over the years John Archer and I (Archer and Lloyd, 1975, 1985) have argued for the importance of keeping in mind both biological and social dimensions in explaining the development of women and men. Indeed we called our 1985 text *Sex and Gender* in an effort to differentiate and to highlight these sources of explanation. But this may be only the tip of the iceberg.

A second consequence of the difficulty in theorizing gender is the partial nature of most psychological accounts of development. By now we are all familiar with approaches which use data gathered primarily from males to propound a general theory, be it of moral development or achievement. Efforts at righting such imbalance, for example, Gilligan's *In a Different Voice* (1982), run other risks. Although the creators of such theories see their task as correcting an earlier mistake, it becomes all too easy to create feminine ghettos and to slip into thinking of gender-segregated moralities, paths to achievement, linguistic codes, identities, etc. Examination of empirical evidence from a range of psychological dimensions indicates that women and men are more similar than different. Social gender categories are discrete and non-overlapping but the behaviour of women and men tells a different story. An adequate social psychological theory must account simultaneously for the considerable behavioural similarity between women and men on the one hand and for the implications of membership in exclusive social gender categories which, through their social construction, define contrasting expectations and performance of women and men on the other.

Social identity theory has seemed a suitable candidate for this task as it appears to provide a model with which to examine the consequences of group membership. It offers principles such as in-group favouritism and strategies for social change when, as in the case of gender group membership, individuals are generally not free to change their group membership. Intergroup theory is abstract and formal and in its original formulations was not tied to any content domain. Its usefulness in analysing gender group membership appears to rest on the assumption that form or process is independent of content. Yet repeatedly the authors of individual chapters challenge its principles and recount its shortcomings. In part these judgements reflect the empirical grounding of intergroup theory in the minimal group experiments but some criticisms relate directly to the difficulty in theorizing gender and in particular gender identity. Thus a frequent assertion in the book is that there is no single social identity of women. Before considering this claim we need to return to the question of an appropriate methodology.

Issues stemming from the formal nature of the model are related to criticisms about appropriate methods for studying the social identity of women and other group identities. In the minimal social situation group membership is arbitrary and the meaning of the group is controlled by the experimenters, who restrict it by providing limited defining characteristics such as the Klee group or the Kandinsky group. This impoverishment of meaning is in sharp contrast with the saturated significance of socially constructed natural groups.

In order to take account of the cultural meaning of social groups Gerard Duveen and I (Duveen and Lloyd, 1986) proposed that social identities be viewed as the internalization of the social representations of the groups in which individuals participate. Although our formulation is tied to the theory of social representations proposed by Moscovici (and it is open to argument whether this is the most appropriate social psychological theory of cultural meaning), we have recognized an important element missing in social identity theory. Highlighting the demand to situate social identities in their cultural context emphasizes a need for methods appropriate to the investigation of culture. Our own solution has been to employ an ethnographic approach alongside the more traditional techniques of developmental psychology (Duveen and Lloyd, in press) but there are other useful methods, as this book illustrates. In a number of chapters criticism about a failure to take account of 'meaning' emerges as one of the crucial limits on the exclusive use of social identity theory. These criticisms and the search for new methods, whether in terms of ideology or of discourse, relate to a need to describe the content of social categories.

An investigation of the cultural meaning of social groups – for example, the values, beliefs and practices which characterize the categories women and men – could be used to address the issue of whether there are single, all-embracing definitions of these categories. In so far as age, race and class are also social categories in which membership is obligatory, their meanings moderate gender group membership along essential dimensions. The nature of this interaction requires further exploration in the light of an understanding of the meanings of these affiliations. There are, as the volume illustrates, additional social group memberships such as professional affiliation, which further influence the social identities of women.

Finally we come to a most important and difficult issue, the definition of the social identity of women. According to intergroup theory social identity derives from group membership and is differentiated from personal identity. The application of these terms in the domain of gender is susceptible to conceptual confusion. The term 'the social identity of women', appears straightforward at first sight, but how are appropriate comparison groups to be identified? Are they women and men, traditional and non-traditional women, women and mothers? The definitional problems do not stop at the issue of groups.

A gendered or sexed self is not unitary at the level of personal identity. Difficulties occur in thinking about a personal gender identity and these rapidly lead to considerations of sex and sexual preference. This common detour serves to illustrate another important limit of social identity theory: it is, as opposed to psychoanalytic formulations of identity, primarily a theory of rational thought. As Gerard Duveen and I noted (1986), social gender identity and a psychoanalytic gender identity belong to different levels of analysis and entail different methodologies. The personal gender identity of intergroup theory represents yet another conceptual mode. All these notions of identity may be usefully employed in exploring different aspects of an individual's sense of being a gendered self, but it is important both conceptually and methodologically to distinguish them clearly. Because sex and gender are such central concerns we are quick to consider them but we may well lack sufficient perspective to analyse them clearly.

This volume serves its readers well by indicating the complexity involved in analysing the social identity of women and in prompting them to explore the concept more critically. In order to develop sound methodologies it is necesssary to clarify the analytic terms of one's discourse. Here we are provided with signposts, if not solutions. The editors have created a context within which to think, not a recipe book.

School of Social Sciences
University of Sussex

References

Archer, J. and Lloyd, B. (1975) 'Sex Differences: Biological and Social Interactions', in R. Lewin (ed.), *Child Alive*. London: Temple Smith.

Archer, J. and Lloyd, B. (1985) *Sex and Gender*. New York: Cambridge University Press.

Duveen, G. and Lloyd, B. (1986) 'The Significance of Social Identities', *British Journal of Social Psychology*, 25: 219–30.

Duveen, G. and Lloyd, B. (in press) 'An Ethnographic Approach to Social Representations', in G. Breakwell and D. Canter (eds), *Empirical Approaches of Social Representations*. Oxford: Oxford University Press.

Gilligan, C. (1982) *In a Different Voice*. Cambridge, MA: Harvard University Press.

The Contributors

Dominic Abrams is a lecturer in social psychology in the Institute of Social and Applied Psychology at the University of Kent.

Deborah Baker is a postdoctoral research officer in the School of Social Sciences at the University of Bath.

Susan Condor is a lecturer in psychology in the Department of Psychology at Lancaster University.

Christine Griffin is a lecturer in social psychology in the Department of Psychology at the University of Birmingham.

Patricia Gurin is professor of psychology in the Department of Psychology at the University of Michigan, Ann Arbor, and at the Russell Sage Foundation, New York.

Hazel Markus is professor of psychology in the Department of Psychology at the University of Michigan, Ann Arbor.

Harriette Marshall is a lecturer in psychology in the Department of Psychology at the Polytechnic of East London.

Suzanne Skevington is a senior lecturer in psychology in the School of Social Sciences at the University of Bath.

Lindsay St Claire is a lecturer in psychology in the Department of Psychology at the University of Bristol.

Margaret Wetherell is a lecturer in psychology in the Department of Psychology at the Open University, Milton Keynes.

For our children

Hannah, Jamie
Rachel and Zoe

Acknowledgements

We would like initially to acknowledge the late Henri Tajfel's contribution to social psychology. His theoretical perspective has enlivened and rejuvenated interest in the 'social' in psychology, and has also made a major contribution to an understanding of the processes underlying social group formation and membership. His work continues to provoke new thinking and to stimulate debate, as is reflected in the chapters of this book.

We warmly thank the authors of these chapters for their continued commitment to the task in hand and for their gracious responsiveness to our editorial comment.

Thanks are also extended to those who facilitated the publishing process, particularly to Farrell Burnett for her encouragement and diligence in the first stages, and to Sue Jones and Nicola Harris, who have followed the project through. The anonymous reviewer of our original proposal also deserves our gratitude for her helpful recommendations as to the organization of the book.

Susan Condor would like to thank Charles Antaki, Michael Michael and Gavin Kendall for their useful comments on drafts of Chapter 2.

Suzanne Skevington gratefully acknowledges helpful comments made by Debbie Baker during the drafting of Chapter 3.

Dominic Abrams' Chapter 4 is partly based on a paper by Abrams and Condor (1984); he would like to thank Susan Condor and Diane Houston for comments on an earlier version, and Michelle Gilbert and Kevin Grady for transcribing the interview material. The work was done at the University of Dundee.

Deborah Baker wishes to thank Suzy Skevington and John Archer for helpful comments on the original version of Chapter 5, which formed part of her Ph.D. thesis. She is also indebted to all the mothers who participated in her study and to the health visitors in Trowbridge, Bradford on Avon and Melksham for their practical assistance with leaflets and questionnaires. The Grid Analysis Package she used was provided by the MRC service for analysing repertory grids (Dr Patrick Slater) and she is grateful to Douglas Clarke and Christopher Bell for their advice about analysis.

Harriette Marshall and Margaret Wetherell would like to thank Halla Bellof and Jonathan Potter for their contribution to the study. The research in Chapter 6 formed part of Harriette Marshall's Ph.D. thesis, and the data were reanalysed and written up by Margaret

xiv   *Acknowledgements*

Wetherell. Harriette Marshall would like to acknowledge the support of the ESRC. The authors would also like to thank the group of lawyers who were participants in this research.

Patricia Gurin and Hazel Markus gratefully acknowledge the helpful criticisms of a draft of Chapter 8 by Robert K. Merton (Columbia University), Sheldon Stryker (University of Indiana), Cynthia Epstein (Russell Sage Foundation and City University of New York), and Robert B. Zajonc and James Hilton (University of Michigan).

1

Introduction

Suzanne Skevington and Deborah Baker

This book presents a wide range of work on social identity and gender taking its original stimulus from social identity theory (Tajfel, 1974, 1978, 1984). It aims to make the ideas expressed by Tajfel more accessible in the context of research focused on a topic familiar to everyone, namely their sex group. We intend to evaluate how far social identity theory can take us in understanding the many faces of womanhood, and also to look at ways in which studies of women can and do challenge the boundaries of such a theory.

We hope that the content of this volume will contribute to debates about the dynamics of intergroup relations between the sexes and the changing social identities of women in contemporary societies.

This first chapter lays the groundwork for the rest of the book with an introduction to the main features of social identity theory, followed by a review of the ways in which this theory has been applied to women. Within this context we outline how the studies in this book have elaborated upon, developed, or sometimes rejected the social identity approach. We then review the kinds of methodologies that have been used by social identity theorists and introduce those used or recommended by the authors in this volume. Our overall emphasis here is that social identity can and should be studied using methods which accommodate the dimensions of real-life situations and the wider social context, so addressing practical and political as well as theoretical issues.

Social Identity Theory

The essence of social identity theory is its concern with those aspects of identity that derive from group memberships. Tajfel (1978; Tajfel and Turner, 1979) stressed the fact that society is composed of social groups that stand in power and status relations to one another; he believed that this group structure has important implications for identity formation. Tajfel followed Festinger (1954) in thinking that identity formation rests on the process of *social comparison*, whereby in order to evaluate their opinions and abilities people compare themselves with similar others in the course of social encounters. However, Tajfel stressed the importance of comparisons between social groups; he theorized that as well as evaluating themselves through interpersonal comparisons, people also need to assess the value of their own group in relation to other similar groups, and they do this by means of *intergroup comparison*. Here, own group or ingroup is compared with similar but distinct outgroups; the dimensions that are used to make these comparisons – that is, to distinguish self and ingroup from other comparable groups – are called *social categorizations*. These are by their very nature stereotypic or consensual constructions since they mark out the agreed boundaries of group membership. *Social identity* is founded on an internalization of these social categorizations.

Turner (1982; Turner et al., 1987) has linked the processes of intergroup and interpersonal comparison to two essentially distinct aspects of self concept. He sees the self concept as consisting of all available constructions of self which fall into two different subsystems: one of these is made up of social identifications derived from ingroup–outgroup categorizations (such as sex, race, occupation and class); the other consists of personal identifications – idiosyncratic descriptions of self which derive from differentiation of self as a unique individual from other individuals.

The primary motivational factor governing the process of intergroup comparison is the need for a positive social identity: that is, one which establishes self and ingroup as positively distinct on the relevant dimensions of comparison (Tajfel and Turner, 1979). Whether this is achievable or not depends initially on the relative status of groups being compared. Hogg and Abrams (1988) clearly describe how the power and status relations between groups bear on social identity: the dominant groups in society have the power and the status to impose the dominant value system and ideology which serves to legitimate and perpetuate the status quo. Individuals are born into this structure and, simply by virtue of their sex, social class and the like, fall into one social group rather than others. By internalization of the social categorizations definitive of these group memberships, they acquire particular social identities which may have a positive or negative value. Members of dominant and higher-status groups gain a positive social identity and high self-esteem from group membership; members of the lower-status or subordinate groups have a less positive social identity and lower self-esteem.

Here the behavioural consequences of social identification come into play. Members of low-status groups may seek to change their position and so attain a sense of positive distinctiveness, whereas members of high-status groups will act to maintain superiority

(Turner, 1982). The sort of action taken by low-status groups depends upon their beliefs about the nature of intergroup relations. If individuals believe that membership of the higher-status group is achievable by individual effort then they will attempt to move upwards into the dominant group by these means. This is referred to as individual upward *social mobility* (Tajfel, 1978), and as Hogg and Abrams (1988) point out, it is a very convenient belief as far as dominant groups are concerned, since it leaves the status quo intact.

However, if individual upward social mobility is impossible and members of low-status groups see the boundaries between groups as impenetrable, they may adopt collective strategies to create a more positive social identity for their group. These strategies are generally encompassed by the term *social change* (Tajfel, 1978). There appears to be a continuum between individual action at one end and collective action at the other, whereby the more difficult it is for individuals to improve their own personal position or status by becoming members of the high-status group, the more likely it is that members of the low-status group will join together to improve the group's status.

The term 'social change' subsumes three main kinds of activity. Firstly there is *assimilation or merger* (Tajfel, 1978) which involves the adoption of the positive features of the high-status group by the low-status group who wish to join them. This strategy effectively dissolves the comparison processes which maintain intergroup tensions by reducing the psychological distance between the two groups, so increasing the similarity. Such a strategy requires cooperation between high- and low-status groups rather than differentiation and competition.

For example, Skevington (1980, 1981) found merger the most important strategy considered by nurses during discussions about changes in the structure of the nursing profession. By merging the low-status State Enrolled Nurses (SENs) with the high-status State Registered Nurses (SRNs) through training, it was intended that the more positive characteristics of the high-status group would be attributed to all nurses. In this case the SRNs felt threatened by the potential loss of their highly valued and positive social identity. They tended to see the inclusion of the low-status members as having a diluting effect, so watering down the positive distinctiveness of their group. In contrast, the low-status SENs generally wished for change and supported the dissolving of status relations through merger.

A second type of action is referred to as *social creativity* (Tajfel, 1978), whereby the subordinate group seeks to create a new and positive image for itself. For example, low-status groups may create brand new characteristics for the group which effectively make it so different from the group it compares itself with that it reduces the need for any further comparisons with the high-status group and hence creates a more positive social identity. Giles (1978) has provided many instances of how language or dialect has been used by ethnic minorities such as the Welsh, French Canadians and American Blacks, to assert their positive distinctiveness from the majority.

Subordinate groups may also reinterpret negative features currently attributed to the group so that they become positive characteristics that enhance their social identity. One of the most quoted examples of this type of activity in recent years relates to the rise in black consciousness in the 1960s, when the negative image of being black was reinterpreted through the 'Black is Beautiful' slogan.

Finally, rather than compare themselves with the superior group, low-status groups may seek comparisons with equivalent or more subordinate groups to themselves in order to enhance their own social identity.

The third type of strategy for social change is *social competition* (Tajfel and Turner, 1979), when the subordinate group challenges the basis of the status hierarchy and seeks to change the relative power and status of groups by active or passive resistance. Good examples of this form of action are the American Civil Rights movement and the Black Panthers, both resisting White domination in the 1960s and 1970s.

These then are the basic tenets of social identity theory. Let us now move on to consider how this theory has been applied to the study of women.

Social Identity and Women

Social identity theory has potential as a way of understanding both the nature and content of women's group identifications in the course of women's lives, and also the intergroup relations between women and men and their consequences in social action. The first and definitive paper in this area was that of Williams and Giles (1978). They saw women as being the disadvantaged gender group, whose social identity derives from comparisons with men. Because men are dominant and more powerful and women are the less powerful and subordinate, group identification brings with it negative characteristics and inferior status. So women need to take action in order to develop a sense of positive distinctiveness.

Williams and Giles illustrate ways in which the strategies of social mobility and social change have been employed by women for this purpose. If women accept their lot they may choose to enhance their personal status by individual means. For instance, by defining themselves in relation to their husband's occupation and position and in devoting their efforts to improving his social status, they may also enhance their own self-image.

On the other hand, if women collectively do not accept their status as a group, they may take action to establish a positive social identity for the group. The aims of the Women's Liberation Movement illustrate this strategy well. Within the broad context of this movement women have fought to establish equality with men in working conditions and in legal and political terms. They have tried to modify the consensual inferiority associated with women's roles by encouraging women to make choices about motherhood and to take control over their own bodies through contraception and abortion. Some writers redefined women's work in the home so that it is valued in the same way as work in the public sphere. Women have also asserted their differences from men in positively valued directions by organizing their groups in a non-hierarchical way. This contrasts with the organizational features often adopted by male groups, using stratification to form hierarchies and to promote leadership qualities.

Williams and Giles' (1978) model of social identity for women forms the starting point for much of the thinking which underlies the chapters in this book. Its limitations highlight the more general problems social identity theory has in explaining group identifications as they are created and recreated within historical and social contexts.

One problem is that Williams and Giles are describing the ideological intergroup relations between men and women from a theoretical rather than an empirical stance. In doing this they make the mistake of assuming that womanhood is perceived by all women in the same way, using the same consensual (and unfavourable) dimensions when comparing themselves with men. So womanhood is presented as a unified social category whose characteristics are well known and accepted. While this paper may have presented the simplest possible case for reasons of theoretical clarity, common sense tells us that this is not the way things are. We have only to look at the many activities women pursue and the changes of role that occur during the course of their lives to appreciate the numerous social identifications that could fall under the umbrella definition of 'womanhood'.

Breakwell (1979) stresses this in her own analysis of social identity for women. She theorizes that it is the lack of consensus as to what actually characterizes 'womanhood' at any one time that gives rise to an unsatisfactory social identity for women, rather than unfavourable comparisons with men. To illustrate this point Breakwell makes the distinction between external and internal criteria for group member-ship. External criteria are often social norms that are personified in stereotypes and that have a consensual objectivity quite independent of fact. Internal criteria are composed of personal knowledge and beliefs about group membership and perceptions of how they relate to self. Breakwell (1979) suggests that for women these two facets of group membership are usually incompatible because there are no static or consensually agreed external criteria for womanhood. Consequently, whenever a woman synchronizes the 'woman' that she is and sees herself to be with 'woman' as society says she should be, the focus is likely to change and the external criteria are amended. Whatever the precise nature of this change – whether, for instance, it is the image of the working woman that is at the forefront, or the mother, or the working mother – this incompatibility gives rise to the subjective experience of marginality, and it is this that Breakwell says leads to unsatisfactory social identity.

The picture that emerges from Breakwell's analysis is one of a social identity which is both multifaceted and transient; this provides the theme for two chapters of this book. Harriette Marshall and Margaret Wetherell look at the identities of a group of students who are training to be lawyers. They draw interesting distinctions between personal identity, social identity derived from occupational status, and gender identity, and look at how these aspects of self concept are interlinked. Debbie Baker looks at one particular group of women, namely first-time mothers, to see how they distinguish themselves from other groups of women, such as working women. She also evaluates the sorts of socio-pyschological factors that influence the extent of a positive social identity for first-time mothers.

The second area of departure from Williams and Giles' model arises from their perception of the relationship between group identification and the dominant ideology governing intergroup relations between the sexes. Williams and Giles assume that only those women who reject the sex-role status quo identify strongly as a group and so adopt the collective strategies of social change to improve their group's status. However, Condor (1983, 1986) and Gurin and Townsend (1986) have argued to the contrary that the extent of gender group identification is not necessarily dependent on group consciousness – that is, on beliefs about the group's position of power and status in the intergroup context. Condor's (1986) empirically based studies of the meaning of womanhood as a social category found that 'traditional women' often identified strongly with their group, seeing their roles as preferable to those of men, and yet at the same time they also accepted the sex-role status quo. They did not, however, conceptualize their relationships with men in terms of intergroup conflict, but as cooperative relationships with husbands in the family context. Gurin and Townsend (1986) concluded from their study of women's group identification and consciousness that group members may identify with other women in terms of personal characteristics, or gender group membership may be a central aspect of self concept, without necessarily involving any awareness of the low status of women as a social group. It is only if women see their group as one which is unfairly treated by society that group consciousness develops and collective discontent brings about the need to change the group's position and status. One function of the consciousness-raising groups of the 1970s was to make women aware of their status as a group within society and thus to provoke action to bring about change.

The theme of group identification and consciousness, and particularly the nature of feminist consciousness, is further addressed in his volume by Patricia Gurin and Hazel Markus, Christine Griffin, and Lindsay St Claire. Patricia Gurin and Hazel Markus further explore ways in which gender identity for women is related to group consciousness, this time focusing on the effect of the centrality of gender identity in the self-schema on feelings about group membership and potential change. Christine Griffin moves on from trying to produce fixed definitions of group identification and consciousness to look at notions of identity and consciousness which are flexible in relation to historical and social contexts. She uses feminism and feminist consciousness as examples of the interaction between identification, consciousness and context. Lindsay St Claire focuses on the group consciousness generated by minority group membership. She feels that the whole notion of women as a minority group should be re-examined and suggests that the application of models developed in research on handicap might lead to a better understanding or consciousness of the disadvantages that accrue from gender group membership for women.

The third strand of development from Williams and Giles' original approach focuses on the intergroup relations between women and men. Williams (1984) has subsequently developed her own analysis by making the important point that the type of social identification outlined in the original version of Tajfel's theory is consistent with an instrumental orientation, more associated with masculine behaviour. In the style of Bakan (1966) she relabels this as agentic social identity, based as it is on the processes of differentiation, comparison and competition. This is only a partial explanation of intergroup relations, since it ignores the importance of affiliation and attachment to others which are the distinct characteristics forming the basis of a woman's social identity. Following on from this, Williams suggests that a group may also be given meaning communally, through relationships with other groups. Self-esteem from this cooperative mode of relating may well be derived from a communal social identity sustained by relationships within the ingroup. While Brown and Williams (1984) have so far been unable to identify empirically these two alternative modes of intergroup relations, there is supporting evidence from other sources outside the theory. Gilligan (1982) in the field of moral development, and Archer (1984) looking at the development of gender identities, give us strong reason to believe that men and women have fundamentally different ways of relating to the world.

In this volume Suzanne Skevington explores this difference and develops Williams' analysis by considering the emphasis of social identity theory on the cognitive (agentic) as opposed to the emotional (communal) aspects of intergroup relations. She then goes on to discuss the affective components of agentic and communal social identities.

Dominic Abrams shows us the difference between female and male sex groups by locating intergroup relations within the developmental context of childhood and adolescence. He demonstrates how gender identity changes with age and in the light of interpersonal relationships between the sexes. In contrast, Susan Condor takes intergroup relations into the historical context. She develops a detailed critique of Tajfel's (1978) conception of 'social change' and points to the essential relativity of current forms of intergroup relations between the sexes.

All these chapters, whether they are theoretically or empirically based, seek to understand what being a woman means to women in contemporary social contexts. The search for an understanding of the various social identifications women may share, group consciousness, and intergroup relations with men, all arise directly from questions about how women think, feel and live their lives today. We believe that it was Tajfel's original intention that social identity should be viewed as a product of group experience (Israel and Tajfel, 1972), but that the original message has been obscured by the need to create 'scientific' knowledge using quantitative data. Methodologies traditionally used by social identity theorists have narrowed the focus of study, reifying process over content, emphasizing the exclusively cognitive as opposed to the social or emotional (see Skevington in this volume for further exposition of this point).

Social Identity: The Methodologies

The dominant research paradigms within social identity theory have in the past focused on the processes of social identification, social categorization and social comparison and their consequences for behaviour using small group laboratory experiments. In this approach, group memberships are assigned for the duration of the experiment, effectively separating participants as far from their actual group experiences as they could ever dream of being.

The classic design illustrating this approach is the minimal group experiment first described by Tajfel et al. (1971), in which participants were placed in separate cubicles and asked to state their preference for pairs of paintings projected on a screen. Later they were privately informed that each pair contained a painting by European artists Klee and Kandinsky, and as a result of their preferences they had been assigned to the Klee or Kandinsky group – in fact group allocation was at random and they did not know who was in their group and who was in the other one. They were then required to share out points (representing money) between two other individuals, who were identified only by their group memberships. These other individuals may belong to the same group as the subject (ingroup) or to a different group (outgroup). Participants indicated how they wished to allocate the money by selecting one of thirteen pairs of numbers, arranged in the form of a distribution matrix. These matrices were presented in a booklet in which there are a number of different formats; for example, the two individuals may both be ingroup members, one may be from ingroup and one from outgroup, and so on.

These matrices can be analysed in terms of four main strategies. They reveal whether participants give most points to their own group (maximum ingroup profit), assign the highest possible profits to both groups (maximum joint profit), emphasize the difference between the two groups, even at the expense of overall profit for the ingroup (maximum difference), or are as fair to both groups as possible (fairness). Results of these group experiments have shown that simply being allocated to a category representing a group about which there is minimal knowledge brings into play the processes of intergroup comparison, competition and ingroup favouritism. Subjects tend to allocate more money to ingroup, thereby attempting to maximize ingroup profit, but more importantly they seek to maximize the difference between the groups, even at the expense of maximum pay off for their own group.

However, these and other similar experiments tell us little about the meaning of group memberships in the real world. How do people conceptualize their group memberships and what accounts for different levels of identification? Why do people belong to one group rather than another? How does group belonging become intertwined with history and ideology? At the other end of the spectrum are workers who seek the answers to such questions, utilizing the social context and linking the concepts and impressions of the participants to the construction of social identity (see, for example, Brown, 1978; Brown and Williams, 1984). Such work requires more qualitative methods; research techniques which are designed to bring to light subjective interpretations of reality and/or which take into account personal history and social existence.

Qualitative measures which probe the meaning of group membership and identification for women are as yet in their infancy. Field studies of social identity and women began by using prescriptive measures based on constructed scales. For example, Condor (1983) in a study of the meaning of womanhood (n = 540) used two measures to assess the relationship between sex group identification and sex group ideology. A sex group identification scale was used containing items 'pertaining to feelings of loyalty and empathy and solidarity with other women' (1983: 11), together with a sex group ideology scale that included 'statements articulating acceptance or rejection of the sex-role status quo' (1983: 11). Condor classified respondents in terms of levels of group identification (high/low) and directions of sex-role ideology (traditional/radical). In this way she was able to distinguish between four types of responses on the two scales: namely women who identified with their group and either accepted or rejected the status quo and women who did not identify with their group and either accepted or rejected the status quo.

Measures have also been devised to look more specifically at the strength of group identification. Skevington (1980, 1981) in her studies of the intergroup relations between high-status State Registered Nurses and low-status State Enrolled Nurses, used 31 subjective characteristics found to be relevant to nurses from previous interviews, which both groups of women were required to rate in terms of their application to 'ingroup', 'outgroup' and self. She evaluated the extent of positive social identity by the degree of correspondence between ingroup and self ratings, and found that for SRNs self and ingroup ratings were almost identical, indicating a highly positive social identity, whereas for SENs ingroup and self ratings differed significantly, indicating a less positive identity.

Gurin and Townsend (1986) used a different method to look at group identification in their study of gender identity and group consciousness. Women participants were presented with 16 category labels including 'women' and were asked 'which of these groups do you feel particularly close to – people who are most like you in their ideas and interests and feelings about things?' After making their choices they were read the names of the categories they had chosen and asked to rank them in relation to how close they felt to each group. The higher the rank for women, the stronger the identification.

It would be a mistake to dismiss these measures as irrelevant simply because they use constructed scales rather than women's accounts to look at social group membership. All were carefully designed as relevant to the situations studied, often utilizing the language of the participants interviewed during pilot work. They present us with valuable insights into how the mechanisms of social identification, comparison and categorization, identified in the laboratory, can actually be applied in field studies. So possibly a combination of qualitative and quantitative techniques will turn out to be the best way of approaching this subject.

Nevertheless, out of such studies has grown a desire for more qualitative accounts of social identification and categorization which arise directly from people structuring their own conceptions of group membership. Older methodologies have often been 'imported' into social identity theory for this purpose.

Brown and Williams (1984), in their search for a way of measuring group identification for groups of workers in a small bread factory, used the Twenty Statements Test (Kuhn and McPartland, 1954). In this 'test' subjects are repeatedly asked 'who am I?' and their answers content-analysed for personal or consensual (that is, social) identity referents. The subjective importance of group identification was then ascertained by asking subjects to rank their responses. Brown and Williams were dissatisfied with the excessively open-ended nature of the task, as participants were confused and baffled about what was required. This measure has the advantage, however, of being able to look at a range of social identifications and their subjective importance in relation to one another. Skevington and Dawkes (1988) used a modified version of this test to greater effect in a study of social identification for female and male nurses. Nurses were asked to list six groups to which they belonged and rank them in order of importance. They found that the group 'nurses' was ranked high in relation to other group memberships, which the authors took to indicate both a strongly positive social identification and the centrality of occupation to the self concept.

Other methodologies have focused on the content of social categorizations and their construction from social experience. Open-ended interviews have been used for this purpose by Condor (1986) to understand the basis of group membership for 'traditional' women, but perhaps the biggest push in this direction has come from the practitioners of discourse analysis, where the emphasis is on the way that social categories are constituted in discourse (that is, conversational materials, scientific and literary documents, media accounts and the like). Potter and Reicher (1987) successfully applied this technique in a detailed analysis of the use of the category 'community' and the notion of 'community relations' in accounts of the St Paul's riot in Bristol in the 1980s. Wetherell (1986) advocates discourse analysis as a means of establishing a more fluid and fragmentary picture of gender identity rather than one based on fixed categories such as feminine/masculine and agency/communion. She believes that by looking at how people talk about their gender we may find that contradictory and inconsistent categorizations underlie gender identity and that its meaning changes from one situation to another.

The impetus for more qualitatively based methodologies in field studies, particularly for women, corresponds with one of the main aims of feminist research, namely to explore 'women's own knowledge and experience in a disciplined, scholarly and rigorous way' (Wilkinson, 1986: 2). We feel that all the chapters in this volume reflect this general aim, whether their approach is theoretically or empirically based.

Harriette Marshall and Margaret Wetherell use discourse analysis, constructing their approach to social identity through the conversations of lawyers about their own qualities, the qualities they need for their jobs and their talk about occupational versus domestic roles. Deborah Baker uses repertory grids as a means of looking at social categorization and social identification for first-time mothers; interviews are also used to relate these data to their historical and contemporary social experience. Both Dominic Abrams and Christine Griffin draw on extensive data from open-ended interviews of children and young people to develop and illustrate their very different approaches to social identity and women, and two more authors, Lindsay St Claire and Suzanne Skevington, recommend alternative methodologies stemming from social constructivism. Patricia Gurin and Hazel Markus, on the other hand, retain more quantitative methodologies, combining self-reported questionnaires and laboratory work, to extend their ideas about gender identity and gender consciousness.

We will now leave the reader to assess, through the chapters of this book, just how far social identity theory can be useful in the study of women's lives today and whether the approaches developed by the authors do enrich and extend the concept of social identity. In the first half of the book, four chapters by Susan Condor, Suzanne Skevington, Dominic Abrams and Deborah Baker raise a variety of issues that arise directly from applying social identity theory to the study of womanhood. In contrast, the following four chapters by Harriette Marshall and Margaret Wetherell, Lindsay St Claire, Patricia Gurin and Hazel Markus, and Christine Griffin apply alternative approaches to the study of women, using these theoretical positions as a means of either enhancing or rejecting the principles of social identity theory. A final chapter sets out our own conclusions.

References

Archer, J. (1984) 'Gender Roles as Developmental Pathways', *British Journal of Social Psychology*, 23: 139–48.

Bakan, D. (1966) *The Duality of Existence: Isolation and Communion in Western Man.* Boston: Beacon Press.

Breakwell, G. M. (1979) 'Women: Group and Identity?' *Women's Studies International Quarterly*, 2: 9–17.

Brown, R. J. (1978) 'Divided We Fall: An Analysis of Relations between a Factory Workforce', in H. Tajfel (ed.), *Differentiation between Social Groups: Studies in the Social Psychology of Intergroup Relations*. London: Academic Press.

Brown, R. J. and Williams, J. (1984) 'Group Identification: The Same Thing to All People?' *Human Relations*, 37: 547–64.

Condor, S. (1983) 'Womanhood as an Aspect of Social Identity: Group Identification and Ideology'. Paper presented at the British Psychological Society Annual Conference, University of London, December.

Condor, S. (1986) 'Sex Role Beliefs and "Traditional" Women: Feminist and Intergroup Perspectives', in S. Wilkinson (ed.) *Feminist Social Psychology*. Milton Keynes: Open University Press.

Festinger, L. (1954) 'A Theory of Social Comparison Processes', *Human Relations*, 7: 117–40.

Giles, H. (1978) 'Linguistic Differentiation in Ethnic Groups', in H. Tajfel (ed.) *Differentiation between Social Groups: Studies in the Social Psychology of Intergroup Relations*. London: Academic Press.

Gilligan, C. (1982) *In a Different Voice: Psychological Theory and Women's Development*. Cambridge, MA: Harvard University Press.

Gurin, P. and Townsend, A. (1986) 'Properties of Gender Identity and their Implications for Gender Consciousness', *British Journal of Social Psychology*, 23: 311–16.

Hogg, M. A. and Abrams, D. (1988) *Social Identifications: A Social Psychology of Intergroup Relations and Group Processes*. London: Routledge.

Israel, J. and Tajfel, H. (eds) (1972) *The Context of Social Psychology*. London: Academic Press.

Kuhn, M. H. and McPartland, T. S. (1954) 'An Empirical Investigation of Self Attitudes', *American Sociological Review*, 19: 68–76.

Potter, J. and Reicher, S. (1987) 'Discourses of Community and Conflict: The Organization of Social Categories in Accounts of a "Riot" ', in *British Journal of Social Psychology*, 26(1): 25–41.

Skevington, S. M. (1980) 'Intergroup Relations and Social Change within a Nursing Context', *British Journal of Social and Clinical Psychology*, 19: 201–13.

Skevington, S. M. (1981) 'Intergroup Relations in Nursing,' *European Journal of Social Psychology*, 11: 43–59.

Skevington, S. M. and Dawkes, D. A. (1988) 'Minorities at Work: Men in a Woman's World', in D. A. Canter, J. C. Jecsuino, L. Soczka and G. M. Stephenson (eds), *Environmental Social Psychology*. London: Kluwer.

Tajfel, H. (1974) 'Intergroup Behaviour, Social Comparison and Social Changes'. Unpublished Katz–Newcombe Lectures, University of Michigan, Ann Arbor.

Tajfel, H. (ed.) (1978) *Differentiation between Social Groups: Studies in the Social Psychology of Intergroup Relations*. London: Academic Press.

Tajfel, H. (1984) *The Social Dimension*, Vols 1 and 2. Cambridge: Cambridge University Press.

Tajfel, H. and Turner, J. (1979) 'An Integrative Theory of Intergroup Conflict', in W. H. Austin and S. Worchel (eds), *The Social Psychology of Intergroup Relations*. Monterey, CA: Brooks–Cole.

Tajfel, H., Flament, C., Billig, M. and Bundy, R. P. (1971) 'Social Categorization and Intergroup Behaviour', *European Journal of Social Psychology*, 1: 149–78.

14   Suzanne Skevington and Deborah Baker

Turner, J. C. (1982) 'Towards a Cognitive Redefinition of the Social Group', in H. Tajfel (ed.) *Social Identity and Intergroup Relations*. Cambridge: Cambridge University Press.

Turner, J. C., Hogg, M. A., Oakes, P. J., Reicher, S. and Wetherell, M. (1987) *Rediscovering the Social Group: A Self-Categorization Theory*. Oxford: Basil Blackwell.

Wetherell, M. (1986) 'Linguistic Repertoires and Literary Criticism: New Directions for a Social Pyschology of Gender', in S. Wilkinson (ed.), *Feminist Social Psychology*. Milton Keynes: Open University Press.

Wilkinson, S. (ed) (1986) *Feminist Social Psychology: Developing Theory and Practice*. Milton Keynes: Open University Press.

Williams, J. A. (1984) 'Gender and Intergroup Behaviour: Towards an Integration', *British Journal of Social Psychology*, 23: 311–16.

Williams, J. A. and Giles, H. (1978) 'The Changing Status of Women in Society: An Intergroup Perspective', in H. Tajfel (ed.) *Differentiation between Social Groups: Studies in the Social Psychology of Intergroup Relations*. London: Academic Press.

2

'Biting into the Future': Social Change and the Social Identity of Women

Susan Condor

Social Change and Contemporary Common Sense

The first attempt to apply a social identity (SI) approach to gender was reported in a chapter entitled 'The Changing Status of Women in Society' (Williams and Giles, 1978). In contemporary Western society it is often the case that a discussion about Women,[1] whether in the context of an academic textbook or in everyday conversation, will involve some reference to 'social change'. Talk about Women may, for example, be structured in the form of a progress narrative. The lives of women today may be compared favourably with a mythical past:

> Females constitute a clear majority of the world's population. Yet, they have often been treated much like a minority in many cultures . . . Fortunately, the situation appears to be changing in many nations. Overt discrimination practices are decreasing, and there has been at least some shift towards more egalitarian sex-role attitudes on the part of both men and women . . . (Baron and Byrne, 1987: 172)

We may allude to an historical trajectory directing human life slowly but inevitably towards a utopian end-point of gender equality:

> I think it is much better now than probably it ever has been but still I don't think it is completely equal. There is still a long way to go before it's anything like really equal, because there are so many prejudices still held. But I think it's good that opportunities are opening up, and as more capable women go into them it's bound to get better in the future when it's shown that women can work as well as men . . . it will become more and more easy and more and more acceptable. (Respondent in Wetherell ct al., 1987)

We may herald the present status of Women as an arrival – the culmination of historical process:

> The day I first sat in this chair, I couldn't believe my luck. Of course I couldn't. A new job, a new role with a new, exciting, totally different magazine, and what's more one that feels so right for now, so in tune with what all new women want. I felt I'd come home. And you will too. (Editorial in *New Woman* magazine, August 1988)

These examples have been taken from a social psychology textbook, a young woman's conversation with a researcher, and an editorial from a women's magazine. Despite their diverse origins they illustrate a common theme which will be the subject of the present chapter: the relationship between representations of Women and change over time.

The view of male–female relations as undergoing progressive change that is illustrated in these examples reflects a more pervasive view of time as linear and irreversible. We regard biological and geological phenomena as temporary stages (species, formations) in an ongoing process of evolution. Similarly, we perceive structures of social life (national boundaries, class relations and the like) to be located historically. This consciousness of progressive movement over time – which is commonly termed 'historicity' – is so central to the way in which people in contemporary Western societies[2] think that we tend to take it for granted. However, anthropologists emphasize that historicity is neither culturally nor historically universal. Our contemporary awareness of change over time needs to be understood in contrast to other views which stress iteration and permanence over time. As Gurevich (1976: 231) notes: 'The consciousness of primitive man [sic] is not directed towards the perception of changes, but inclines to find the old in the new. This explains why the future, for him, is not differentiated from what has already been.'

It is outside the scope of the present chapter to consider this issue in any detail.[3] The point I wish to make here is simply that an awareness of 'the changing status of women in society' should be regarded as historically and culturally specific. Moreover, our present awareness of change over time needs to be understood in the more general context of human activity and social structure in modernizing societies. The development of a linear time consciousness has been traced, for example, to technological advances enabling the measurement of time and to the growth of literacy. The relevance of the preceding discussion to Tajfel's model of intergroup relations becomes clear when we consider how theorists have related changes in Western ideas about history to changes in the way in which social structures are reproduced. Social theorists often draw a distinction between 'cold' and 'hot' societies, which to some extent parallels Tajfel's (for example, 1974, 1978a, 1978b) distinction between 'stable' and 'unstable' intergroup settings. In cold (pre-industrial) societies an emphasis on tradition, routine and social reproduction over time serves to stabilize social organizations and practices. This is not to say that changes do not occur in such societies. However, change tends to be gradual, or to be brought about by external forces. We may note, for example, how gender relations in pre-industrial societies have been upset by contact with, and pressure from, industrialized Western nations (Jayawardena, 1986).

These traditional conditions of social reproduction are altered by an awareness of change over time. In hot (fast-changing, post-industrial) societies an awareness of different forms of social organization (drawn, for example, from a knowledge of the past) means that the status quo can no longer be taken for granted. People become conscious of the possibility of change and attempt to control the pace and direction of social transformation. A tendency to differentiate the present from the past not only enables, but also justifies, action directed towards implementing change. As Giddens (1987: 148) notes, 'it becomes possible to use knowledge of the past to "bite into" the future, thereby mobilizing the present'. Awareness of change is accompanied by an acceleration in the pace of social transformation in post-industrial societies – as Tajfel (1978a: 1) noted, 'We live in a world in which the process of unification and diversification proceed apace, both of them faster than ever before.'

I will return to the distinction between contemporary historicity and earlier views of time in the third section of this chapter, in which I assess the contribution of Tajfel's work for an analysis of social change. Here I consider in a little more detail the use of notions of 'change' and 'continuity' in contemporary thought about Women.

In his discussion of the Enlightenment Becker (1932: 19) suggested that an awareness of change over time might be incompatible with essentialist categorical thought:

> Historical-mindedness is so much a preoccupation of modern thought that we can identify a particular thing only by pointing to those various things it successively was before it became that particular thing which it will presently cease to be.

Whilst accepting Becker's point, I will argue that we should not assume that a linear time consciousness has simply replaced an earlier emphasis on circular or reversible time. The coexistence of linear and recursive views of time may be reflected in contradictory maxims of common sense: whilst we know that 'you can't turn the clock back', we are also aware that 'history repeats itself' (see Billig et al., 1988 for a discussion of contradictions of common sense). This dual notion of time – embracing both continuity and change – is reflected in contemporary ideas about Women as a social category. On the one hand we can identify statements (such as those quoted at the beginning of this chapter) which suggest that people view the present nature and status of Women as a transient stage between the past and the future. On the other hand we may also find contemporaneous statements which apparently subscribe to a circular notion of time and to a view of Woman as historically continuous:

The psychological attachment and lack of separation between mothers and daughters and daughters and mothers continues through generations of women. The daughter becomes involved in a cycle that is part of each woman's experience: attempting to care for mother. As the daughter learns her role as nurturer, *her first child is her mother*. (Eichenbaum and Orbach, 1983: 57; their italics)

The contemporaneous coexistence of two different ideas about Women – as changing over time (the New Woman), and enduring across time (the Eternal Feminine) – would pose a problem for those theorists who posit consistency in belief-systems.[4] Social scientists often suggest that these apparently contradictory ideas may be characteristic of distinct, internally consistent attitudes or ideologies. For example, some social psychologists have suggested that an emphasis on change over time is characteristic of feminist political orientations, and that ideas which stress social continuity are charac-teristic of antifeminist positions (see Condor, 1984).[5] Similarly, in her historical analysis, Banks (1981: 3) suggested that 'Any groups that have tried to *change* the position of women, or ideas about women, have been granted the title feminist' (her italics).

Such assumptions may appear reasonable in the light of the fact that political groups may have characterized their own views along these lines. Feminists may point to historical disjunction in order to emphasize the instability of present social arrangements, 'If women were powerful once, a precedent exists; if female biology was ever once a source of power, it need not remain what it has since become: a root of powerlessness' (Rich, 1976: 85). Feminism as a social movement is obviously directed towards transforming society in accord with women's interests. However, some feminist writers have identified the goals of their movement with 'social change' *per se*. For example, Collins et al. (1978) entitled their feminist handbook *Directory of Social Change*, and one feminist organization calls itself simply 'Change'.

Conversely, positions opposed to feminist views may stress the enduring nature of feminine character, value the past (for example, Doane and Hodges, 1987), and represent change as degeneration:

If the young women of the twenties had a serenity that their descendants lack that was surely because they were more at peace with themselves. Their position in society, if in many respects less equal, was more clearcut. They might be flappers but they were never bimbos. They might not earn as much and they were less independent, but their menfolk treated them with respect. (*Daily Mail*, editorial comment, 15 August 1988)

These examples notwithstanding, to identify feminism with a belief in social change, and non-feminist positions with an assumption of historical continuity, would greatly oversimplify the issue. It seems that *both* a belief in, and a rejection of, change over time constitute widely available maxims of common sense which may be invested with different meanings and used for different rhetorical ends. Feminist rhetoric does not *always* identify and value the occurrence of social change. For example, rhetoric directed towards the collective mobilization of Women may refer to an essential, unchanging Female Nature which unites all women across space and time. Raymond (1986: 44), for example, argues for this sort of perspective on the basis that 'Women have always been enjoined to be be discontinuous with our original Selves, with a female and feminist past whose continuities we have never known. In some contexts feminists may deploy a cyclical view of time (see, for example, the quotation from Eichenbaum and Orbach above) and use nostalgic imagery:

> In the new science of the twenty-first century, not physical force but spiritual force will lead the way . . . Extrasensory perception will take precedence over sensory perception. And in this sphere woman will again predominate. She who was revered and worshipped by early man because of her power to see the unseen will once again be the pivot . . . about whom the next civilization will, as of old, revolve. (Davis, 1971: 339)

Conversely, any attempt to identify the political Right simply with a belief in, and a value for, historical continuity is evidently problematical. Even people who express vehement opposition to the Women's Movement would be unlikely to contend that no 'change' has ever occurred in the nature and the status of women. Neither would they necessarily regard those changes which have occurred as a bad thing. Winship (1987: 18), for example, notes how traditional British women's magazines like *People's Friend* and *Woman's Own* may 'celebrat[e] just how far women have travelled along the line of history' using progress narratives similar to those quoted at the beginning of this chapter. Moreover, it is clear that even 'conservative' political rhetoric is directed towards shaping the course of history and hence necessarily rests upon a desire for *some* form of future change.

The commitment of the political Right to transform (rather than simply to maintain) existing social structures and processes has become more transparent in recent years because of changes which have taken place in the language used by political groups.[6] The rhetoricians of the British Right, for example, are increasingly using words such as 'change' and 'progress' to describe their goals. Borrowing from the language of the Left, members of the British Conservative Party re-present themselves as the 'radical' (sometimes 'revolutionary') proponents of 'change'. The identification of the Right with a value for change is also apparent in the way in which they characterize their opponents as resisting 'progress' and 'seeking to turn the clock back'. To return to the issue of gender relations, we may note how an opposition to feminism may be legitimated with reference to notions of 'progress' and 'social change'. Consider, for example, the following comment made by a young female student in response to a question about whether her university should have a Women's Week:

> I think that ideas like this were probably OK ten years ago, but I don't think it would really be relevant to students nowadays. Probably a few strident feminists would like it, but what they fail to recognize is that most women at university are not discriminated against any more. I don't think it will improve things any more to keep harping back to these old ideas. What is more important now is that women capitalise on the freedoms which we have got now, and drop all the feminist stuff.

This woman presents a view of society as having already progressed so far that the things which feminists were demanding in the 1960s and 1970s have now been achieved. Hence feminism is no longer 'relevant', it is old-fashioned ('harping back') and future progress depends on leaving these outmoded ideas behind.

Up to this point I have considered the way in which contemporary talk about Women may embrace ideas both of transience and of permanence, and suggested that neither position can be associated reliably with particular political goals. I have illustrated these general points with short quotations. However, I would emphasize that use of short quotations to illustrate ideal types has some important drawbacks. In particular, this may lead us to overlook the co-presence of themes *within* accounts. Take, for example, the following extract from an advertising feature in *Wedding and Home* magazine (Autumn 1988) entitled 'Victorian Values':

> Many modern day brides are putting their everyday, extrovert images aside and looking to their great-grandmothers for inspiration on their wedding day. Debbie Djordjevic selects a timeless, Victorian collection, and captures them in the magnificent surroundings of the Natural History Museum in London.

Images of permanence and transience are so intertwined in this text that a thorough account would require a more detailed analysis than is possible here. For present purposes we may note the references to change over time (the historical category Victorian; the distinction between modern-day brides and their ancestors; the allusion to evolutionary Natural History). Within the same text, however we may identify themes pointing to a recursive view of time (the 'wedding day' rendered meaningful through its difference from 'everyday' routine; the 'timeless' dress evoking an identity between the modern-day bride and her great-grandmother; the setting in a Museum). We can appreciate how the author plays upon the contradiction between old and new, continuity and change, for rhetorical force. A similar juxtaposition may be identified in political slogans which uses images of tradition to promote social change, such as 'Nostalgia dell'Avvenire' (Nostalgia for the Future) used in the 1970s by the Italian neo-fascist party, the MSI (Cheles, forthcoming), and 'The New Traditional Woman' used by the New Right in the USA (Klatch, 1988).

I would like to take the consideration of co-presence one stage further and suggest that, even when a statement about Women appears to emphasize transience *or* permanence, an interpretation needs to go beyond what is visible in the text. Any contemporary statement about time is made in a context in which people share an awareness of both continuity and change. Consequently, even an apparently straight-forward reference to transience (or permanence) in fact rests upon, and evokes, the unspoken position. We would not need the maxim that 'history repeats itself' if we did not, at some level, recognize that time is irreversible. Similarly, the warning that one 'cannot turn the clock back' is only meaningful when set against a valorization of tradition. Reference to an Eternal Feminine reflects an unspoken assumption that some things about Women have changed. The concept of a New Woman evokes notions *both* of change and of continuity since the use of the same category label ('Woman') to identify the supposedly New phenomenon implies some essential continuity with what went before. Just as we can assume that the 'New Blue Whitener' we see advertised will not differ essentially from the washing powder previously sold under the same brand name (at the very least we would expect the two products to share a common lavational affordancy), 'New' Women, however they may differ from their great-grandmothers, remain Women.

If we reconsider the quotations cited earlier in the light of the co-text from which they were drawn, and with a view to the wider ideological/ historical context in which they were produced, the problem of interpreting any statement as simply asserting historical continuity *or* change becomes clear. Take, for example, nostalgia. On the one hand, nostalgic statements appear to give voice to a circular view of time – the assumption that a Paradise Lost may be Regained. On the other hand, nostalgia rests upon a linear view of time – the idea that present conditions represent a radical break from the past. In the classical context it would be appropriate to regard these ideas of change as being subordinated to a recursive view of history in which (for all the appearance of change) the wheel of fate ultimately turns full circle. This sort of reading would not, however, be appropriate for contemporary texts which are made and read by people who are historically minded. Speakers may use a classical genre, yet their aim is not to construct a future which simply regains or reproduces a mythical past, but to appropriate old ideas and practices for a future in which they will be invested with a new meaning. Similarly, it would be a mistake to treat the earlier quotation from Eichenbuam and Orbach as if it was essentially similiar to those circular views of time described by Gurevich as typical of traditional societies. Whilst Eichenbaum and Orbach stress the reproduction of femininity across generations they do so against a background awareness of the possibility of social change. Their analysis of the mechanics of social reproduction is neither intended nor read as a legitimation of the present. Rather, the process of social reproduction is regarded as a problem which needs to be explained in order to suggest ways of effectively biting into the future.

Permanence, Transience and 'The Social Identity of Women'

I have already noted, in passing, how a concern for change over time may be implicit in the writing of academic social psychologists. Paradoxically, however, many mainstream approaches to social psychology have been subject to criticism for their apparent failure to theorize change (for example, Gergen, 1973; Moscovici, 1972; Sampson, 1977). Tajfel (1972), like many other authors writing around the time of the crisis debates, was critical of what he regarded as static approaches to social psychology. He was concerned to contrast these 'static' approaches with his own dynamic SI perspective:

> The 'dynamic' approach to the problems of social identity adopted in this discussion is based on several considerations. First, it is unlikely that there exist many examples of intergroup situations which are static in the sense that they consist of an unchanging set of social relationships between the groups. We are, however, less concerned here with social situations than with their psychological counterparts; these are bound to be even less static. (Tajfel, 1974: 77)

Tajfel stressed how social identification may be subject to temporal fluctuation: 'the psychological existence of a group for its members is a complex sequence of appearances and disappearances, of looming large and vanishing into thin air . . .' (Tajfel, 1982: 485), and this consideration has been taken up in Turner's (1982, 1985, 1988; Turner et al., 1987) self-categorization approach to social identification:

> The model proposed by [self-categorization theory] is by no means static, fixed, global, reified. The opposite is the case: a fundamental idea is the rejection of self-categories as 'absolutes': the self is dynamic, relational, comparative, fluid, context-specific and variable. Self-categorizations are part of the process of relating to the social world, not 'things'. (Turner, 1988: 144)

Many authors (for example, Billig et al., 1988; Gergen and Gergen, 1984; Potter and Wetherell, 1987; Sampson, 1981) have suggested that a tendency to overlook the flexibility of social perception and the possibility of change over time may be traced, in part, to a reliance on positivist–empiricist language and methodology amongst social psychologists. It is, however, worth noting that SI theory and research has remained firmly wedded to the positivist–empiricist tradition (see Turner, 1981). Tajfel specifically argued that '[our] selection of problems and research perspectives seems to have been of much greater importance in restricting our interests than our choice of methods' (1975a: 3). SI researchers have not generally recognized any need to develop new methods to deal with the dynamic aspects of human cognition and social activity. Most existing work applying SI perspectives to gender, for example, employs standard experimental (for example, Bond et al., 1985) and survey (for example, Abbondanza et al., 1980; Gurin and Townsend, 1986) techniques. Researchers typically use tests to measure phenomena such as gender salience (D. Abrams et al., 1985; Oakes and Turner, 1986), self-stereotyping (Hogg and Turner, 1987; Smith, 1980), and social perception (Condor, 1984; Dubé and Auger, 1984; Kalmuss et al., 1981). In the following pages I will argue that this reliance on traditional methods may have limited the development of a dynamic SI approach to Women. Since it is not possible to consider the complexities of this field in any detail I will summarize work which applies the SI perspective to Women in terms of three main approaches.

The first of these approaches assumes the objective existence of Women as a group. This is apparent in Williams and Giles' (1978) original article, in which social change is conceptualized purely in terms of a shift in the relative status of Women *vis-à-vis* Men. These authors do not allow for the possibility that, in the future, the categories Man and Woman might simply not exist. A similiar a priori assumption of the objective existence of Women as a group may be identified elsewhere in the SI literature. For example, some writers assume that Women have certain common interests despite the fact that individual women may not be 'conscious' of them (Kalmuss et al., 1981). Moreover, even those theorists who talk of the fluctuating salience of sex (see below) still report the sex of their subjects as a timeless fact. They assume that – however variable gender may be as a system of self-categorization – their subjects are, and remain, objectively male or female.

In some respects it is not surprising that SI theorists should assume the existence of the gender categories. Evidence certainly suggests that gender dualism represents a moral requirement of contemporary thought.[7] However, even if we accept that 'Woman, as a group, is never lost to the cognitions . . .' (Breakwell, 1979: 15), this does not justify SI theorists simply presupposing knowledge of Woman as a social identity. The fact that gender-dualistic thought may be inescapable in contemporary Western societies does not mean that we should take this for granted: many contemporary feminist accounts attempt to construct gender-free utopias. Moreover, this does not mean that gender dualism is always explicit in our dealings with the world, or that we always define the male–female distinction in the same way, or imbue it with the same meanings (Breakwell, 1979; Condor, 1986; Wetherell, 1986).

A second sort of perspective focuses on relatively stable differences in self- and social perception. Most of the work that I would include in this category measures social identification using variants of standard attitude and personality scaling techniques. For example, D. Abrams et al. (1985) have measured individual differences in gender salience; Smith (1980) measured social identification in terms of self-stereotyping; and Gurin and Townsend (1986) have used questionnaire responses to categorize subjects according to various facets of gender identification. This is broadly similar to the type of research that I conducted for my Ph.D. thesis, in which I constructed a scale designed to distinguish women manifesting 'high' and 'low' levels of group identification (see Condor, 1984). In addition to questionnaire-based studies, I would include Williams and Giles' (1978) analysis of the contemporary Women's Movement in this category. Williams and Giles imply that an awareness of Woman as a social identity will co-vary with (relatively stable) political consciousness. On one hand, these authors suggest that an awareness of Woman as a social (collective) identity is peculiar to contemporary feminist consciousness. *Only* the activity of the women in the Women's Movement is granted the label 'acting in terms of group' – women in the past, and those not currently supporting the aims of the Women's Movement, are deemed to 'act individualistically'. On the other hand, Williams and Giles are more specific, implying that a commitment to Woman as a social identity is characteristic of only some types of Women's Movement strategy. Following Tajfel (1978a, b) they distinguish between strategies which differentiate between the sexes and stress the positive distinctiveness of Women ('redefinition' and 'social creativity') and strategies which minimize male–female distinction and downplay or deny the distinctiveness of Women ('assimilation'). In this respect, Williams and Giles' account parallels feminist formulations which distinguish between different types of Women's Movement activity on the basis of whether it emphasizes Male–Female similarity or difference (for example, Kahn and Jean, 1983; McFadden, 1984).

The major advantage of this type of approach is that it complies with Tajfel's (1978a,b) demand that group membership be understood with a view to the subjectivity of the people involved. The major disadvantages arise from the way in which this subjective awareness is understood. Researchers often assume that responses to questionnaires reflect reliable individual differences in attitude or personality. This necessarily underestimates the potential for flexibility in social and self-perception. Any approach to the social identity of women which attempts to classify individuals as 'high' or as 'low' group identifiers conflicts with Tajfel's argument that social identification is flexible and that individuals cannot be said to simply 'have' stable group identifications.

A second problem with this work concerns the *way* in which variation in the social identity of women is conceptualized. Generally, this work conceives of variation in terms of quantity ('strength') rather than quality. Individual differences are *measured*: the question is 'how much' social identification a woman displays, rather than 'in what way' it is manifested.[8] In its extreme form, this involves distinguishing between those individuals for whom gender 'is' or 'is not' a salient aspect of self-perception (D. Abrams et al., 1985) and those who 'do' or 'do not' identify with their sex (Condor, 1984). This is, of course, in accord with Tajfel's notion of social identification 'looming large' and 'vanishing into thin air'. There is, however, as we have already seen, a problem in assuming that people are ever unaware of, or unconcerned with, gender distinction. When a woman describes herself as 'different from other women', or claims that 'I often find it difficult to understand other women' (two of the items which I used on my questionnaire) she is still acknowledging some identification with the label 'Woman'. Of course, part of the problem here is that identification is assumed in the way in which the questions are posed in the first place ('other women'). However, in open-ended interviews I conducted subsequently, it seemed that, on those occasions in which a woman did not make explicit reference to her sex, this was because the fact that she 'was' a woman was being taken for granted (Condor, 1984).

Similiar problems may be identified in Williams and Giles' distinction between strategies of gender assimilation and differentiation. Even assimilation strategies (which deny the validity and legitimacy of beliefs in male–female difference) do not escape gender-dualistic thought. At the very least, the claim of feminists to speak with a distinctive Female voice in the interests of Women as a political group depends on the acceptance of difference. As an example of the problems of positing a 'pure' assimilationist position on gender distinction, let us consider Radical Feminist rhetoric. On the one hand, the separatist strategies and the valorization of the feminine apparent in much Radical Feminist rhetoric would appear to provide almost a prototypical example of a strategy of differentiation. On the other hand, Radical Feminists often make it clear that the ultimate aim of an approach which valorizes the feminine is to break down the assumption of gender dualism on which the category Woman depends:

> the end goal of feminist revolution must be . . . not just the elimination of male *privilege* but of the sex *distinction* itself. (Firestone, 1979: 19)

> We believe that the male world as it now exists is based on a corrupt notion of 'maleness vs femaleness', and that the oppression of women is based on this very notion and its attendant institutions . . . We must eradicate the sexual division on which our society is based. (Kreps, 1973: 239)

However, it is not possible to suggest simply that, within Radical Feminist theory, a recognition of Woman as a (presently existing) social category is used as a strategic device which is, in the last analysis, to be subordinated to the ultimate goal of assimilation. Paradoxically, in the act of criticizing the 'male habit of setting up boundary lines between imagined polarities [which] has been the impetus for untold hatred and destruction' (Roszak, 1969: 304), Radical Feminists implicitly accept the terms of the debate they are rejecting. One could not posit the original existence of Men as a group who could draw up boundary lines in their own interest without assuming a pre-existing gender distinction.

A tendency to conceive of flexibility in terms of variations in the *strength* of category identification has led to a tendency to underestimate the potential for flexibility in the *meaning and use* of the category Woman. Hence, for example, Williams and Giles imply that the category Woman is peculiar to *feminist* self-awareness. However, these authors are, at the same time, implicitly aware that the category Woman exists independently of its use in any *particular* form of political rhetoric. They recognize how the Women's Movement may use strategies of 'social creativity' which attempt to attach new meanings to an *already existing* social distinction. Historically, the notion of a collective female identity was not the invention of feminist politics. Mary Wollstonecraft did not have to create Woman as a social category: her argument was based on the fact that this category already existed and was incommensurate with dominant values of individualism.

However, Williams and Giles are, in one sense, correct. When feminists speak as Women they are not simply using an already existing identity but are transforming its meaning: the very attempt to co-opt the category Woman represents a claim to female power which 'violates the reality structure' (Campbell, 1973). This does not, however, imply that the category Woman cannot still be associated with different meanings, and deployed for different rhetorical ends. Texts which Williams and Giles would not consider examples of

Women's Movement activity often construct a collective female subject. For example, Winship (1987: 67) notes of a variety of women's magazines: '[e]ach engages and embraces readers in a world of "we women" but assumes and constructs different definitions of who "we" are . . .' Despite feminist attempts to co-opt and redefine Woman as a social identity, the meaning of this identity remains essentially contestible. Antifeminist movements may, in turn, co-opt feminist slogans and re-work them for their own political ends. A good example provided by Cheles (in press) is a poster produced for the 1984 Euro-elections by the MSI, a far-right Italian organization, which co-opted the graphics and the language ('Let's build a Europe that is also "Woman-Centred"') originally used in a poster produced for a feminist organization.

The third approach to the social identity of women also focuses on the representation of gender in the awareness of the research 'subject'. Research on gender 'salience' (for example, Oakes, 1983, 1987; Oakes and Turner, 1986) does not assume that Woman may constitute a social identity to some women all of the time, but rather suggests that Woman constitutes a social identity to all people some of the time. Research from this perspective is concerned largely with the question of *when* it is that people use gender categories as a system of self-definition and social perception.[9] This sort of work certainly seems to be closer to Tajfel's original idea of social identification as variable across situations. However, in common with the 'individual differences' perspectives, it also assumes that this flexibility is best understood quantitatively. In this case there is a tendency to distinguish between presence (salience) *or* absence (non-salience) rather than more subtle gradients of strength in group identification. This, once again, raises the problem of absence: is it ever the case that gender distinction is simply 'not salient'? Turner (1988: 115) recently commented: 'Thinking of men as emotional, I may compare myself to other men in terms of the stereotypical trait and conclude that I am unemotional (but still see "us men" as emotional when I compare men to women).' This does not seem to posit a simple salient/non-salient distinction with respect to gender as a means of self-categorization. Even when this hypothetical individual is not seeing himself as 'us men' he is still implicitly aware of his gender – he does not compare himself with 'other women'. Again, it may be that on those occasions in which we do not specify a view of ourselves as a Woman or a Man, we are simply taking it for granted.

The assumption that variability in gender categorization can be understood primarily in terms of a distinction between presence and absence again precludes a consideration of the potential flexibility of the *meanings* associated with the social category Women. Salience research is often based on an a priori assumption that gender categories are associated with a fixed stereotype which is evoked every time gender becomes a salient aspect of self- or social categorization. The salience of a particular ingroup–outgroup distinction is explained partly in terms of the fit of this predefined category content to a particular situation (Oakes, 1987). In the experimental research setting the salience of gender distinction may be *operationally defined* in terms of description of others or self in terms of predefined structures of sex stereotypes (see, for example, Oakes and Turner, 1986).

This sort of perspective overlooks the possibility that the meanings of the category Woman may vary according to context. Take, for example, images of female driving ability: 'Women drivers' are notoriously bad, but when we buy cars we are prepared to accept that the same 'lady owners' have not damaged their vehicles. Which is 'the' stereotype of Women? In some respects, salience research actually precludes us from ever recognizing flexibility in thought about gender categories. Any evidence which might lead us to suggest that a female 'stimulus person' may, on some occasions, *not* be regarded as a 'bad driver' is liable to be interpreted simply as evidence that, in this situation, her gender was 'not salient'. The fact that we may hold contradictory images of Women does not, however, mean that the gender of an actor is irrelevant to the way in which we perceive their behaviour. The label Woman acts as co-text, qualifying our interpretation of 'a bad driver', 'a car owner' and so on (Condor, 1986).

Salience research also limits our conceptualization of psychological flexibility to the presence or absence of a *particular* social category. Oakes and Turner (1986: 323) pose the question, 'When does a black British woman feel strongly 'British' as opposed to 'black' or 'female' . . .?' This question reflects a commitment to a positivist research tradition which assumes that the world may be carved up into discrete, 'independent' variables (in this case, gender, race, nation). In contrast, most other (for example, social anthropological, sociological, semiological) analyses of the same phenomena are far more attuned to the fact that gender, race and nation constitute aspects of an intermeshing system of identities and abstract social symbols and values (Ortner and Whitehead, 1981). To regard Black and British identities as simply 'opposed to' the category Woman can only lead us to overlook the way in which gender boundaries are implicated in nationalist and racist rhetoric and imagery. Historical analyses indicate, for example, the importance of gender identities in Nazi ideology (Koonz, 1987), and the way in which the status of Women was used to symbolize national progress in nineteenth-century nationalist movements (Jayawardena, 1986). The female form is typically used to portray a whole variety of (often contradictory) abstract values and social identities. Is it the case that the national symbolism of Britannia or the Statue of Liberty is diminished when we become aware of its manifestation in a *female* body (see Warner, 1985)?

The Changing Status of Women in Society

The problem I will be addressing in the final section of the chapter relates to Williams and Giles' original aim – to explain 'the changing status of women in society' and, more particularly, to consider the activities of the Women's Movement:

> [Tajfel's] theory . . . not only clarifies the strategies women are currently using to assert themselves in society, but also allows us to examine more closely the dynamics of the situation. Such an approach, it is felt, does not offer a substitute for others; but it does compensate for some of their deficiencies, the most prevalent of which is their failure to account adequately for the process of change. (Williams and Giles, 1978: 432)

Williams and Giles were not alone in looking to Tajfel for 'a theory of social change'. Reicher, for example (1984), identified Tajfel's Katz–Newcombe lecturers of 1974 as 'the most explicit attempt to deal with large scale social change' to arise from the European critique, and Turner and Giles (1981) inform us that Tajfel 'employed the developing theory [of Social Identity] to analyse intergroup conflict and social change in stratified societies'. More cautiously, Eiser (1986: 333) suggested that Tajfel's 'ultimate goal' was 'a theoretical account of the psychological processess involved in social change *over time* . . .'

Williams and Giles' article, however, might lead us to question whether SIT does provide a basis for historical analysis. Given its title, their article is curiously lacking in analysis of changes in the status of women in Western (or any other) society. Nor do the authors demonstrate any particular concern over this omission. At the time when the article was written, a large body of historical literature was available on just this issue. However, Williams and Giles appear to skip over the question of 'the changing status of women in society' to get to the major subject of their article – an analysis of Women's Movement activity. Once again the reader is provided with little in the way of historical analysis. The article generally provides a static description of the strategies used by European and North American feminists in the mid-1970s.

It might, of course, be argued that Williams and Giles simply failed to capitalize on the ability of the SI model to provide an historical perspective on gender relations. Taylor and McKirnan (1984), for example, have since adopted SIT to develop a diachronic account of social movement activity.[10] However, a careful re-reading of Tajfel's work suggests that this was never intended as a 'theory of social change'. From the quotation on page 22 we can see that, although

Tajfel certainly *acknowledges* the occurrence of social change over macro-time, his 'dynamic' approach in fact focuses on social cognitive plasticity in micro-time. Similarly, existing work on category salience is concerned only with social psychological flexibility; it is not concerned with ideological transformations, let alone changes in social structure. Even if we overcome some of the problems outlined in the last section of this chapter, and consider flexibility in the use and the meaning of the category Woman, there is nothing in SI theory which would help us go about relating this new 'dynamic' understanding of the social identity of women to power relations or to the process of social transformation. Of course, we might posit some relationship between the flexibility of human thought and wide-scale change over time, but this relationship is in no way a simple one. Tajfel made it clear that a certain amount of dynamic movement in our perception of social structures is characteristic of 'stable' as well as 'unstable' intergroup settings: 'even in the most rigid caste system . . . the social distinctions which may appear very stable are related to a continuously dynamic psychological situation in which a superior group can never stop working at the preservation of its distinctiveness' (Tajfel, 1978a: 88).[11] Furthermore, it may be that a theoretical focus on social psychological flexibility in micro-time may actually undermine an attempt to document historical changes in social beliefs and practices. Historical analysis which considers 'change' over time relies upon an ability to bracket flexibility. Unless one can define what a belief or practice 'is' at time 1, one cannot contend that it has 'changed' by time 2.

There is another reason why the SIT model seems unlikely to provide a basis for historical analysis of change in gender relations. Despite paying lip-service to the need to consider 'historical context', SI approaches are largely ahistorical. The postulated distinction between 'social' and 'personal' identity is assumed to constitute a universal psychological fact (Turner, 1981), as is the postulated search for positive ingroup distinctiveness (Tajfel, 1981; cf. Wetherell, 1982). At the beginning of this chapter I noted a parallel between Tajfel's (for example, 1978a, b) description of 'unstable' intergroup settings and sociological and social anthropological accounts of the process of social change in 'hot' societies. There is, however, one crucial difference between these accounts. Social theorists such as Lévi-Strauss (1966) and Giddens (1979) are acutely aware of the *historical specificity* of 'hot' societies in which people act in a conscious attempt to change (or maintain) the course of history. Tajfel demonstrates no such awareness of the historical specificity of those situations in which 'some awareness that the existing social reality is not the only possible one and that alternatives to it are conceivable and perhaps attainable ...' (1974: 82). Similiarly, other theorists have identified the current tendency towards rapid transformation in social category boundaries with a specific historical context (modernity), and have attempted to charter the history of this phenomenon (for example, Berman, 1982). In contrast, Tajfel's recognition of the increased pace of social change in contemporary life (cited on page 17) appears little more than a platitude serving to emphasize the timely nature of his own discussion of differentiation between social groups.

To the extent that they fail to consider the specific historical location of unstable intergroup settings, SI theorists are in danger of representing what is, in fact, a description of social relations in modernity, as transhistoric truth. Despite their aim to 'look historically at the situations in which women have become "rebellious" about their status in society' (1978: 436), Williams and Giles focus only on contemporary forms of protest, and apparently assume that these illustrate some more general phenomenon. In this respect, Williams and Giles' account parallels certain forms of feminist historiography that attempt to construct a vital, enduring, feminist identity by seeking links between contemporary Women's Movement activity and protest behaviour by women in the past:

> If we ... discover that even in long dead society there were women who resisted ... restriction of their identity and that these women were in fact accepted as proclaiming great truths ... is not this discovery as potentially exhilarating and encouraging as discovering our contemporary sisters? (Ker, 1983: 43)

We should, however, recognize that practices which Tajfel (1978 a, b) describes as 'minority group strategies' are not transhistoric or transcultural. Indeed, the term 'minority group' itself embodies the assumptions of liberal democracy (Meyers, 1984). Historians have shown how the Woman Question could only have been raised in post-industrial society (Ehrenreich and English, 1979).[12] The strategies outlined by Williams and Giles as characteristic of Women's Movement activity in Britain and the USA in the middle to late 1970s reflect, and build upon, culturally and historically specific traditions of rationalism and romanticism in European thought. In particular, much of the rhetoric of the contemporary women's movement (which deploys notions such as 'equality', 'individuality' and 'human rights') is understandable only as part of the language of the revolutionary bourgeois tradition in Western thought (Mitchell, 1976, 1986). It is easy for us to overlook this fact, since the language and assumptions of the Enlightenment have become an accepted part of the way in which we understand the world in which we live. The people quoted at the beginning of this chapter were probably unaware that the notions of 'minorities', 'discrimination', 'egality', 'equality', 'prejudice' and, of course, progressive 'social change', which inform their common-sense accounts of Women were once revolutionary concepts. That we assume that the concepts which we now take for granted have always been part of the way in which people view the world is understandable in everyday life. This assumption is, however, inexcusable in social theory which is supposedly concerned with historical context and with social change.

Up to this point, I have been arguing that Tajfel's 'dynamic' approach to social identity was primarily a critique of reification and not an attempt to construct a theory of social change. Moreover, in assuming the immutability (cf. Gergen, 1984) of phenomena such as 'social identity', and 'intergroup differentiation', and in failing to consider the historical specificity of 'unstable intergroup settings' and contemporary minority group movements, Tajfel's perspective may even be seen as antithetical to historical analysis. If this is the case, the question arises as to why so many authors have attributed Tajfel with a 'theory of social change'. I would suggest that this may have arisen, in part, from terminological confusion. Tajfel often used the term 'social change', in his writing but *not* (usually) in it sociological sense (that is, pertaining to transformation in ideas and social structures over macro-time). Rather, he used the term to refer to a *belief in ascribed category membership* (see Tajfel, 1975b for a clear statement of this distinction). Tajfel (1975b) pointed out that situations of 'social change' were just as likely to accompany 'stable' as 'unstable' intergroup settings. However, when describing behaviour in 'situations of social change', Tajfel (1978a, b) sometimes focused on unstable intergroup settings and, under the heading of 'strategies of social change', discussed the activities in which members of low-status groups may engage in the pursuit of social transformation. What seems to have happened is that some subsequent theorists – including Williams and Giles – have misinterpreted Tajfel's description of such 'strategies of social change' as an account of the *process of social transformation*. This misinterpretation of Tajfel's phrase 'strategies of social change' has two important consequences for Williams and Giles' analysis of 'the changing status of women'.

First, identifying pressure for social change with the activity of disadvantaged ('minority') groups can lead to an assumption that *all* current efforts for social change come from subordinate social groups. I noted earlier how, particularly in the 1960s and 1970s, left-wing movements sometimes identified their aims with 'change' and the Right with a mere preservation of the status quo. It seems that Tajfel's work reflected this form of political rhetoric which was current at the time he was writing. Tajfel suggested that motivation to transform social hierarchies would come from *low-status* groups, and that high-status groups would be motivated to maintain the status quo. Similarly, Williams and Giles assumed that high-status group activity (in this case the activity of men) is confined to maintaining the status quo or, when necessary, 'reacting' to 'minority' group activity in order to restore the status quo (see, for example, Giles and Johnson, 1981 – an example of this supposition in the context of ethnolinguistic change). In the first section of this chapter I suggested that it was unlikely that any political group in contemporary society is simply motivated to 'maintain the status quo'. Moreover, historical analyses provide examples of situations in which motivation for social trans-formation may come from high-status groups. For example, pressures towards the 'liberation' of Women in the Middle East in the nineteenth century can be traced, in part, to the activity of Western imperialists (Jayawardena, 1986). In many parts of the world today pressure for 'change' comes not only from oppressed 'minority' groups, but also from groups such as the New Right religious fundamentalists and those pursuing the interests of international capital.

A second, related problem which arises from any attempt to use Tajfel's list of 'minority group strategies' as an account of social change is that this obscures the complex relationship between history and human agency. Williams and Giles not only assume that all efforts towards change in gender relations will come from the Women's Movement, but they also overlook the possibility that strategies undertaken by (some) women to improve the status of their group may not succeed or that they might have unintended outcomes. Hence, these authors assume that all 'change' will be in Women's interests (or rather, in the interests of Women as defined by the Women's Movement). Williams and Giles (1978: 446) concede only that:

> Social change by use of the strategies outlined above will be slow and accompanied by concomitant strategies to maintain male superiority on old and newly-created dimensions.

Tajfel's (1978a, b) analysis of 'minority group reactions' was, however, clearly limited to the *intention* of social activists. He speculated as to why people might *try* to maintain or change the status quo, but the actual outcome of these ideas and practices he left entirely untheorized.

To suggest that human beings do not always realize their intentions (for example, that social movements and/or established social forces may fail in their aims) is not to deny that people 'make their own history' (to borrow Marx's famous phrase). However, historical analyses demonstrate that many social changes have represented the *unintended* consequences of human actions (see P. Abrams, 1982: Giddens, 1984). The characteristics of modern industrialized society could not have been foreseen, let alone intended, by those individuals who developed the technology which, with hindsight, we regard as pioneering developments of the Industrial Revolution. With respect to gender relations, Bryant (1979) describes the profound changes which took place in the education of women in the nineteenth century as an 'unexpected revolution'. Mitchell (1986) notes that women's lives in the late 1980s may be affected by a rise in the rate of female participation in the labour force coinciding with an increase in male unemployment. It seems unlikely that any changes in gender relations which may result from this were intended by social planners. Mitchell also notes that feminist activity may have unintended consequences noting, in particular, how attempts during the 1970s to focus on gender as the primary social division may have contributed to a developing ideology which underplayed class differences.

The greatest contribution to any historical analysis is, of course, the gift of hindsight. In the ten years since the publication of Williams and Giles' article times have changed. Some of these changes are traceable to Women's Movement activity in the 1970s (see Segal, 1987), whilst other aspects of social change appear to have been less in accord with the demands of Western feminists (see Allen, 1986). Feminists are becoming increasingly aware that even when their demands are met, these may not have the consequences which were anticipated.

Since the time when Williams and Giles were writing it has become rare for feminist historiography to take the form of a simple progress myth ('things are getting better all the time') that simply assumes that the movement will succeed. These revisions in historiography are not intended to deny, but rather to promote, feminist agency to change the world. The kind of 'happy ending' narrative reflected in Williams and Giles' article may have been useful as a mobilization device for social movements in a liberal political climate. However, in a situation in which the Right has political power and may (barring unforeseen circumstances) control the pace and direction of social transformation, the complacency generated by progress myths may prove positively dysfunctional to oppositional social forces.

Notes

1   I will be using a capital 'W' to distinguish Women as an abstract social category from particular category members ('women' with a lower case 'w').

2   For the sake of simplicity I am referring to a homogeneous 'contemporary Western society'. However, notions of social continuity and change are likely to vary within 'society'. The ideas that I am describing are particularly characteristic of Judeo-Christian thought.

3   In order to maintain simplicity of style I will not pepper the following discussion with specific reference to existing analyses of social representations of time. The

ideas presented in this chapter have been taken from various sources, including historical analyses of notions of time in political rhetoric (White, 1973) and scientific thought (e.g. Gould, 1988); anthropological analyses of time in primitive (e.g. Lévi-Strauss, 1966) and contemporary (e.g. Leach, 1971) society; and sociological analyses of time and social structure (e.g. Giddens, 1979, 1984, 1987).

4 The assumption of cognitive and ideological consistency in social psychological theory and research has recently come under attack from a number of theorists who have suggested alternative analyses based on poststructuralist views on language (e.g. Potter and Wetherell, 1987; Billig, 1987; Billig et al., 1988). The following discussion is based largely on these recent critiques although, again, for stylistic reasons, I will not necessarily refer to this work directly.

5 The problems involved in trying to reach a baseline definition of what 'is' and 'is not' feminism have been discussed by Delmar (1986) and I will not repeat this argument here. In the present chapter, I am using the term 'feminism' to denote ideas and actions which are *consciously directed towards* increasing the authority and autonomy accorded to women. Since the strategies used to achieve this end may vary in the course of a debate (see Cott, 1986), the term 'feminism' is intended to indicate rhetorical goal(s) rather than the manifest *content* of an argument.

6 It is unlikely that these sorts of changes are a 'new' phenomenon. Similar examples of co-option in political rhetoric may be identified in different historical and political contexts (see e.g. Cheles, in press). An account of recent changes in British political rhetoric has been provided in a special edition of *Marxism Today* (October 1988).

7 The omnipresence of gender-categorical thought has been the subject of a good deal of recent literature. The present discussion is based on perspectives from ethnomethodology (Kessler and McKenna, 1978), social psychology (Billig et al., 1988), literary criticism (Derrida, 1967) and feminism (Cixoux, 1975). These perspectives emphasize, however, that the omnipresence of gender dualism does not imply that the category 'Woman' is always visible. Poststructuralist feminists in particular (see e.g. Weedon, 1987) argue that this 'absence' of Woman as a stated social category represents an important aspect of patriarchal ideology.

8 Some theorists do suggest that a woman's identification with her sex may be a multifaceted phenomenon. For example, Gurin and Townsend (1986) distinguished a priori between three aspects of group identification. Similarly, on the basis of factor analysis of questionnaire responses, I discovered two empirically distinct aspects of social identification. However, this work still assumes that these various forms of social identification will remain stable over time.

9 Although extant research on gender salience poses the question of when it is that an individual uses gender as a means of *self* reference, much of the research in this area focuses on the way in which we use gender categories to interpret the behaviour of others.

10 Taylor and McKirnan (1984) also emphasized that Tajfel's 'strategies of social change' are peculiar to modernity. However, this account also suffers from problems as an historical analysis since it apparently assumes a universal 'world history'. Like some crude Marxist formulations, Taylor and McKirnan's account presents industrialization as a universal, inescapable, aspect of social evolution: 'all intergroup relations follow a similar sequential course' (Taylor and McKirnan, 1984: 292).

11 Similarly, Billig's (1987) elegant discussion of the flexibility of human thought does not address the issue of social change. It is significant that many of the examples

which Billig provides of the flexibility of human thought (taken, for example, from the Talmud, and from Ancient Greek texts) occurred in cold (stable) societies. The fact that people may be able to argue with one another and to change their mind does not mean that, in so doing, they will necessarily be changing the world.

12   The relationship between the development of modernity and changes in the behaviour and status of Women is a complicated one, since Women's history tends not to fit neatly into the conventional timetable normally used in the analysis of European history (see Branca, 1978).

References

Abbondanza, M., Simard, L. and Guimond, S. (1980) 'A Personal and Collective Look at the Situation between the Sexes'. Paper presented at the 41st Annual Convention of the Canadian Psychological Association, Calgary.

Abrams, D., Sparkes, K. and Hogg, M. (1985) 'Gender Salience and Social Identity: The Impact of Sex of Siblings on Educational and Occupation Aspirations', *British Journal of Educational Psychology*, 55: 224–32.

Abrams, P. (1982) *Historical Sociology*. Bath: Open Books.

Allen, J. (1986) 'Evidence and Silence: Feminism and the Limits of History', in C. Pateman and E. Gross (eds), *Feminist Challenges: Social and Political Theory*. London: Allen & Unwin.

Banks, O. (1981) *Faces of Feminism*. Oxford: Martin Robertson.

Baron, R. and Byrne, D. (1987) *Social Psychology*, 5th edn. Boston: Allyn and Bacon.

Barrett, M. (1985) 'Ideology and the Cultural Production of Gender', in J. Newton and D. Rosenfelt (eds), *Feminist Criticism and Cultural Change*. London: Methuen.

Becker, C. (1932) *The Heavenly City of the Eighteenth Century Philosophers*. Yale: Yale University Press.

Beddoe, D. (1983) *Discovering Women's History: A Practical Manual*. London: Pandora.

Berman, M. (1982) *All that is Solid Melts into Air: The Experience of Modernity*. New York: Simon & Schuster.

Billig, M. (1987) *Arguing and Thinking: A Rhetorical Approach to Social Psychology*. Cambridge: Cambridge University Press.

Billig, M., Condor, S., Edwards, D., Gane, M., Middleton, D. and Radley, A. (1988) *Ideological Dilemmas: A Social Psychology of Everyday Thinking*. London: Sage.

Bond, M., Hewstone, M., Kwock-Choi, W. and Chi-Kwan, C. (1985) 'Group-serving Attributions across Intergroup Contexts: Cultural Differences in the Explanation of Sex-typed Behaviours', *European Journal of Social Psychology*. 15: 435–51.

Branca, P. (1978) *Women in Europe since 1750*. London: Croom-Helm.

Breakwell, G. M. (1979) 'Women: Group and Identity?' *Women's Studies International Quarterly*, 2: 9–17.

Bryant, M. (1979) *The Unexpected Revolution*. London: University of London Institute of Education.

Campbell, K. (1973) 'The Rhetoric of Women's Liberation: An Oxymoron', *Quarterly Journal of Speech*, 59: 74–86.

Cheles, L. (in press) ' "Dolce Stil Nero?" Images of Women in the Graphic Propaganda of the Italian Neo-fascist Party' in Z. Baranski and S. Vinall (eds), *Donna: Women and Italy*. London: Macmillan.

Cheles, L. (forthcoming) ' "Nostalgia dell'Avvenire": The New Propaganda of the MSI' in R. Ferguson, M. Vaughan and L. Cheles (eds), *Neo-Fascism in Europe*. London: Longman.

Cixoux, H. (1975) *La Jeune Née*. Paris: UGE.

Collins, W., Friedman, E. and Pivot, A. (1978) *Women: The Directory of Social Change*. London: Wildwood House.

Condor, S. G. (1984) *Womanhood as an Aspect of Social Identity*. Unpublished Ph.D. thesis, University of Bristol.

Condor, S. (1986) 'From Sex Categories to Gender Boundaries: Reconsidering Sex as a "Stimulus Variable" in Social Psychological Research', *BPS Social Pyschology Section Newsletter*, Spring.

Condor, S. (forthcoming) 'Gender, Ideology and Intergroup Relations', *British Journal of Social Psychology*.

Cott, N. F. (1986) 'Feminist Theory and Feminist Movements: The Past before Us', in J. Mitchell and A. Oakley (eds), *What is Feminism?* Oxford: Basil Blackwell.

Davis, E. (1971) *The First Sex*. Harmondsworth: Penguin.

Delmar, R. (1986) 'What is Feminism?', in J. Mitchell and A. Oakley (eds), *What is Feminism?* Oxford: Basil Blackwell.

Derrida, J. (1967) *L'Écriture et la Différence*. Paris: Seuil.

Doane, J. and Hodges, D. (1987) *Nostalgia and Sexual Difference*. London: Methuen.

Doise, W. (1988) 'Individual and Social Identities in Intergroup Relations', *European Journal of Social Psychology*, 18: 99–111.

Dubé, L. and Auger, L. (1984) 'Identité féminine dans un monde de changement: étude des processus d'identité sociale', *Canadian Journal of Behavioral Science*, 16: 298–310.

Ehrenreich, B. and English, D. (1979) *For Her Own Good: 150 Years of the Experts' Advice to Women*. London: Pluto Press.

Eichenbaum, L. and Orbach, S. (1983) *Understanding Women*. Harmondsworth: Penguin.

Eisenstein, H. (1984) *Contemporary Feminist Thought*. London: Allen & Unwin.

Eiser, J. R. (1986) *Social Psychology*. Cambridge: Cambridge University Press.

Firestone, S. (1979) *The Dialectic of Sex*. London: Virago (originally published 1971).

Gergen, K. (1973) 'Social Psychology as History', *Personality and Social Psychology Bulletin*, 2: 373–83.

Gergen, K. (1984) 'An Introduction to Historical Social Psychology', in K. Gergen and M. Gergen (eds), *Historical Social Psychology*. Hillsdale, NJ: Erlbaum.

Giddens, A. (1979) *Central Problems in Social Theory*. London: Macmillan.

Giddens, A. (1984) *The Constitution of Society*. Cambridge: Polity.

Giddens, A. (1987) *Social Theory and Modern Sociology*. Cambridge: Polity.

Giles, H. and Johnson, P. (1981) 'The Role of Language in Ethnic Group Relations', in J. Turner and H. Giles (eds), *Intergroup Behaviour*. Oxford: Basil Blackwell.

Gould, S. (1988) *Time's Arrow, Time's Cycle: Myth and Metaphor in the Discovery of Geological Time*. Harmondsworth: Pelican.

Gurevich, A. (1976) 'Time as a Problem in Cutural History', in L. Gardet et al. (eds), *Cultures and Time*. Paris: UNESCO.

Gurin, P. and Townsend A. (1986) 'Properties of Gender Identity and their Implications for Gender Consciousness', *British Journal of Social Psychology*, 25: 139–48.

Hogg, M. and Turner, J. (1987) 'Intergroup Behaviour, Self-stereotyping and the Salience of Social Categories', *British Journal of Social Psychology*, 26: 325–40.

Jaggar, A. M. (1983) *Feminist Politics and Human Nature*. Brighton: Harvester.

Jayawardena, K. (1986) *Feminism and Nationalism in the Third World*. London: Zed.

Kahn, A. and Jean, P. (1983) 'Integration and Elimination or Separation and Redefinition: The Future of the Psychology of Women', *Signs: Journal of Women in Culture and Society*, 8: 659–71.

Kalmuss, D., Gurin, P. and Townsend, A. (1981) 'Feminist and Sympathetic Feminist Consciousness', *European Journal of Social Psychology*, 11: 131–47.

Ker, M. (1983) 'Brides of Christ and of Poor Mortals: Women in Medieval Society', in P. Crawford (ed.) *Exploring Women's Past*. London: George Allen & Unwin.

Kessler, K. and McKenna, W. (1978) *Gender: An Ethnomethodological Approach*. New York: Wiley.

Klatch, R. (1988) 'Coalition and Conflict among Women of the New Right', *Signs*, 13: 671–92.

Koonz, C. (1987) *Mothers in the Fatherland: Women, the Family and Nazi Politics*. London: Methuen.

Kreps, B. (1973) 'Radical Feminism', in A. Koedt, E. Levine and A. Rapone (eds), *Radical Feminism*. New York: Quadrangle Books.

Leach, E. (1971) 'Two Essays concerning the Symbolic Representation of Time', in *Rethinking Anthropology*. University of London: Athlone Press.

Lévi-Strauss, C. (1966) *The Savage Mind*. Chicago: University of Chicago Press.

McFadden, M. (1984) 'Anatomy of Difference: Toward a Classification of Feminist Theory', *Women's Studies International Forum*, 7: 495–504.

Meyers, B. (1984) 'Minority Group: An Ideological Formulation', *Social Problems*, 32: 1–15.

Mitchell, J. (1976) 'Women and Equality', in J. Mitchell and A. Oakley (eds), *The Rights and Wrongs of Women*. Harmondsworth: Pelican.

Mitchell, J. (1986) 'Reflections on Twenty Years of Feminism', in J. Mitchell and A. Oakley (eds), *What is Feminism?* Oxford: Basil Blackwell.

Moscovici, S. (1972) 'Society and Theory in Social Psychology', in J. Israel and H. Tajfel (eds), *The Context of Social Psychology: A Critical Assessment*. London: Academic Press.

Oakes, P. (1983) 'Factors determining the Salience of Group Membership in Social Perception'. Unpublished Ph.D. thesis, University of Bristol.

Oakes, P. (1987) 'The Salience of Social Categories', in J. Turner et al., *Rediscovering the Social Group*. Oxford: Basil Blackwell.

Oakes, P. and Turner, J. (1986) 'Distinctiveness and Salience of Social Category Memberships: Is there an Automatic Perceptual Bias towards Novelty?' *European Journal of Social Psychology*, 16: 325–44.

Ortner, S. and Whitehead, H. (eds) (1981) *Sexual Meanings*. Cambridge: Cambridge University Press.

Potter, J. and Wetherell, M. (1987) *Discourse and Social Psychology: Beyond Attitudes and Behaviour*. London: Sage.

Raymond, J. (1986) *A Passion for Friends*. London: Women's Press.

Reicher, S. (1984) 'Social Identity and Social Change'. Paper presented at the Annual Conference of the Social Psychology Section of the British Psychological Society, Oxford, September.

Rich, A. (1976) *Of Woman Born*. London: Virago.

Roszak, B. (1969) 'The Human Continuum', in B. Roszak and T. Roszak (eds), *Masculine/Feminine*. New York: Harper & Row.

Sampson, E. (1977) 'Psychology and the American Ideal', *Journal of Personality and Social Psychology*, 35: 767–82.

Sampson, E. (1981) 'Cognitive Psychology as Ideology', *American Psychologist*, 36: 730–43.

Segal, L. (1987) *Is the Future Female?* London: Virago.

Smith, P. (1980) 'Language Variables in Intergroup Relations: The Voices of Masculinity and Femininity', Unpublished Ph.D. thesis, University of Bristol.

Tajfel, H. (1972) 'Introduction: Experiments in a Vacuum', in J. Israel and H. Tajfel (eds), *The Context of Social Psychology: A Critical Assessment*. London: Academic Press.

Tajfel, H. (1974) 'Social Identity and Intergroup Behaviour', *Social Science Information*, 13: 65–93.

Tajfel, H. (1975a) 'Social Psychology and Social Processes'. Paper presented at the Methods in Social Psychology conference, Bologna, December.

Tajfel, H. (1975b) 'The Exit of Social Mobility and the Voice of Social Change', *Social Science Information*, 14: 101–18.

Tajfel, H. (1978a) *Differentiation between Social Groups: Studies in the Social Psychology of Intergroup Relations*. London: Academic Press.

Tajfel, H. (1978b) *The Social Psychology of Minorities*. London: Minority Rights Group.

Tajfel, H. (1981) *Human Groups and Social Categories*. Cambridge: Cambridge University Press.

Tajfel, H. (1982) 'Instrumentality, Identity and Social Comparison', in H. Tajfel (ed.), *Social Identity and Intergroup Relations*. Cambridge: Cambridge University Press.

Taylor, D. and McKirnan, D. (1984) 'A Five-Stage Model of Intergroup Relations', *British Journal of Social Psychology*, 23: 291–300.

Turner, J. (1981) 'The Experimental Social Psychology of Intergroup Behaviour', in J. Turner and H. Giles (eds), *Intergroup Behaviour*. Oxford: Basil Blackwell.

Turner, J. (1982) 'Towards a Cognitive Redefinition of the Social Group', in H. Tajfel (ed.) *Social Identity and Intergroup Relations*. Cambridge: Cambridge University Press.

Turner, J. (1985) 'Social Categorization and the Self-concept', in E. Lawler (ed.), *Advances in Group Processes*, Vol. 2. Greenwich, CT: JAI Press.

Turner, J. (1988) 'Comments on Doise's "Individual and Social Identities in Intergroup Relations"', *European Journal of Social Psychology*, 18: 113–16.

Turner, J. and Giles, H. (1981) 'Introduction', in J. Turner and H. Giles (eds), *Intergroup Behaviour*. Oxford: Basil Blackwell.

Turner, J., Hogg, M., Oakes, P., Reicher, S. and Wetherell, M. (1987) *Rediscovering the Social Group: A Self-Categorization Theory*. Oxford: Basil Blackwell.

Warner, M. (1985) *Monuments and Maidens: The Allegory of the Female Form*. London: Pan.

Weedon, C. (1987) *Feminist Practice and Poststructuralist Theory*. Oxford: Basil Blackwell.

Wetherell, M. (1982) 'Cross-cultural Studies of Minimal Groups: Implications for the Social Identity of Intergroup Relations', in H. Tajfel (ed.), *Social Identity and Intergroup Relations*. Cambridge: Cambridge University Press.

Wetherell, M. (1986) 'Linguistic Repertoires and Literary Criticism: New Directions for a Social Psychology of Gender', in S. Wilkinson (ed.), *Feminist Social Pyschology: Developing Theory and Practice*. Milton Keynes: Open University Press.

Wetherell, M., Stiven, H. and Potter, J. (1987) 'Unequal Egalitarianism: A Preliminary Study of Discourses Concerning Gender and Employment Opportunities', *British Journal of Social Psychology*, 26: 59–71.

White, H. (1973) *Metahistory: The Historical Imagination in Nineteenth Century Europe*. Baltimore: Johns Hopkins University Press.

Williams, J. and Giles, H. (1978) 'The Changing Status of Women in Society', in H. Tajfel (ed.), *Differentiation between Social Groups*. London: Academic Press.

Winship, J. (1987) *Inside Women's Magazines*. London: Pandora.

Wollstonecraft, M. (1792) *Vindication of the Rights of Woman*. Reprinted 1978, Harmondsworth: Penguin.

3

A Place for Emotion in Social Identity Theory

Suzanne Skevington

While the subject of emotions pervades the content of the broad field of intergroup relations, affect has never been fully integrated into the study of the intergroup theory of social identity, which has used essentially cognitive methods to investigate intergroup conflict. In this chapter I first present evidence to suggest that there is an important place for the study of emotions within social identity theory, and then go on to indicate why, as a topic, emotions are particularly appropriate to studies of intergroup relations between the sexes.

Emotions and Intergroup Relations

Readers only need to pick up their daily newspaper to know about the range of emotions that can be expressed when intergroup behaviour is present. Emotive language used by religious groups in Northern Ireland, talk of the relations between Arab and Jew, football supporters commenting on their teams and other supporters after a match, and striking workers expressing their views about the management and other groups of workers in pay disputes provide a wealth of examples. These spontaneous accounts are certainly cognitive, but observation suggests that it is the powerful language of the emotions which seems to drive the hostility and animosity between groups to further and further episodes. So how is it that social identity theory is devoid of an analysis of emotions when it was designed directly to address these conflicts (Tajfel, 1972, 1974, 1978, 1982; Tajfel and Turner, 1979)?

Recently some authorities have recognized the omission of affect in relation to several areas of intergroup relations outside social identity theory. In an appraisal of the contact hypothesis, which looks at the effects of contact on relations between groups, Pettigrew (1986) has argued that emotions should be an integral part of its analysis. He describes (1986: 181) the seriousness of this omission for the contact hypothesis which deals primarily with antipathy towards groups: 'To treat intergroup contact as if it were dealing solely with cold cognition is to slight what makes the entire area of intergroup conflict problematic – its *heat*.' The same could be said of social identity theory.

The recent literature on intergroup behaviour too has been largely socio-cognitive, littered with only passing references to issues concerning the expression of emotions, and few researchers have devoted their efforts to investigating affect. An exception is the work of Konecni (1979), who believes that intergroup conflict is frequently precipitated by aversive events. He demonstrates how cognitions and affect are dynamic and interactive in the intergroup context, and sees emotions as a product of being able to ascribe a label to psychological and subjective changes associated with an increase in the level of arousal. He has shown that aversive events influence arousal and emotional states and also 'represent information that affects thoughts and attitudes, including those concerning the members of a group other than one's own' (Konecni, 1979: 85). These resulting schemata need to be incorporated into the attitudinal structure before they are acted on. So there is often a delay between the occurrence of an aversive event and its effects on aggression and conflict in intergroup situations. The residual effects of anger are usually negative responses, such as beliefs that others are threatening and feelings of resentment. Acknowledging Tajfel et al.'s (1971) powerful cognitive findings that merely dividing people into ingroups and outgroups is sufficient to lead to discriminative behaviour (see below), he does not claim that emotions are the exclusive answer to an analysis of intergroup conflict.

Another theory which has sought to integrate cognitions and emotions is realistic group conflict theory (RCT). Emphasizing the importance of goal relationships in intergroup relations it looks at whether people respond competitively or with cooperation to real or imagined group interests (Brown, 1988b). For instance, in a classic quasi-experiment on intergroup hostility and friendliness, boys in US summer camps were first grouped into teams to establish a social identity, then these teams engaged in a series of competitive activities which were followed by a period when superordinate goals were evoked to create cooperative situations (Sherif, 1966). Here cooperation increased friendliness following the hostilities of the competitive phase. Although competition and cooperation have been investigated within a social identity framework, this theory has never been fully displaced by social identity theory. RCT attempts to integrate affective with cognitive material, so concurring with observations of intergroup behaviour in real life as well as making scientific sense of these conflicts – Brown (1988b) provides a readable account of these two theories.

Turning to the literature of emotions, facets of intergroup relations have been investigated there which might have been more fully developed within social identity theory. An example is an analysis of emotions associated with relative deprivation (RD) by Mark and Folger (1984). Runciman (1966) distinguishes fraternal deprivation (social discontentment arising from comparisons between the ingroup with outgroups) from egoistic deprivation (personal discontentment which can occur when individuals compare their own situation with that of an individual ingroup or outgroup others). Relative deprivation in general was recognized as a precursor of intergroup conflict by Tajfel (1978), and Skevington and Lodge (1983) went on to point out that fraternal RD is probably more applicable to the development of social identity than egoistic deprivation.

So not only are intergroup theorists *outside* the social identity field considering the role of emotions in conflict, but some experts on affect perceive intergroup conflict to be an apt area for study. In the next section social identity theory and the role of emotions is examined.

Emotions and Social Identity Theory

In a major statement about social identity theory, Tajfel (1978: 63) defined social identity as 'that part of an individual's self-concept which derives from his (or her) knowledge of his (or her) membership of a social group (or groups), together with the value and emotional significance attached to that membership'. Tajfel also refers to the 'sense of belonging' reported by people who belong to groups (Tajfel, 1974), and this concept of attachment also has affective connotations. The intensity and qualities of these attachments were deemed to form the basis of the discriminatory behaviour which is at the heart of social identity theory. However, the emphases of laboratory studies which followed from this original definition were concerned more with the cognitions of discrimination that result from the processes of categorization and comparison (see Tajfel, 1978), while the important affective component in this definition was largely neglected. Relevant key volumes by Tajfel and others bear witness to this essentially cognitive history of laboratory work (Tajfel, 1978: Turner and Giles, 1981; Tajfel, 1982; Hogg and Abrams, 1988) and this line of thought still persists. For instance, Turner et al.'s (1987) self-categorization theory has recently reaffirmed and refined the exclusively cognitive stance *par excellence*. The pursuit of 'cold' cognitions continues in some quarters.

It is not clear how far Tajfel originally intended to integrate emotions into his theory. Finely articulated descriptions of intergroup conflict in real life pervade his writings (for example, Tajfel, 1978; Tajfel and Fraser, 1978) and suggest that he was exquisitely aware of the power of emotions in these situations. However, some of his earliest work with Wilkes on the categorization and evaluation of coin-sized objects indicates an initial interest in socio-cognitive phenomena that was to continue in the years that followed (Tajfel and Wilkes, 1963).

But at the same time that Tajfel's definition of social identity was being created, a new innovative methodology capable of assessing cognitive strategies of intergroup discrimination was published in a seminal paper demonstrating the design and use of matrices (Tajfel et al., 1971). This technique dominated the style of laboratory work in Bristol for much of the 1970s, so sustaining the socio-cognitive tradition in social identity research to the exclusion of many other potential methods.

The methodology consisted of several types of distribution matrices which were designed for use in 'minimal categorization' studies (see the Introduction to this volume); their results were compelling. They showed that 15-year-old boys were willing to discriminate against members of other groups even when they had no information about the groups other than which group they themselves belonged to. Furthermore, following allocation to a group, the boys not only discriminated against the outgroup, but did so even at the expense of their own group. These experiments were conducted so that the boys had no means of knowing the membership constitution of the ingroup or outgroup. Face-to-face interaction between members was prevented: the aim being to examine social categorization and social comparisons in their purest sense, so excluding the possibility that any sort of relationship between participants might be formed, no matter how temporary or superficial. Such relationships might have elicited emotions, thereby contaminating the power of these cognitive results.

While it was vital to the purposes of the 1971 study to exclude any affective elements to demonstrate the point that emotions are not quintessential to the expression of discrimination, this experimental departure served the purpose of perpetuating more laboratory work within a similar exclusively socio-cognitive mould. By concentrating on the cognitive aspects of differentiation and discrimination at the expense of affect, the laboratory studies which used the new methodology effectively operationalized only *half* the concept of social identity as originally defined (see page 42).

An integral part of any study of intergroup relations must take account of stereotyped attitudes which arise from categorizations and comparisons of social phenomena (Brown, 1988a; Tajfel and Fraser 1978, Chapter 17). Within social identity theory ideas about social categorization were underscored by parallel developments in the categorization of objects in the cognitive field (for example, Rosch, 1978). Stereotypes, like other attitudes, have three components which are cognitive (opinions, beliefs and ideas about the object of the attitude), affective (evaluative feelings of liking and disliking), and behavioural (involving verbal statements about behavioural intentions and overt actions) (Rosenberg and Hovland, 1960). While Tajfel (1982) rightly criticized investigations of stereotypes for providing an overly individualistic view of social behaviour (which is anathema to the much more social approach taken by social identity theory), he acknowledged stereotyped attitudes to be a valuable aid to explanations of social events and justifications for ingroup action. So while Tajfel (1978, Chapter 2) rejects this approach as a starting point for his intergroup theory, he does integrate two elements of their approach, namely cognitive and verbal aspects of the behavioural components, yet fails to tackle affect (Tajfel, 1982, Chapter 17).

A closer inspection of social identity theory shows that affective concepts pervade many of its paradigms and in most cases these have tended to remain peripheral without being developed empirically or theoretically. Scope for a study of emotions within a social identity framework is illustrated below. The first example is of a study where aspects of affect were measured but not acknowledged. Turner and Brown (1978) looked at the impact of in/stability and il/legitimacy on cognitions about social identity. They provided Visual Analogue Scales of dimensions such as friendly/unfriendly, warm/cold and likeable/unlikeable which they claimed were neither socio-emotional dimensions nor personality measures. Consequently, they did not use their results to develop theory on affect from these ostensibly affective measures. In any study of groups facing unstable and insecure conditions it is questionable how far it is possible to fully appraise actions without evaluating emotions such as collective fear and anxiety. Measures of these emotions need to be included in future studies.

Further examples indicate some areas of the theory where studies of affect might be profitably performed. For instance, social identity theory predicts that when low-status groups attempt to create social change and fail, a similar and comparable high-status group may respond in uncharacteristic fashion by being psychologically 'generous' to the lows, in what Tajfel (1978) describes as a *prise de conscience*. This *prise de conscience* is known to be cognitive from studies which show that under these conditions the highs are more positive about the lows than formerly, but this concept also implies a collective emotion of guilt although this has not been investigated.

To take a final example, high-status members identify more strongly with their group than lower-status members, and this degree of attachment contributes to the positivity of a group's social identity (Skevington, 1981). Consequently, in the event of attempts to change the status relations between groups, high-status groups may lose the valuable positive social identity that they have acquired and maintained and so tend to feel threatened by the potential loss of status (Tajfel, 1974). Loss of a positive social identity has powerful emotional consequences as the term 'threat' itself implies, and while Breakwell (1986) has looked at how people cope with threatened identities at a personal and interpersonal level, she has fallen short of developing affect at an intergroup level in her model of identity, threat and coping. These 'gut reactions' associated with achieving a better place for your group in society, and those evoked in defence of the group from impending change, seem to be focal to an understanding of the processes involved in social identification, so underlining the omission of a systematic approach to the integration of affect in the theory.

Having looked at a variety of laboratory studies on social identity theory, we go on to examine evidence of emotions in field studies of the theory.

Incorporating Emotions into the Social Context

Tajfel was part of an influential vanguard that succeeded in persuading British social psychologists of the 1970s to put back the social context into social psychology (Tajfel, 1972). So alongside the carefully designed and controlled studies emerging from the Bristol laboratory at that time grew a series of field studies conducted within their social context that were designed to test in practice what had been derived in theory. The theory was geared to resolving intergroup problems such as those found in race relations, but rather than examine conflict between blacks and whites in British cities like Leicester (where to investigate at that time might have fanned the flames of discontent), workers chose less contentious settings for ethical reasons, such as pay disputes between engineers (Brown, 1978) and changes in the training of nurses (Skevington, 1980, 1981).

An important characteristic of emotions is that they are situation-specific and therefore tend to be recognized by the situations in which they occur. This is known from studies which have looked at how people commonly deal with emotions: for example, one strategy of coping is explicitly designed to divorce the emotion from its situation or social context (Strongman, 1987). Affect is automatically introduced, therefore, by including the social context in studies of intergroup relations. Acknowledging the presence of affect expressed in a particular context is only one strand of this debate: a separate issue is whether or not this affect is measured. So if the measures chosen for field studies remain entirely cognitive, thereby imitating the style of laboratory methods, it becomes impossible to tap the important affective aspects of behaviour arising from the presence of a social context.

While laboratory workers aimed to remove or reduce the social context and largely ignored the contribution of emotions, field-workers were faster to recognize this omission as they were often confronted by evidence of affect in their data. Integrating the findings of field and laboratory studies in a review of similarity in intergroup relations, Brown (1984) focused on liking arising from attraction and frustration/aggression. He observed that 'it has usually been assumed, although on unclear theoretical grounds, that affective responses would simply covary with these . . . (cognitive aspects of intergroup behaviour)' (Brown, 1984: 610). Supporting the idea that cognition and affect are orthogonal dimensions, Brown cites data from outside social identity theory, using results on evaluation and attraction reported by Brewer and Campbell (1976) from a study of tribal groups in East Africa. While his review thoroughly examines liking and attraction (and to a lesser extent frustration), we remain in the dark about the gamut of other emotions known to arise from intergroup encounters, so an investigation of this range of emotions within the theory is overdue.

Some field studies have included measures of emotion. Skevington (1980) conducted a quasi-experimental study of social change between trained nursing groups. Cognitive ratings of ingroup, outgroup and self on relevant subjective characteristics were obtained, with estimates of the extent to which groups perceived the situation to be legitimate. Additionally, she included two affective measures of hostility from the Hostility and Direction of Hostility Questionnaire, which evaluates hostility towards self and others. The results showed that low-status nurses expressed more hostility than the highs, and an unpredicted finding was that lows expressed more hostility in cooperative than competitive situations. However, it is debatable how far this measure embraces the collective concept of intergroup hostility because it was designed for investigations of personality. The development of appropriate measures to examine affect in intergroup situations remains a challenge to those working in the area.

Some attempts have already been made in this direction. Brown et al. (1986) designed a comprehensive measure of group identification – probably the best so far available, and one which also incorporates affect. This 10-item scale integrates the three facets of social identity directly derived from Tajfel's (1978) definition quoted earlier, namely awareness of group membership (2 items) and evaluation and affect (4 items each). Two items of positive affect indicated 'gladness' to be a group member and 'having strong ties' with it. Negative affect was reflected by 'feeling held back' by the group and annoyance with it. It is debatable whether item 10, which deals with criticism of the group, might also have been included in the affective subgroup, as it seems to reflect negative affect as well as evaluation.

Studying factory workers, Brown et al. (1986) found only weak evidence to support the contention of social identity theory that strong identification predicts marked differentiation. Looking more closely at the identification process they found that 'the single most important and recurring aspect of group membership for our respondents were the interpersonal relationships within the group' (Brown et al. 1986: 284). They specify friendships with particular individuals and 'more general affiliative tendency' in support of this statement, and go on to suggest that an emotional attachment to the group and a cognitive self-definition of membership are necessary precursors to intergroup behaviour but 'are not in themselves sufficient to produce or explain the variety of different group responses in any particular context'. This research seems to point to the importance of investigating affect at all levels within social identity theory.

It is not just within their own familiar social context that people feel emotional about intergroup behaviour. Participants in laboratory studies can and do feel passionately about issues, particularly where meaningful and pertinent topics are chosen for discussion with the aim of engaging participation. In this way, quasi-experimental procedures bring aspects of real life into the laboratory by introducing an abbreviated form of the social context, and so provide a bridge between laboratory and field investigations. Examples of laboratory studies which seem likely to have generated a range of emotions which were not directly measured are provided by Reicher, where students with opposing views discussed vivisection or the Campaign for Nuclear Disarmament (Reicher, 1984, 1987). While Reicher's work provides good examples of the way the social context can be profitably integrated into a laboratory study to produce a more social social psychology (Armistead, 1974), at the same time it exemplifies a paradox within social identity theory, namely that while workers were trying to put the social context back into social psychology, they were also developing and pursuing cognitive methods and theory to the exclusion of affect. In doing this they remained blind to the fact that cognitive methods would only tap one element of the social context. To formalize the development of affect in the theory demands at best the development of new non-cognitive methods or, alternatively, modifications and adaptations of existing methods for investigating the type of collective affect appropriate to the more global and less individualistic demands of social identity theory. Without these affective measures the 'heat' generated by the social context in quasi-experimental and field studies will continue to be treated in a descriptive manner; as acknowledged background 'noise' which does not readily lend itself to analysis but which, optimistically, might help to interpret the findings of cognitive measures.

Those wishing to fully integrate an analysis of the different dimensions of the social context into social identity theory might derive useful skills from environmental psychologists about how to categorize relevant aspects of the social environment. At present there are no agreed rules which could be used firstly to guide selection of intergroup contexts suitable for specific purposes, and secondly to identify key variables that would enable systematic comparisons to be made of contextual material from different studies. Any such analytical framework would naturally need to be grounded in the theory itself.

Social identity theorists have not, of course, been unique in following the tradition of social cognition which dominated the social psychology of the 1970s, and recently interest has been revived in the interaction between cognitions and emotions outside the social arena. It has been suggested that emotional imagery and its meaning is stored in an emotion prototype (Lang, 1984) in much the same way as cognitive prototypes are stored. Also, there is evidence for emotion nodes in the memory with connections to facial muscles and the autonomic nervous system as well as to cognitive nodes (Gilligan and Bower, 1984). This appears to be one way of explaining how cognitions and emotions interact at an individual level and may serve as a basis for work looking at the integration of similar material at higher-order social levels. So a fusion between cognitions and emotions seems timely when looking at intergroup behaviour. Before developing theory about the emotions within social identity theory, the methods which might be suitable for use in studies of emotion in intergroup relations must be considered. But first the case for studying emotions in intergroup relations, particularly with reference to gender, will be elaborated.

Gender in Social Identity Theory

A theoretical statement by Williams and Giles (1978) was the first attempt to apply gender relations to the main features of social identity theory (see the Introduction to this volume), and their assumption that men are perceived as high-status and women as low-status groups has been commented on elsewhere in this book. Since then, Williams (1984) has developed a more elaborate thesis about sex differences in social identification. She shows how the style of social identity theory defined by Tajfel (1978), Turner (1981) and others was based on the assumption that differentiation arising from competition is quintessential to the expression of intergroup conflict. Adopting Bakan's terminology, she relabels this original formulation an *agentic* social identity, which she says, represents an individual or personal style of identification more commonly displayed by men. Contrasted with this she presents a case to show that groups may gain their social identity from relations with other social groups, not just from identification with the ingroup. While individuals do value aspects of being ingroup members, as Tajfel suggests, at the same time they may also value the relationships or affiliations they develop with members of relevant outgroups, and additionally from relationships which ingroup and outgroup may have with a third party. These valued relationships or attachments are described as a source of *communal social identity*, and Williams indicates that women are more likely to express this style of social identification than men.

While this concept of communality is a new and interesting idea in intergroup relations, the observation that women value personal relationships more than men is not completely new to social psychology. For example, women derive greater social self-esteem, by developing social relationships with others, than personal self-esteem (which is more individualistic), on scales such as the Carlson Adjective Checklist where it is possible to measure these components separately. Furthermore, Fransella and Frost (1977) suggest that one contributory reason for the 'underperformance' of women in their careers may be that they are more interested in developing successful social relationships with others, rather than working towards those goals which traditionally define job success for men; this is because developing relationships represent a major source of positive self-esteem for women. These investigations, arising from a more individualistic social psychology, appear to lend some validity to Williams' statement about sex differences in the processes of social identification.

In an empirical investigation of Williams' ideas, Skevington and Dawkes (1988) compared women in nursing with a male minority, looking at patients as a third party. Using samples carefully matched for age, qualifications and job status they found evidence of communal *and* agentic styles of identification in both sexes. The balance of the two styles for these groups appears to be determined not by sex *per se* but by the sex-role of the occupational group to which they belong. So, because nursing is seen as women's work, both women and men in nursing expressed high levels of communality in accordance with this female orientation. Additionally, they both showed low levels of agentic identification; men expressed slightly higher levels of agency than women, presumably as a result of their sex-role socialization. The data therefore indicate a more complex pattern than the one originally theorized by Williams, as both sexes express identifications which are agentic *and* communal, and the sex-role of the occupation they choose seems to influence whether agency or communality predominates within the group. As a consequence of these findings, groups where women are in a *majority* (as distinct from all-women groups) will be referred to as women-orientated groups (similarly male-orientated groups are those in which there is a majority of men) because the majority appear to have an important influence in determining which style of social identity predominates in the group. In the case of women-orientated groups this would be a communal social identity.

The concept of valuing relationships enshrined within the definition of a communal social identity certainly implies an evaluative aspect of intergroup relations, but in addition this concept implicitly involves an affective dimension. A contrast drawn from Williams' dichotomy concerns on the one hand positive affect associated with valuing relationships as an integral part of communality, and on the other negative affect arising from the hostilities of competition and discrimination associated with agency. So where intergroup relations are concerned, the world of women's work would seem to be a more affectively positive place to be (regardless of the person's sex) than the less affectively positive climate of groups where men are a majority. Unpublished data by Skevington and Dawkes show that men and women in nursing believe they do get on very well with each other, but the affective atmosphere of male-orientated groups needs to be examined more thoroughly in the future.

But is the positive affect arising from a communal social identity the result of being a part of a women-orientated group or because many such groups are also of low status? In one of the earliest field studies of social identity theory, Skevington (1981) selected two groups of women nurses in training and examined evidence for each of the main paradigms of the theory. She found that more positive characteristics were attributed to the high-status Registered nurses than to lower-status Enrolled nurses. A closer look at the data showed that characteristics attributed to the highs were more *task-related*, such as being intelligent, organized, confident and responsible, while the low-status group were mutually acknowledged to be superior on *socio-emotional* dimensions, such as being cheerful, thoughtful and happy (Brown, 1988a, b). In a Dutch study of nurses, Van Knippenberg and van Oers (1984) report similar results where higher-status academic nurses were viewed as superior on theoretical skills and lower-status psychiatric nurses on interpersonal skills. More detailed comparisons, separating sex from status, are not available as the sex breakdown of these groups was not recorded (Van Knippenberg, pers. comm.), but it is worth noting that in both these studies the socio-emotional characteristics recorded tend to reflect positive rather than negative affect. This suggests that low-status groups are more likely to express positive affect in a context where a communal social identity is evident.

This discussion of emotionality in women-orientated groups might, however, lead to the erroneous conclusion that women (and/or low-status groups) are more emotional than men. While it is impossible to make a definitive statement about low-status groups in this respect because the research is inconclusive, there is plentiful research on emotionality in women. Strongman (1987: 224) summarizing the position, says that

> There is very little evidence to support the view that women are more emotional than men. However they do tend to pay more attention than men to other people's emotions . . . they are more affected by them and perhaps might be regarded as more emotionally sensitive than men, although this is more speculative.

From a review he concludes that men react to emotion-evoking experiences primarily with physiological responses, whereas women are more likely to respond through verbal/cognitive channels. So, because men and women react differently to emotional experiences, it is impossible to say which sex reacts more, or which type of reaction is preferable.

We may learn from this that women are probably more aware of their emotions, have a capacity to express emotional reactions to situations and events, and value highly the emotionally bound relationships they create with others. Affective aspects of everyday life are particularly salient to women, and presumably this extends to the climate of women-orientated groups. To clarify, a higher level of emotionality is *not* being attributed to women and their groups here: the key issue is the high *degree of importance* that people in women-orientated groups give to affective aspects of their lives. It therefore seems likely that the extensive use of cognitive methods that has so far overshadowed studies of social identity effectively leaves untapped a major aspect of intergroup behaviour, namely emotions. And while most previous studies of social identity would have benefited from the inclusion of affective measures, it appears that this may have been a more serious omission for the study of some types of groups than others.

The way researchers conceptualize problems and the methods they ultimately choose reflect their ideology and interests within intergroup relations, as in other areas of social science. So it is perhaps not insignificant that sex differences, valued relationships, communality and, related to this, the emotions, have been identified and explored mainly by women researchers in this area. In contrast, studies of cognitions of social identity which have led the field so far have tended to remain the preoccupation of male researchers. It would also be fair to say that regardless of sex, research on social identity also tends to reflect white Anglo-Saxon thought and would benefit from a more pluralistic approach.

To examine the above ideas empirically, new methodologies incorporating dimensions of emotions seem to be called for in future studies of the valued relationships of a communal social identity. These techniques would need to tap representations of intergroup relations (Moscovici, 1988), rather than be unsuitably individualistic like the majority of techniques currently available for measuring emotions in social psychology. They would also need to complement appropriate cognitive techniques not displace them, so that an integrated socio-cognitive affective view of intergroup behaviour could be obtained.

Social Identity, Gender and Emotions

Studying emotions in intergroup relations presents difficulties because social psychologists researching emotions have tended to do so from the viewpoint of the individual person rather than from a truly social perspective. The field of social emotions has tended to reflect concerns with physiological, subjective and behavioural measures of emotions overlaid with a social flavour, instead of being geared to capture emotions generated by groups or in intergroup situations. In this section I present a case in support of the use of a social constructivist position in understanding and measuring emotions in intergroup relations. For social constructivists the meaning of the social context is paramount to their analysis, and this desire to integrate the social context concurs with one of the two original aims of social identity theory (Tajfel, 1972), although with references to the latter, it is debatable how far this aim has been achieved.

Constructivists like Coulter (1986) believe that people know about their own emotions better than observers, not because they have private access to their internal feelings (a traditional view in psychology), but because they cannot ignore the context of their own behaviour; while any observer must necessarily be ignorant of much of this context as it involves the person's history. Because of the context, in certain circumstances people feel 'entitled' to be angry rather than sad, for example. It therefore seems inappropriate for social identity researchers merely to describe the social context as they as observers perceive it, but techniques need to be found to enable the participants to record the context of their emotions and cognitions.

Using a constructivist perspective, Averill (1986) indicates occasions when affect can become particularly salient for group members. He suggests that people feel the need to access their emotions or 'get in touch with their feelings' when they move from one socio-cultural context to another. These shifts can take the form of a physical relocation such as immigration, economic movement such as in promotion or redundancy, or ideological moves such as a political or religious conversion. Emotional readjustments are required as old values are abandoned and new standards established and this process stimulates questioning about how far people are still in contact with their 'true' feelings. Acceptance by the new reference group involves authentication of the newly emerging emotions.

These changes in the context inevitably involve a concomitant shift between groups and, as a result of altered group membership, adjustments in intergroup relations. Strategies of social change between groups like the merger can require movement between contexts. In this case, both groups shift into a single new context which combines them both, and it seems possible that under these changing circumstances those merging may feel the need to get in touch with their feelings, so enhancing the affective component of intergroup relations at this time. Similarly, some differentiation strategies of social change which involve competition may also require movements into a new context. For this reason it seems particularly important to include affective measures in studies of social change.

Some methods of the social constructivists seem particularly adaptable to investigating the emotions in intergroup relations in general and social identity in particular. Using past experience to offer insight into the ways in which people construct themselves into existing relations, these techniques seem appropriate to investigations of sensitive issues such as gender relations, where it can be difficult to encourage self-disclosing accounts. Kippax et al. (1988) have adapted a new methodology called 'memory work' to look at how the cognitive features of knowing and understanding are intimately connected with emotions. Their rationale for using this method is that they believe that 'cognitivism fails to come to terms with the essentially social aspects of emotion since it is unable to shift the level of analysis from the individualistic or interindividualistic to the genuinely social' (Kippax et al., 1988: 20).

An established group generated their data by writing their memories of past experiences on a mutually negotiated topic or episode. Accounts of an early experience were written in the third person and (as far as possible) from the viewpoint of an outside observer. Collective reflections and theorizing allowed the processes involved to be revealed, and common factors running through the different accounts were noted, as well as contradictions, clichés, gaps and 'cultural imperatives'. This led to revisions of the group's ideas on this topic until an end-point was reached where a coherent picture emerged from the negotiations. The authors claim their method is sensitive to historical aspects and is based on shared feelings and the shared significance given to a shared circumstance. Furthermore, it enables participants to relate the unfamiliar to familiar aspects of their lives. They say we know about emotions because we actively search for meanings to life, negotiate these meanings with others, and reflect on these emotions using our own experience and by looking at the way others express their own experiences. They believe that this process is responsible for constructing the identity. If this is so, then social identities may be similarly constructed.

To give more details of Kippax et al.'s (1988) methodology: five academic women researchers (aged between 40 and 60) met fortnightly for 2 to 3 hours over 18 months. At each meeting they wrote an account of a memory and between meetings read the literature on emotions. From each session emerged a topic for discussion at the following session. Data for a discussion based on the topic of transgressions were appraised at two levels of analysis. Instead of the expected emotional themes of guilt and shame, the recollection revealed widespread puzzlement, hurt and indignation in accounts of events which had gone badly wrong at ages 4 to 11. These data were used to show how the emotions of self-righteousness and injustice are constructed.

The technique was designed to look at the creation of identities and it seems suitable for eliciting detailed collective information about social identities. One feature it shares with social identity theory is that it is designed to facilitate *comparisons* of experience, so eliciting valuable social comparisons. Memory work could be used to examine the varied range of social identities associated with particular groups by looking at representations of the ingroup and outgroups, thereby incorporating the emotions associated with these cognitions. A study of this nature is currently in progress. Elsewhere in this book (see Condor) social identity theory has been criticized for failing to take account of the history of people's social identities, and this technique seems particularly well-suited to remedy this omission.

Integrating Emotions into Gender Relations in Social Identity Theory

In a previous section it was shown how, regardless of their sex, people who work in a women's world have a predominantly communal social identity, and that this distinguishes them from male-orientated groups who are more likely to express the agentic style of social identity described by Tajfel. The key to this distinction appears to be whether within these groups there is an ethos of valuing the relationships with outgroup members and other third parties, or whether such relationships are seen as unimportant. We have seen that, at an individual level, women value social relationships more highly than men, so it is not surprising that these particular values are also a prevailing influence in the intergroup relations of women-orientated groups. These valued relationships appear to be more central to the social identity of women when they are working in occupations where women form a majority (in the numerical sense at least); and men who work beside them in such jobs seems to absorb these values too, presumably to become more acceptable as a minority (Skevington and Dawkes, 1988).

It is suggested here that in a context where relationships beyond the ingroup are valued, more positive emotions will be expressed than in contexts where groups do not value extragroup relationships. In order to value relationships between groups it is necessary to select positive information about those outside the ingroup to develop a positive affective scheme. In turn, this affective atmosphere may set the scene for the type of social change strategy which is ultimately adopted if status relations between the two groups become unstable. Groups who value relations with other groups are more inclined to cooperate rather than compete possibly because, in valuing the links, they seem likely to be more attracted to outgroup and third-party members than groups who are more orientated towards discrimination and competition. This positive affect generated by cooperation could also predispose such groups towards a merger in preference to other strategies of social change, given the precedent of working together rather than separately.

In groups expressing a predominantly agentic social identity, who do not value relationships with members of a similar outgroup or third-party member, the intergroup context may be affectively less positive or even negative. Negative affect among ingroup members seems more likely to facilitate competition and discrimination between groups than cooperation, and this affective climate may predispose groups to chose a strategy of distinctiveness to create social change, as extensively exemplified in studies by Tajfel and associates. In this atmosphere too, aversive events could precipitate greater hostility and greater differentiation between social groups, and act as an irritant in a context which is already negative – hence increasing the negativity of the affect in this context.

To summarize: it is being suggested here that the ethos of creating valued relationships, or not doing so, provides a collective schema for the group which is responsible for the affective atmosphere in intergroup relations, and enables the group to sift information and events connected with other groups. The nature of this powerful combination of socio-cognitive schema and emotions determines the

56 *Suzanne Skevington*

strategy of social change that the group might subsequently choose to use if unstable conditions arise. The empirical testing of these ideas calls for a suitable socio-cognitive affective technique and I believe that 'memory work' may be appropriate for this purpose. Investigations of women in intergroup relations and theorizing about them seems to have brought to light the shortcomings of using only cognitive measures to operationalize social identity when measures of affect are so clearly demanded. Because women are more inclined to value relationships with other people from groups other than their own, it seems possible that groups where women are in a majority may well turn out to provide a more positive climate in which to work for both sexes.

References

Armistead, N. (ed.) (1974) *Reconstructing Social Psychology*. Harmondsworth: Penguin.
Averill, J. R. (1986) 'The Acquisition of Emotions during Adulthood', in R. Harré (ed.), *The Social Construction of Emotions*. Oxford: Basil Blackwell.
Breakwell, G. (1986) *Coping with Threatened Identities*. London: Metheun.
Brewer, M. B. and Campbell, D. T. (1976) *Ethnocentrism and Intergroup Attitudes: East African Evidence*. New York: Halstead Press.
Brown, R. J. (1978) 'Divided we Fall: An Analysis of Relations between Sections of a Factory Workforce', in H. Tajfel (ed.), *Differentiation between Social Groups: Studies in the Social Psychology of Intergroup Relations*. London: Academic Press. pp. 395–430.
Brown, R. J. (1984) 'The Role of Similarity in Intergroup Relations', in H. Tajfel (ed.), *The Social Dimension*, vol. 2. Cambridge: Cambridge University Press. pp. 603–23.
Brown, R. J. (1988a) 'Intergroup Relations', in M. Hewstone et al. (eds), *Introduction to Social Psychology: A European Perspective*. Oxford: Basil Blackwell. pp. 381–412.
Brown, R. J. (1988b) *Group Processes: Dynamics within and between Groups*. Oxford: Basil Blackwell.
Brown, R. J., Condor, S., Mathews, A., Wade, G. and Williams, J. A. (1986) 'Explaining Intergroup Differentiation in an Industrialist Organization', *Journal of Occupational Psychology*, 59: 273–86.
Coulter, J. (1986) 'Affect and Social Context: Emotion Definition as a Social Task', in R. Harré (ed.), *The Social Construction of Emotions*. Oxford: Basil Blackwell.
Fransella, F. and Frost, K. (1977) *On Being a Woman: A Review of Research on how Women see Themselves*. London: Tavistock.
Gilligan, S. G. and Bower, G. H. (1984) 'Cognitive Consequences of Emotional Arousal', in C. E. Izard, J. Kagan and R. D. Zajonc (eds), *Emotions, Cognitions and Behaviour*. Cambridge: Cambridge University Press.
Hogg, M. A. and Abrams, D. (1988) *Social Identifications: A Social Psychology of Intergroup Relations and Group Processes*. London: Routledge & Kegan Paul.
Kippax, S., Crawford, J., Benton, P., Gault, U. and Noesjirwan, J. (1988) 'Constructing Emotions: Weaving Meaning from Memories', *British Journal of Social Psychology*, 27: 19–33.
Konecni, V. J. (1979) 'The Role of Aversive Events in the Development of Intergroup Conflict', in W. G. Austin and S. Worchel (eds), *The Social Psychology of Intergroup Relations*. Monterey, CA: Brooks-Cole.

A Place for Emotion in Social Identity Theory 57

Lang, P. J. (1984) 'Cognition in Emotion – Concept and Action', in C. E. Izard, J. Kagan and R. B. Zajonc (eds), *Emotions, Cognitions and Behaviour*. Cambridge: Cambridge University Press.

Lazarus, R. S. (1976) *Patterns of Adjustment*, 3rd edn. London: McGraw-Hill/ Kogakusha.

Mark, M. M. and Folger, R. (1984) 'Responses to Relative Deprivation: A Conceptual Framework', in P. Shaver (ed.), *Review of Personality and Social Psychology: Emotions, Relationships and Health*, vol. 5. Beverly Hills: Sage. pp. 192–218.

Moscovici, S. (1988) 'Notes towards a Description of Social Representations', *European Journal of Social Psychology*, 18: 211–50.

Nicholson, J. (1984) *Men and Women – How Different are They?* Oxford: Oxford University Press.

Pettigrew, T. F. (1986) 'The Intergroup Contact Hypothesis Reconsidered', in M. Hewstone and R. J. Brown (eds.), *Contact and Conflict in Intergroup Encounters*. Oxford: Basil Blackwell. pp. 169–95.

Reicher, S. (1984) 'Social Influence in the Crowd: Attitudinal and Behavioural Effects of De-individuation in Conditions of High and Low Group Salience', *British Journal of Social Psychology*, 23: 341–50.

Reicher, S. (1987) 'Crowd Behaviour as Social Action', in J. C. Turner et al. *Rediscovering the Social Group: A Self-Categorization Theory*. Oxford: Basil Blackwell. pp. 171–202.

Rosch, E. (1978) 'Principles of Categorization', in E. Rosch and B. B. Lloyd (eds), *Cognition and Categorization*. Hillside, NJ: Erlbaum.

Rosenberg, M. J. and Hovland, C. I. (1960) 'Cognitive, Affective and Behavioural Components of Attitude', in C. I. Hovland and M. J. Rosenberg (eds,), *Attitude, Organization and Change*. New Haven, CT: Yale University Press.

Runciman, W. G. (1966) *Relative Deprivation and Social Justice*. London: Routledge & Kegan Paul.

Sherif, M. (1966) *Group Conflict and Cooperation*. London: Routledge & Kegan Paul.

Skevington, S. M. (1980) 'Intergroup Relations and Social Change within a Nursing Context', *British Journal of Social and Clinical Psychology*, 19: 201–13.

Skevington, S. M. (1981) 'Intergroup Relations in Nursing', *European Journal of Social Psychology*, 11: 43–59.

Skevington, S. M. and Dawkes, D. A. (1988) 'Minorities at Work: Men in a Woman's World', in D. A. Canter et al. (eds), *Environmental Social Psychology*. London: Kluwer. pp. 272–80.

Skevington, S. M. and Lodge, E. (1983) 'Choices in Intergroup Relations'. Unpublished manuscript, University of Bath.

Strongman, K. T. (1987) *The Psychology of Emotion*, 3rd edn. Chichester: Wiley.

Tajfel, H. (1972) 'Experiments in a Vacuum', in J. Israel and H. Tajfel (eds), *The Context of Social Psychology: A Critical Assessment*. London: Academic Press.

Tajfel, H. (1974) 'Intergroup Behaviour, Social Comparison and Social Change'. Unpublished Katz–Newcombe lectures. University of Michigan, Ann Arbor.

Tajfel, H. (ed.) (1978) *Differentiation between Social Groups: Studies in the Social Psychology of Intergroup Relations*. London: Academic Press.

Tajfel, H. (ed.) (1982) *Social Identity and Intergroup Relations*. Cambridge: Cambridge University Press.

Tajfel, H. and Fraser, C. (eds) (1978) *Introductory Social Psychology*. Harmondsworth: Penguin.

Tajfel, H. and Turner, J. C. (1979) 'An Integrative Theory of Social Conflict', in W. Austin and S. Worchel (eds), *The Social Psychology of Intergroup Relations.* Monterey, CA: Brooks-Cole.

Tajfel, H. and Wilkes, A. L. (1963) 'Classification and Quantitative Judgement', *British Journal of Psychology*, 54: 101–14.

Tajfel, H., Flament, C., Billig, M. and Bundy, R. P. (1971) 'Social Categorization and Intergroup Behaviour', *European Journal of Social Psychology*, 1: 149–78.

Turner, J. C. (1981) 'The Experimental Social Psychology of Intergroup Behaviour', in J. C. Turner and H. Giles (eds), *Intergroup Behaviour.* Oxford: Basil Blackwell.

Turner, J. C. and Brown, R. J. (1978) 'Social Status, Cognitive Alternatives and Intergroup Relations', in H. Tajfel (ed.), *Differentiation between Social Groups: Studies in the Social Psychology of Intergroup Relations.* London: Academic Press.

Turner, J. C. and Giles, H. (eds) (1981) *Intergroup Behaviour.* Oxford: Basil Blackwell.

Turner, J. C., Hogg, M. A., Oakes, P. J., Reicher, S. and Wetherell, M. (1987) *Rediscovering the Social Group: A Self-Categorization Theory.* Oxford: Basil Blackwell.

Van Knippenberg, A. and van Oers, H. (1984) 'Social Identity and Equity Concerns in Intergroup Perceptions', *British Journal of Social Psychology*, 23: 351–61.

Williams, J. A. (1984) 'Gender and Intergroup Behaviour: Towards an Integration', *British Journal of Social Psychology*, 23(4): 311–16.

Williams, J. A. and Giles, H. (1978) 'The Changing Status of Women in Society: An Intergroup Perspective', in H. Tajfel (ed.), *Differentiation between Social Groups: Studies in the Social Psychology of Intergroup Relations.* London: Academic Press. pp. 431–46.

4

Differential Association: Social Developments in Gender Identity and Intergroup Relations during Adolescence

Dominic Abrams

An emphasis on male–female relations has recently become more popular in the gender literature, in which the theorizing tends to focus on personal relationships, sex stereotypes and gender identity (Ashmore and Del Boca, 1986). There is also a tacit acceptance of developmental stage type models which explain changes in relations between the sexes during adolescence and beyond in terms of intra-individual changes, rather than vice versa (Katz, 1986). The purpose of the present chapter is to re-examine the nature of some of these changes, and to suggest that they may be understood in terms of more *social* psychological processes than current theories consider. The focus is not so much on cognitive, moral or sexual development, as on the way that social context and intergroup relations between the sexes may shape gender identity over time. As gender is often one of the core aspects of identity it is obviously important to understand the way that it becomes incorporated into the self-concept. The term 'gender identity' in this chapter is used to refer to subjective femininity and masculinity. In turn, what individuals perceive to be masculine and feminine is based on their beliefs about the social categories (men/boys and women/girls).

This definition accepts both that sexuality is an historically constructed social phenomenon (Weeks, 1986)[1] and that people and cultures combine to produce many different definitions of gender-related dimensions. Thus, gender identity – 'a basic phenomenological sense of one's maleness or femaleness' (Spence, 1985: 92) – cannot be measured against the yardsticks of social consensus (for example, global sex-stereotypes), biology (sex), or distributional data (psycho-metrics). It is essentially a matter of social comparison in specific contexts, as I shall go on to suggest.

Sex categorization enables people to behave towards one another on the basis of cultural stereotypes concerning the associated sex-roles and characteristics (cf. Tajfel, 1978, 1981). The *development* of gender identity and behaviour in terms of sex categories is of particular interest because the content and relevance of gender stereotypes may change as the individual grows older (cf. Del Boca and Ashmore, 1981). People are categorized both by sex and age, and must maintain a sense of self which is congruent with their present age and social context, while at the the same time preparing for *change* in what they are expected and allowed to do by others. Thus, developmental 'tasks' of understanding self and society (Hart and Damon, 1985) are overlaid with the social tasks of establishing public personae, anticipating future roles, maintaining a satisfactory self-image, and acting as a social agent who has relationships, commitments and interests in common with others.

Given that changes in the content of self-categorization, and its relationship to identity may be central features of adolescent development, it seems appropriate to explore Tajfel and Turner's (1979) social identity theory as a framework for understanding how and why such changes occur. Another reason for adopting a social identity theory approach is that it explicitly raises the problem of how individuals relate to society in terms of both their group memberships and as individuals. In so doing, it can go beyond cognitive-developmental (Kohlberg and Ullian, 1974), social learning (Mischel, 1966), or social cognition (Bem, 1981) perspectives on gender identity. For example, emphasis on cognitive processes leads to rather bizarre suggestions such as raising 'gender aschematic children' as a way of reducing the gender schematizing influences of culture and biology (Bem, 1985), and thus eventually eliminating sexism. This seems somewhat akin to proposing that conflict can be resolved by making opposing parties 'conflict aschematic'. Moreover, the idea that thinking in terms of gender is purely a cognitive-developmental process misses the point that people can be, and are, led to think of themselves as members of new social categories all the time (witness the rise in hostility towards Argentinians amongst English people during the Falklands war). Therefore, the content and form of self-categories are established through *social* processes, while it is their sophistication which may depend on an individual's cognitive development (see Emler, 1987, for similar ideas). Perceiving the world in terms of gender *may* reinforce traditional distinctions, but it can equally be the basis for recognizing inequalities and striving for change. Bem's (1985) ideas would seem to depict gender schematicity as an individual difference variable over which people have no control. It entails a cognitive orientation which traps individuals. This view ignores both the child's active participation in constructing gender, and the existence of a real intergroup relationship between males and females. As M. Sherif (1966) pointed out, intergroup relations have properties of their own and are not the product of individual group member's personalities. From a social identity perspective, relations between the sexes can be seen as an integral part of the construction of gender identity, not simply a consequence of it.

C. Sherif's (1982) point that there has been relatively little research on intergroup relations between the sexes reflects the fact that there has been little theorizing at the intergroup level of analysis, and that which has appeared considers rarely the actual nature of relations *between* males and females (but see Ashmore and Del Boca, 1986), preferring to concentrate on the processes underlying the maintenance of positive female identity (for example, Condor, 1984; Huici, 1984; Williams, 1984; Williams and Giles, 1978). That there has until recently been relatively little work on gender identity among social identity researchers also reflects the fact that the theory was not originally developed to deal with social relations as complex as those between the sexes (Condor and Abrams, 1984). It seems reasonable to argue that the utility and generality of the social identity approach would benefit from such an analysis. This may contribute to a fuller social psychological model of gender identity.

Social Identity Theory

Tajfel and Turner (1979) proposed that behaviour can be conceptualized as lying on a continuum – from group/intergroup to personal/interpersonal. At the group end, actions are determined by social identity – identification with social groups or categories. At the interpersonal end, actions are determined by 'personal identity' – idiosyncratic aspects of the self, personality and so on. Most of the theoretical work has concerned intergroup contexts, and much of the empirical work has involved experimentally created groups (for example, see Hogg and Abrams, 1988 and Turner and Giles, 1981 for reviews). Owing to this emphasis there has been a tendency for group identification to be viewed as a transient phenomenon whose impact on behaviour is a function of factors such as situational salience (Oakes, 1983) and focus of attention (Abrams, 1985). When a social identification is salient individuals are said to behave in terms of their group membership. They regard both others and themselves in terms of the stereotypical attributes of the groups to which they are perceived to belong (Turner, 1985). The theory also embraces more enduring social identifications (Tajfel, 1978), such as with an ethnic group. Irrespective of the groups or categories providing the content of social identity, a fundamental motivation is a need for positive self-esteem (Tajfel and Turner, 1979). This creates a desire for positive distinctiveness for the ingroup, *vis-à-vis* the outgroup. That is, individuals seek to make their group different from and better than the outgroup on dimensions which are of importance or value to the ingroup. It is this need for positive distinctiveness which is said to underlie mutual ingroup favouritism and intergroup discrimination between equal status groups.

Social identity theory also deals with relations between unequal groups, particularly minority/majority groups. Members of minority groups are motivated to achieve a positive identity but may be denied the material resources necessary to compete with the majority. Within such contexts, minority members' actions may reflect one of two 'belief structures'. A 'social mobility' belief structure has as its premise a belief that boundaries between the groups are permeable, and that it is possible for individuals to 'pass' from one group to the other (by fulfilling entrance requirements, for example). However, when the boundaries are believed to be fixed it is more likely that group members will hold a 'social change' belief structure. This is based on the view that the individual can only improve his or her self-image if the group as a whole can raise its status in certain ways. It has been argued that social mobility beliefs typically precede social change beliefs, and that the latter are the basis for collective action (Taylor and McKirnan, 1984). The forms of action outlined by Tajfel and Turner (1979) include assimilation of the group as a whole; 'social creativity' (redefining the dimensions which are relevant for intergroup comparisons to provide a more favourable outcome for the ingroup, or changing the value attached to existing dimensions to regard them more positively); and 'social competition' (trying to excel on consensually valued dimensions so as to beat the outgroup). Where groups are perceived as being relatively similar, or the differences as being illegitimately favourable towards one group, or relations as lacking status stability (that is, 'insecure'), social comparison between groups and social change belief structures are most likely to arise (Turner and Brown, 1978).

This theoretical framework has not totally escaped criticism. For example, Brown and his colleagues (Brown and Williams, 1984; Williams, 1984) have noted that identification with a group does not always lead to intergroup differentiation or discrimination. Furthermore, Abrams and Hogg (1988) have argued that there is no *necessary* link between differentiation and self-esteem. A variety of other motives may quite easily mediate between group identification and intergroup behaviour. With regard to the sexes, Williams (1984) has argued that research has been biased towards a male 'agentic' model of social identity and intergroup relations, and has not systematically explored or explained sex differences in intergroup behaviour. Williams' view is that male groups adopt intergroup strategies which enhance their distinctiveness whereas females tend to concentrate on strengthening intragroup cohesiveness and communality (cf. Bakan, 1966; Gilligan, 1982; but also see Turner's, 1984, argument that intergroup distinctiveness and ingroup cohesiveness are part of the same process).

Along with these considerations there are three other extensions to the theory that contribute to the present analysis of gender identification. The first of these is that it may be feasible to treat interpersonal behaviour/personal identity and intergroup behaviour/social identity as orthogonal continua (Stephenson, 1981) and not as opposite ends of a single dimension (Brown and Turner, 1981). It is likely that individuals engage in and display both personal and social categorical aspects of their identity at the same time, not only in bargaining and negotiation (Stephenson, 1981), but also when relating to members of the opposite sex (Abrams and Condor, 1984). For example, a man could be an utterly devoted husband (interpersonal relationship), but refuse to allow his wife to pursue a career because he feels that as a man he should be the breadwinner (intergroup relationship).

The second extension is to dissociate identification with a group from any particular ideology concerning that group (Condor, 1984). Condor and Abrams (1984) argue that the feminist sociologist division of women into identified (radical) and non-identified (traditional) sub-groups (Firestone, 1970) represents an unwarranted imposition of Marxist class interpretation on to women's sex group identification. The implication is that those with traditional sex-role ideology, in failing to perceive socio-economic inequalities between the sexes, will not have any collective consciousness or social identification with women. However, evidence suggests that holding a traditional/radical sex-role ideology can be orthogonal to adopting a collective/individual orientation. Thus, treating women as a minority group (for example, Hacker, 1951) with, at one extreme, no collective consciousness (Simmel, 1955) or with negative social identity (Federici, 1975) and, at the other, a radical 'social change' orientation (Williams and Giles, 1978) misrepresents the facts (see Condor, 1986).

The third extension concerns the developmental aspects of social identity. Social identity theory is avowedly *dynamic*, but its proponents have tended to depict intergroup relations as snapshots rather than motion pictures. Intergroup behaviour is often seen as based on motives and desires in the *present*. Yet, in the case of sex group membership and gender identification, the constraints are quite different since the nature of identification with one category (sex) is continually modified by identification with another (age), and membership of both is inescapable. More crucially, individuals are *aware* that they must undergo transitions in role and that the likely future is already mapped out through observable relations between older people.

Beyond these extensions the problem for social identity theorists is to account for the way that one of the clearest criteria for distinctive group memberships (sex) can also be the basis of the most intimate human relationships. An examination of the social developmental aspects of relations between the sexes and gender identification seems likely to illuminate the relevant processes.

The Development of Gender Identity in Childhood and Adolescence

From a social identification perspective several questions arise. What changes occur in the nature of identification with one's sex between the ages of 7 and 17? How do these changes relate to the onset and establishment of attraction to members of the opposite sex? What is the nature of the relationship between gender identification and feelings of self-worth? To what extent do the answers to these questions differ for males and females? Del Boca and Ashmore (1981: 190) have noted that

> cognitive-developmental theorists concerned with sex-role development agree that beliefs regarding the characteristics of the sexes are closely related to gender identity. Very little research, however, has been directed at explicating the nature of the relationship between these constructs.

It is also true that the connection between gender identity and intersex behaviour has not been researched in much detail, despite the good theoretical reasons for doing so. An overview of two developmental patterns which are of particular importance (gender and sex-role development; and same-sex and opposite-sex friendships among males and females) is presented below.

Development of Identity and Concurrent Friendship Patterns
Research on gender identity development in childhood seems to show that both males and females follow a similar pattern up to the age of about 11. At about the age of 6, gender is seen by the child as immutable and is linked to specific physical attributes: 'When Jimmy abandons the belief that he can be a mother, he also abandons the belief that he can be a nurse or a secretary or can wear girl's clothes or play with feminine dolls' (Kohlberg and Ullian, 1974: 212). At this age gender may prescribe activities but it does not appear to be a conscious part of the self-concept; it is not spontaneously mentioned in children's self-descriptions (McGuire and McGuire, 1982). Children of both sexes tend to be identified mostly strongly with mother and/or with significant other individuals (Lynn, 1969, 1981). Essentially, children

know what gender category they belong to but do not appear to have a sense of identification with that category (McGuire and McGuire, 1982), Nevertheless, even at the age of six, children tend to ascribe socially desirable attributes more to their own than to opposite gender (Albert and Porter, 1983). As they get closer to the age of 11 or so, children seem to attach increasing emotional significance to their gender, perhaps in response to the combination of parental reinforcement of sex-role differentiation, the influence of teachers (Fagot, 1979), television (Durkin, 1985), siblings (Katz and Rank, 1981), and peers. Social behaviour rather than physical attributes becomes the most important focus of sex differentiation. There is increasing intolerance of, and unwillingness to engage in, 'cross-gender' behaviour (Carter and McCloskey, 1984). Friendship patterns also change during childhood. Among 6-year-olds, mixed-sex friendships are not uncommon (Kanous et al., 1962), but among 11-year-olds friendships are almost totally limited to same-sex peers (Broderick, 1966; Dunphy, 1972; Katz, 1979).

An interview study of 100 primary school children's perceptions of boys and girls (Abrams, in preparation) revealed that sex differentiation is not a unidimensional process. Its content changes with age, and it operates differently at intergroup and interpersonal levels. Representative examples illustrate this point. In the extracts which follow each quote in response to a particular question is from a different speaker.

The majority of 5-year-olds when asked 'what do you think about boys/girls?' gave descriptive, rather than evaluative, answers. Liking was based on behavioural similarity, and past/future relationships were explained as relational 'facts' without reference to process. It is *because* they are different that boys and girls don't mix. In girls' views,

'boys scratch, fight and wear trousers', 'boys are naughty'; 'they're horrid'; 'girls are better than boys, girls can all skip and boys can't'; 'girls are gooder than boys'; 'girls wear pretty clothes and bumble bee dresses.'

Boys think themselves better too:

'[Boys] do things quite like I do, and girls don't'; 'boys can run faster, they have shorter hair, they're much stronger than girls'; 'boys are better than girls, I think. Girls have got dollies and boys haven't'; 'Girls are different to boys, I hit them sometimes'. 'Boys don't have dolls, girls have dolls'. 'Girls have long hair'; 'I don't think girls are very good, I only like Rebecca'; 'I don't think girls are strong enough'; 'girls are sometimes a bit bossy.'

By the age of 8, children are more sophisticated. Girls see boys as

'OK, sometimes'; 'there are some I don't like because they're a bit babyish'; 'they're messy'; 'they're tougher'; 'some are nice and some are horrible';

'most of them are horrid . . . because they're naughty all the time'; 'they fight more than girls do.'

Boys maintain that girls are

'Dumb'; 'rubbish'; 'horrible'; 'they can be a menace or nice'; 'they're not very good, they're teacher's pet'; 'some are quite nice'; They're 'not that bad, I don't like them that much . . . Boys are excellent'. Girls are 'a little bit soppy'; 'they muck up games.'

There is agreement about the nature of differences but a sharp division on the value attached to those differences. Boyishness and girlishness are only attractive to boys and girls, respectively.

By the age of 11, girls are more generous and more circumspect:

Boys are 'alright'; 'depends what boys'; 'some are a bit rough . . . I'm a bit rough myself . . . some are quite fun, they don't say "you're a girl so you're quite stupid"'. Girls are 'not so boisterous as boys, and seem to like girly things like dolls and things like that, but I don't like those very much'; 'they're good fun, I don't like them when they're playing with dolls and everything. They don't get into a bad mood like boys.'

Boys too are less dogmatic:

Girls are 'alright'; but 'not as good as boys, they're not so good at football'; 'I don't see what's wrong with them but they sometimes get in my way.'

Despite this increase in generosity of spirit children also gain a greater appreciation of an intergroup divide and the complexity of future interpersonal relationships.

The majority of 5-year-olds either did not know what 'boys think about girls' (and vice versa), or reiterated their personal views. The 8-year-olds were aware that 'most boys think they're better than girls', while girls 'think they're better than boys', that boys are 'wallies' who 'think [girls] are stupid'. The two groups think the other is 'horrible'. The 11-year-olds, in contrast, recognize the *basis* for antipathy. Boys think girls

'may not like us very much – we do things that are different to them . . . they always think they push us around a lot, we think they're soppy' . . . 'some girls like boys if they've got a boyfriend', while boys 'don't mix with [girls] – because they're girls, I suppose'; 'they don't really like them spoiling their games and things.'

Girls know that boys see them as

'soppy'; 'dainty'; 'pretty and sheepish, [girls] play with dolls all the time, and they're tell-tale-tits'. Some boys are seen to 'like girls, but not very many – they sort of go around kicking you'. Meanwhile, girls think boys are 'horrible, because they're too rough'; 'not very nice – all my friends think that'; 'they normally hate them, but Kate doesn't. She loves them, she's got a lot of boyfriends.'

The distinction between boys and girls and boyfriends and girlfriends is an important one, as it paves the way for the maintenance of intersex relations in both intergroup and interpersonal terms simultaneously. The children were asked if they had any opposite-sex friends; if they had more, the same or fewer when they were younger; and if they would have more, the same or fewer as they got older.

Five-year-olds tend to say they have fewer opposite-sex friends than before they started school, citing physical separation from old friends as the reason. There was no consensus on what the future held, nor any appreciation of what would determine any changes. The 8-year-olds begin to refer to contexts and relationships in accounting for changes. Opposite-sex friends are more often relations or friends from preschool days. They are aware that the sexes are segregated, and that this is more intense than when they were younger:

> 'I used to play with younger boys but I play with girls now'; I don't know them [opposite sex] any more'; 'I was kissed once when I was little'; 'I used to have more when I was a baby'; I knew them better when I was little, I saw them more'; 'I don't know her any more, even though she's in the same class.'

Meanwhile, the future also involves changes but the majority are unclear about them:

> 'You do more things with a boy'; 'because I'll know more, probably'; 'maybe more, maybe less'; 'less, because you don't meet them very much'. 'I expect [to know more]... because you get married when you're older'; 'you have a house and all different friends'; 'most people have at least one, I don't know whether I will or won't'; 'I've got one girlfriend and she's a lady – we went on a picnic, [but] I hope not [to have more] – I don't like girls.'

These references to heterosexual and romantic relationships are infrequent, but the 8-year-olds do seem to be conscious of the changes in patterns of sociability which accompany changes in age and circumstance.

The 11-year-olds are quite clear that their social patterns are changing, reflecting on their previously small number of opposite-sex friends:

> 'I mix better'; '[girls] like me more. In the first year they weren't like that because they always played silly games like skipping and we played football'; 'when I was younger I used to think it was stupid having friends who were girls'; 'I was very shy, so I just played with my friends – they were all girls'; 'I've grown up quite a bit. I like more boy things.'

They are also alert to the role constraints of growing older, establishing relationships and so on:

> 'After I'm grown up I'd get them'; 'when you get to know friends now, when they grow up you get to know their sisters; and other friends you make, you

know their wives and children'; 'If I was married I wouldn't have so many girlfriends'; 'I hope I have more because I don't want to stay stuck at home all the time'; 'you just get more mature – to like them – it's just a sort of acting'; 'in the seniors they don't say "oh well, you're boys, don't play with girls", so there will be more boys to play with.'

These data are consistent with those of Newson and Newson (1986) who reported that around the age of 11 most friends were same sex, but a number of children had *a* 'romantic' opposite-sex friend. That is, an interpersonal, primarily partner-orientated, layer of relationship becomes both acceptable and socially sanctioned (for example, by parents in Newson and Newson's study). As Schofield (1981: 71) found, children 'do not seem concerned about the potential contradiction that boys and girls are not sufficiently similar to be friends, and their intention to form deep and long lasting romantic and sexual relationships in the future'.

In general, it seems that both the gender identities and friendship patterns of boys up to the age of 11 simply mirror those of girls. Models of adolescent development converge in claiming that, between the ages of 10 and 18, identification moves from parents to peers (Broderick, 1966: Coleman, 1980; Elkind, 1967; Erikson, 1968; Rosenberg, 1985). However, the work of the McGuires (McGuire and McGuire, 1982) on the self-concepts of children in the USA, and of Coleman (1974) in Britain, suggests that male and female identities begin to emerge in different *ways*. While both sexes perceive themselves more in terms of broad social categories as they get older, girls become more 'people-orientated' than boys (Gilligan, 1982; Hendry, 1983). They dissociate themselves from their parents at a slightly younger age (11) (Lynn, 1969; Musgrove, 1964), as well as doing so in a less overtly conflictual way, focusing more on being oneself and having 'some autonomy with respect to one's feelings and thoughts' (Coleman, 1974: 39). The evidence suggests that girls may learn to adopt a different orientation to dealing with potential conflict than boys do, consistent with Williams' (1984) ideas.

It appears that the age of 12 is generally a watershed. Children begin to doubt the immutability of their sex-roles (Kohlberg and Ullian, 1974) and to demonstrate a growing concern with how they wish to enact their role. For example, they become increasingly concerned with physical attractiveness and sexuality (Hendry, 1983; Katz, 1979) and, later on (from the age of 15 upwards) with issues such as careers (in males) and marriage (in females) (Eccles, 1985; Hesse-Biber, 1985; Katz, 1986). Of course, there are variations from this pattern.

Katz (1986: 43) has argued that in early adolescence (12 to 15 years old) the earlier onset of puberty among girls 'makes within-sex bonding more likely during this time because same-sex developmental experiences are more similar'. However, since similarity within sex continues to increase and that between sex to decrease, Katz's reasoning does not fit with the subsequent establishment of pair relationships. Moreover the pattern is asymmetrical for boys and girls. Heterosexual contacts increase for both sexes after the age of 14, but there seems to be a two-year lag. For example, Broderick (1966) found that 13-year-old girls were going out with (older) boys, whereas 13-year-old boys retained exclusively same-sex friendships. Douvan and Adelson (1966) also observed that while girls were actively dating by the ages of 15 or 16, boys were not catching up until the ages of 17 to 19, by which time both sexes have many heterosexual friendships and a reduced dependence on the same-sex peers (Abrams, 1988). Heterosexual couples become the norm (Katz, 1986). There appears to be no generally accepted explanation for either the apparently dramatic change in friendship preferences or the lag between males and females in this change (Johnson and Aries, 1983; Whiteley et al., 1984). Moreover, there seems little apart from socialization theories to explain the persistence of different values among males and females, through adolescence (for example, Eccles, 1985; Ford and Lowery, 1986; Mackie, 1983).

An Intergroup Perspective

Research into normal adolescent social development has previously focused mainly on personal and interpersonal behaviour (for example, Leahy, 1985). The emphasis was on reference persons rather than reference groups (for example, Rosenberg, 1985). Clearly, this underemphasizes the inter*group* consequences of belonging to a sex category. One of the few authors, apart from C. Sherif (1984), to address the intergroup dimension of relations between boys and girls is Schofield (1981). She has compared black/white and male/female relations, and concludes that 'whereas relations with gender outgroups are profoundly influenced by the expectation of future positive ties, relations between blacks and whites are shaped by the history and present existence of racial separation, hostility and discrimination in our society' (Schofield, 1981: 85). While it is doubtful that the history and existence of racial antipathy is more deep-rooted than that of sex differentiation, it is interesting to note that childhood relationships are in fact more segregated by sex than by race or ethnicity. Schofield, moreover, had probably underestimated the degree of sex segregation in adulthood.

From the point of view of social identity theory, sex category identification and intergroup social comparison would make it increasingly important to make one's own category distinctive and positive in relation to the other category. Achieving this over a period of time depends on collaboration among all those who share a given category. This may be the motivation behind the degree of 'mutual antagonism' which seems to exist between boys and girls up to the age of 13 or so. Intersex antagonism between children appears to involve 'social' rather than 'realistic' competition (Turner, 1975) as the stakes are symbolic (ingroup kudos, self-esteem, affirmation of self-concept as 'male' or 'female') and neither group has much to gain in real terms. Such antagonism would be predicted by social identity theory to occur between groups which perceived themselves as having an *equal* claim to positively valued resources.

Boys and girls up to this age feel they may legitimately compete (in education, for example) on equal terms. Girls are often initially more successful than boys but, later on, lag behind in educational attainment (Anyon, 1983; Mahoney, 1985; Sutherland, 1981). Furthermore it has been proposed that from the ages of 11 to 14, boys become relatively more positive about their gender than do girls (Lynn, 1969; McGuire and McGuire, 1982). What is happening, according to some theorists (for example, Sarah et al., 1980; Shaw, 1976) is that males are encouraged to adopt characteristics which are socially valued, such as ambitiousness and determination, whereas females are ascribed less desirable characteristics such as compliance, passivity and deference. Although this picture may be biased by the fact that most of the relevant research has focused only on educational and occupational indices, it does suggest that changes occur at the group level. During adolescence, the 'criterial' stereotypic attributes of the sexes seem to diverge dramatically, one consequence being that it is no longer perceived as consensually legitimate (or stereotypically appropriate) for girls to engage in explicit intergroup competition and conflict with boys.

Traditionally, this divergence has been described in terms of women's individual responsibilities (such as in relation to their family or home) as against the corporate responsibilities of men (government, defence, unions). For example, Simmel (1955) pointed out that men engage in conflicts and sustain memberships of male groups through work and leisure (cf. Willis, 1977), whereas women adopt specific roles which are usually defined by interpersonal rather than group relations (see also McPherson and Smith-Lovin, 1986). They are likely to use their gender identity to invoke normative interpersonal behaviour rather than as a source of positive distinctiveness (Mackie, 1983). Other evidence suggests that from the age of about 13, boys retain a belligerent intergroup orientation towards girls, whereas girls begin actively to establish interpersonal relationships with older boys. This is consistent with an assumption that boys' gender contributes positively to their self-image because it allows them to compare themselves favourably with girls (Shaw, 1976). This comparison is presumably based not on the performances of individual boys and girls in the classroom, but on the stereotypic characteristics of boys and girls and men and women in general (Fennema, 1980). Here, social identity is the crucial factor. It is by comparing at the *intergroup* level that boys are able to gain their positive academic self-image in relation to girls (Abrams et al., 1985; Eccles, 1985).

Correspondingly, some evidence suggests that girls are *decreasingly* likely to make competitive comparisons with boys in traditionally masculine-valued areas because to do so at the group level may produce a negative self-image (Blackstone, 1976). However, at least initially, it is the *nature* of girls' intergroup comparisons which changes, rather than the extent of those comparisons. It would be a mistake simply to equate winning and losing in the educational field with the presence of 'negative' or 'positive' social identity. The developmental differences in association and attraction between the sexes provides a normative context which prescribes future 'positive' attributes for each sex.

Thus it is also necessary to explain why it is that one category appears to behave as a cohesive social group while the other does not. Obviously, the notion of intergroup relationships between the sexes is inappropriate if, as some of the literature suggests, females adopt a purely interpersonal orientation. A closer inspection of the two groups helps to resolve this problem.

Females
To the casual observer, the two-year lag between males' and females' shift to heterosexual relationship preferences could be entirely attributable to girls' earlier onset of puberty (cf. Katz, 1986). In fact, this pubertal lag is relevant, but neither a necessary nor sufficient cause of the social lag (for a summary of arguments surrounding biological explanations see Kenrick, 1987). The McGuires' studies of children's 'spontaneous self-concepts', in which they asked children to answer the question 'tell us about yourself', are relevant here. Children defined themselves by their more distinctive characteristics. Thus, for example, being the only black, the only person who had red hair, or being a member of a numerical minority would mean that those aspects of oneself featured more saliently in the self-concept.

Critics of the distinctiveness explanation of identity salience have argued that salience does not have direct implications for social behaviour (Abrams, 1985); that the self-categorization in question must have social meaning and relevance (Oakes, 1983); and that self-image salience is more likely to be socially created than determined by objective distinctiveness (Condor, 1984). Nevertheless, it seems probable that girls' earlier sexual development sensitizes them to their sex identity since it represents both a further departure from their broad physical similarity with boys, and a departure from their previous self-image. At the group level sexuality may become defined as a 'criterial attribute' of being female just *prior* to the average age of onset of puberty. This is because group attributes can come to be 'prototypical' not because they represent the average position but because they best represent the way *that* group is different from other groups (Turner, 1985). Both early and later developers among girls are likely to regard themselves in sexual terms once sexuality becomes a salient feature of their group.

If the onset of puberty in girls acts as a social marker which catapults them into a new subjective age category, it may in turn alter the stereotypic attributes of their sex category. It is no longer a simple matter of competing with boys across the board. Instead, most girls seem to polarize towards 'femininity' and away from 'masculinity'. For example, girls tend to withdraw from the arena of academic competition for career-orientated skills between the ages of 12 and 16, particularly if they are working class (King, 1987). This does not mean, though, that girls withdraw from all intersex comparison. Instead it seems likely that they attempt to gain positive distinctiveness over own-aged boys in terms of feminine-valued characteristics (typically including beauty, gentleness, supportiveness, sensitivity and so on). Among aspiring middle-class youth this is reflected by differentiation in choice of academic subjects. Females veer towards arts and males towards science and maths, despite the lack of objective differences in ability in these domains (Abrams et al., 1985; Eccles, 1985). Among the most important of the criteria for becoming a 'woman' may be the establishment of interpersonal relationships with men (Schofield, 1981). Thus, issues of attractiveness, desirability, sexuality, and so on become more relevant for females (Huston and Ashmore, 1986), and suitability for the role of 'female partner' is increasingly salient. However, it could be argued that this orientation may lead to the female 'group' becoming dissipated and less cohesive (counter to Katz's assumption that puberty could make girls more cohesive).

In fact, although girls do tend to spend decreasing amounts of time in groups (Hendry, 1983) it would be a mistake to regard this a reduction in group salience. Group cohesiveness is not only derived from interdependence, interpersonal attraction or face-to-face communication, but from the perception of shared category membership. Indeed, that one does not have to be among women to feel like a woman is illustrated by research such as that on distinctiveness and solo status (Cota and Dion, 1986): one's gender tends to be *more* salient when one is in the gender minority. Moreover, the existence and nature of the category 'women' is continuously reinforced, sustained and redefined through media images, discourse and practice. Even among girls who cease to relate to each other in physical groups it is likely that identification with their sex category is possible, thus sustaining it as a 'psychological group' (Hogg and Abrams, 1988).

The nature of girls' interpersonal relationships creates an additional possibility; that they maintain intergroup superiority over own-aged boys, even in terms of some 'desirable' masculine traits. Girls may achieve this in part by 'basking in the reflected glory' of their (generally older) boyfriends. Going out with older boys may create a positive gender identity for girls both by providing external validation of girls' femininity, and because associations with high-status older boys provide confirmation of maturity over own-aged boys.

It is also possible that affiliation with older boys might eventually result in a negative sense of sex identity for girls. They may find that, because they are younger than their boyfriends, they are also subordinate. Taken together with an awareness that most males eventually attain higher status than most females, girls may begin to experience increasing dissatisfaction with traditionally defined gender identity. Gender comes to denote status, and in turn be defined by status (Wagner et al., 1986).

The psychological possibilities raised by the process of restructuring aspects of being female, and doubts over the appropriateness of the nature of previous intergroup comparisons, can be represented by the four sex-role ideology/sex-role identification quadrants outlined by Condor and Abrams (1984). These are traditional–non-identified, radical–non-identified, traditional–identified and radical–identified. First, within a traditional ideology, if 'negative' aspects are properties of the group, rather than the individual, it would be possible to not identify with the category 'women', to operate purely on an inter-personal level; to identify with a male partner (de Beauvoir, 1968); to treat the family as the prime social group (cf. Stroebe and Stroebe, 1984); and to ignore the possibility of comparing with men at the level of the group. Data from a large-scale survey of 16- to 19-year-olds in Britain (Bynner, 1987) revealed that those spending more time in traditional domestic relationships expressed more traditional sex-role attitudes (Abrams, 1988). In contrast, within a more radical ideology, a non-identified girl could decide to strive to succeed purely as an individual, to challenge attempts to treat her in a sex-typed way, but not wish to engage in collective action to change the position of women in general (Kalmuss et al., 1981).

Positive identification with the group may be expressed in quite different ways. In the context of a traditional ideology there will be a polarization towards extreme femininity, valuing the traditional differences between sex groups (having a sense of 'womanhood' (Chafe, 1977)), and perhaps even emphasizing them in order to increase attractiveness to boys at the interpersonal level. Identification with the group in this way will not entail any sense of intergroup conflict with males (cf. Mummenday and Schreiber, 1983). Studies in which female subjects have been found to hold traditional sex-role attitudes support the idea that when their gender is salient they are more likely to adopt traditionally sex-typed behaviour and attitudes (Abrams et al., 1985; Abrams, Thomas and Hogg, in submission; Hogg and Turner, 1987). In contrast, those with a radical or feminist sex-role ideology see their future position in society as being constrained by an iniquitous intergroup relationship. Condor (1984) found that individuals in this quadrant favoured social comparison with men and supported moves towards greater equality of roles and status (that is, they had more 'social change' type of belief structures). Moreover, radical sex-role attitudes sem to be more extreme in 16- to 19-year-old females among those who spend time in groups rather than with partners or family (Abrams, 1988), suggesting that group processes may sustain this ideology.

Given that traditional sex-role ideology is dominant in Western culture, it is understandable that the potential disparity between interpersonal and intergroup relations between males and females is not usually apparent. At the intergroup level social identity may operate to preserve the distinctions between roles of the sexes (cf. Huici's 1984 discussion of the justification functions of sex-role stereotypes), and the dissimilarities may even serve to reduce the likelihood of competitive intergroup comparison arising (Brown and Abrams, 1986). Within a complementary intergroup relationship, which discriminates against females economically, interdependent interpersonal relationships are built up in which each partner supplies the needs of the other. However, the traditional economic dominance of men may also render them less materially dependent on interpersonal relationships with the opposite sex, which may be one reason why the development of sex identification among boys is less orientated towards establishing such relationships.

Males
It is likely that the onset of girls' puberty also increases the salience of sexuality in the eyes of boys. At 13, boys view same-age girls predominantly in terms of developing sexuality (Broderick, 1966; Schofield, 1981). There are strong pressures to maintain maximum differentiation from same-age girls whose entry into puberty may pose a threat that accentuates the intergroup division. Indeed, boys of this

age (13) appear to be overtly and blatantly sexist, to become increasingly clannish and to spend all of their time with same-sex peers. Initially, it is likely that they deride the girls in order to both gain ingroup esteem *and* to devalue the status of older boys. Hence at the age of 13, boys' antipathy towards girls may increase.

The secure and dominant male group identity probably becomes consolidated when males reach puberty and gender identity reaches maximum salience (Leventhal, 1970). Unlike females, males only stand to gain from continuing to make intergroup comparisons between the sexes on previously established consensually valued dimensions. By the age of 15 or so, boys are 'allowed' to engage in heterosexual relationships at the interpersonal level without having to compromise their intergroup orientation to girls. If anything, it is likely that the redefinition of self which follows from the change in age category tends to enhance the positive aspects of being traditionally 'male'. Boys will perceive and anticipate increasing power, responsibility and status *vis-à-vis* girls. Certainly, between 16 and 19, males in general maintain a very significantly more traditional sex-role ideology than females (Abrams, 1988). Having a younger (less statusful) female partner becomes one of the criterial attributes of being a 'man' (Spence, 1985). Although there appear to be few data available it seems likely that male sex group identification is greatest among those holding a traditional sex-role ideology, as it is the males spending time in groups who hold the most traditional attitudes (Abrams, 1988). In contrast, a radical sex-role ideology may entail some degree of disidentification since it implies a belief in the loss of status and security of the position of the ingroup. It also tends to be associated with greater personal commitment to non-masculine activities such as housework (Abrams, 1988).

Into Adulthood

While sexual maturation is not necessarily a main determinant of gender identity, it provides a focal point around which the intergroup and interpersonal *construction* of gender identity takes place. Sexual maturity is important in gender identity development only to the extent that it is salient and imbued with social meaning. Age-related changes in identity may be inevitable, but the transition points are rather arbitrarily defined by events such as changes of school level, leaving school, starting work and so on (Honess, 1985). Among young adolescents, for whom representations of gender are simplified and sometimes extreme, the abstract intergroup relationship is realizable as the two groups find themselves to be of equal size, status and power, while also forced into daily 'contact' (even if this contact is actually only proximity). As they get older, far from dissolving, the intergroup tension becomes refocused in terms of role differentiation (Mackie, 1983; Parsons and Bales, 1955), and takes different forms. Primary friendships are overwhelmingly same-sex, even into very late adolescence (Silbereisen et al., 1986), and males are consistently more likely to hold traditional sex-role attitudes than females (Abrams, 1988).

Perhaps the most significant evidence is the massive degree of sex segregation both in the occupational structure (Bielby and Baron, 1984) and in the voluntary sector. McPherson and Smith-Lovin (1986: 77) conclude that voluntary organizations 'act to maintain the status differences that such segregation implies, by creating networks of weak ties that restrict men's and women's resources to the domains that are traditional for each'. Yet this begs the question of *why* men and women find such segregation rewarding or valuable, and why they become involved in sex-segregated activities despite commitments to the opposite sex in the roles of spouse and parent. It seems reasonable to suggest that social identification is a powerful force in sustaining the segregation of the sexes.

In arguing that a social identity approach is most usefully adopted in conjunction with a developmental perspective a number of problems for the theory have also been highlighted. For example, it lacks any model of how members of social groups deal with predictable and inevitable change in their nature over time. Gender is cross-cut by age and eventually by marital and parental status, each of which are anticipated and prepared for, albeit unrealistically. Furthermore, change and development in gender identity probably continues throughout the lifespan and a social identity approach could be applied usefully at later life stages (Condor and Abrams, 1984).

The present characterization of sex group relations has employed Condor's (1986) analysis in suggesting that reactions to these changes depend partly on sex-role ideology and identification. However, no attempt has been made to explain in any detail from where these ideologies emerge (cf. Anyon's 1983 discussion of sex roles and social class) nor to explore the problem of change in the status quo. The dominant ideology of some cultures precludes the possibility or relevance of making intersex comparisons (see Kahn's 1976 discussion of purdah in Asia). Under such conditions sex-segregation seems not dissimilar to racial segregation and slavery. Yet, unlike most other intergroup situations, that between sexes involves intimate contact. Perhaps there is a lesson for researchers on the contact hypothesis here (see Hewstone and Brown, 1986). Contact between men and women seems to have little impact on intergroup differences in power and status, but that may be because the contact is confined to interpersonal domains where the intergroup aspects are concealed.

Salient intergroup differences often produce a polarization between each group (Skinner and Stephenson, 1981). There are some data which tentatively support this assumption with regard to the sexes where being in a numerical minority can increase gender salience. For example, Leventhal (1970) found that men who only had sisters were more masculine than were men who only had brothers. Dworkin and Dworkin (1983) found that the presence of all-male sexist groups produced increased cohesion, approval of feminine attributes, and anti-male feelings among groups of women with whom they were competing. Finally, Abrams et al. (1985) found that females the majority of whose siblings were male were particularly likely to have abandoned science subjects at school (a polarization effect). Intersex relations are unique in that they involve interaction at both the intergroup and the interpersonal levels at the same time. Yet previous allusions to this fact have tended to emphasize the concrete nature of interpersonal relationships and the abstract nature of the intergroup dimension, which has been used to represent society, culture and so on (Archer and Lloyd, 1982; Del Boca and Ashmore, 1986). It is more probable that both levels coexist and have a psychological reality. Indeed, the interpersonal relationships seem to play an important part in sustaining the intergroup relationship and vice versa. Role differentiation and interdependence evidently reinforce intergroup differentiation, often to the dissatisfaction of women in traditional relationships (Belsky et al., 1986; Mackie, 1983).

The evidence discussed above raises problems for Brown and Turner's (1981) characterization of personal and group relations as falling on opposite ends of a continuum, as it is by no means clear that one implies the opposite of the other, especially in terms of relations between the sexes. It would seem necessary to employ a model which accounts for the simultaneous existence of both forms. This is certainly possible in Stephenson's (1981) formulation whereby group and personal relationships (and identifications) can be orthogonal, but it may also be compatible with Turner's (1985) self-categorization theory if one accepts that different levels of self-categorization (from the broad and abstract 'female', through sub-categories such as 'girl', to idiosyncratic self-schema such as 'ballerina') are compartmentalized and remain psychologically discrete. This latter view would lead to a greater emphasis on issues of variations and changes in salience, whereas Stephenson's requires a more textured view of group and personal relations in varying status of convergence and divergence. It is difficult, at present, to decide which model will be most useful as no direct comparisons have yet been published.

In conclusion, intergroup relations between the sexes can be seen to be an important part of the social construction of gender identity. The intergroup dimension increasingly becomes interwoven with inter-personal relationships with age, and the consequences of this appear to differ for males and females. Specific social contexts (such as sibling constellation, sex segregation of schooling and patterns of affiliation) modify the form and outcome of these processes, as reflected in variations in degrees of sex identification, sex-role ideology and behaviour. Throughout all this is sustained a simultaneous intergroup and interpersonal relationship between the sexes. Thus, a problem is posed for theories at each level.

It is hoped that this chapter has gone part of the way in answering C. Sherif's (1982) explicit call for an understanding of gender identity in intergroup terms, and that this perspective will provide an exciting and fruitful set of questions for future research.

Note

1. No attempt has been made to include homosexuality in the present outline, but there is no reason why it can not be seen in its intergroup dimensions (Abrams, Carter and Hogg, in press).

References

Abrams, D. (1985) 'Focus of Attention in Minimal Intergroup Discrimination', *British Journal of Social Psychology*, 24: 65–74.

Abrams, D. (1988) 'Sex Role Ideology, Siblings and Educational Attainment: Social and Psychological Factors'. Paper presented at the ESRC 16–19 Initiative First Findings Workshop, Harrogate, July 8–11.

Abrams, D. (in preparation) 'Boys and Girls: The Group and Individual Aspects of Gender Differentiation'.

Abrams, D. and Condor, S. (1984) 'A Social Identity Approach to Understanding Sex-identification in Adolescence'. Paper presented at the International Conference on Self and Identity, Cardiff, July.

Abrams, D. and Hogg, M. A. (1988) 'Comments on the Motivational Status of Self-esteem in Social Identity and Intergroup Discrimination', *European Journal of Social Psychology*.

Abrams, D., Carter, J. and Hogg, M. A. (in press) 'Perceptions of Male Homosexuality: An Application of Social Identity Theory', *Social Behaviour*, special issue on Male Sexuality.

Abrams, D., Sparkes, K. and Hogg, M. A. (1985) 'Gender Salience and Social Identity: The Impact of Sex of Siblings on Educational and Occupation Aspirations', *British Journal of Educational Psychology*, 55: 224–32.

Abrams, D., Thomas, J. and Hogg, M. A. (in submission) 'Numerical Distinctiveness, Social Identity and Gender Salience'.

Albert, A. A. and Porter, J. R. (1983) 'Age Patterns in the Development of Children's Gender-role Stereotypes', *Sex Roles*, 9: 59–67.

Anyon, J. (1983) 'Intersections of Gender and Class: Accommodation and Resistance by Working Class and Affluent Females to Contradictory Sex-role Ideologies', in S. Walker and L. Barton (eds), *Gender, Class and Education*. Lewes: Falmer Press.

Archer, J. and Lloyd, B. (1982) *Sex and Gender*. Harmondsworth: Penguin.

Ashmore, R. D. and Del Boca, F. K. (eds) (1986) *The Social Psychology of Female–Male Relations: A Critical Analysis of Central Aspects*. New York: Academic Press.

Bakan, D. (1966) *The Quality of Human Existence*. Chicago: Rand McNally.

Belsky, J., Lang, M. and Huston, T. L. (1986) 'Sex-Typing and Division of Labour as Determinants of Marital Change across the Transitions to Parenthood', *Journal of Personality and Social Psychology*, 50: 517–22.

Bem, S. L. (1981) 'Gender Schema Theory: A Cognitive Account of Sex-typing', *Psychological Review*, 88: 354–64.

Bem, S. L. (1985) 'Androgyny and Gender Schema Theory: A Conceptual and Empirical Integration', in R. A. Sonderegger (ed.), *Nebraska Symposium on Motivation, 1984*. Lincoln, NE: University of Nebraska Press. pp. 179–226.

Bielby, W. T. and Baron, J. N. (1984) 'A Woman's Place is with Other Women: Sex Segregation in Organizations', in B. Roskin (ed.), *Sex Segregation in the Workplace: Trends, Explanations, Remedies*. Washington DC: National Academic Press.

Blackstone, T. (1976) 'The Education of Girls Today', in J. Mitchell and A. Oakley (eds), *The Rights and Wrongs of Women*. Harmondsworth: Penguin.

Broderick, C. B. (1966) 'Socio-sexual Development in a Suburban Community', *Journal of Sex Research*, 2: 1–24.

Brown, R. J. and Abrams, D. (1986) 'The Effects of Intergroup Similarity and Goal Interdependence on Intergroup Attitudes and Task Performance', *Journal of Experimental Social Psychology*, 22: 78–92.

Brown, R. J. and Turner, J. D. (1981) 'Interpersonal and Intergroup Behaviour', in J. C. Turner and H. Giles (eds), *Intergroup Behaviour*. Oxford: Basil Blackwell.

Brown, R. J. and Williams, J. A. (1984) 'Group Identification: The Same Thing to All People?' *Human Relations*, 37: 547–64.

Bynner, J. (1987) 'Coping with Tranisition: ESRC's New 16–19 Initiative', *Youth and Policy*, 22: 25–8.

Carter, D. B. and McCloskey, L. A. (1984) 'Peers and the Maintenance of Sex-typed Behaviour: The Development of Children's Conceptions of Cross-gender Behaviour in their Peers', *Social Cognition*, 4: 294–314.

Chafe, W. H. (1977) *Women and Equality: Changing Patterns in American Culture*. New York: Oxford University Press.

Coleman, J. D. (1974) *Relationships in Adolescence*. London: Routledge & Kegan Paul.

Coleman, J. D. (1980) *The Nature of Adolescence*. London: Methuen.

Condor, S. G. (1984) 'Womanhood as an Aspect of Social Identity'. Unpublished doctoral thesis, University of Bristol.

Condor, S. G. (1986) 'Sex Role Beliefs and "Traditional" Women: Feminist and Intergroup Perspectives', in S. Wilkinson (ed.), *Feminist Social Psychology*. Milton Keynes: Open University Press.

Condor, S. G. and Abrams, D. (1984) 'Womanhood as an Aspect of Social Identity: Group Identification and Ideology'. Paper presented at the International Conference of Self and Identity, Cardiff, July.

Cota, A. A. and Dion, K. L. (1986) 'Salience of Gender and Sex Composition of Ad-hoc Groups: An Experimental Test of Distinctiveness Theory', *Journal of Personality and Social Psychology*, 50: 770–6.

de Beauvoir, S. (1968) *The Second Sex*. New York: Jonathan Cape.

Del Boca, F. K. and Ashmore, R. D. (1981) 'Sex Stereotypes through the Life Cycle', in L. Wheeler (ed.), *Review of Personality and Social Psychology*, vol. 1. London: Sage.

Del Boca, F. K. and Ashmore, R. D. (1986) 'Male–Female Relations: A Summing Up and Notes towards a Social-Psychological Theory', in R. D. Ashmore and F. K. Del Boca (eds), *The Social Psychology of Female–Male Relations: A Critical Analysis of Central Concepts*. New York: Academic Press. pp. 311–32.

Douvan, E. and Adelson, J. (1966) *The Adolescent Experience*. New York: Wiley.

Dunphy, D. C. (1972) 'Peer Group Socialization', in F. J. Hunt (ed.), *Socialization in Australia*. Sydney: Angus & Robertson.

Durkin, K. (1985) *Television, Sex Roles and Children*. Milton Keynes: Open University Press.

Dworkin, R. J. and Dworkin, A. G. (1983) 'The Effect of Intergender Conflict on Sex-role Attitudes', *Sex Roles*, 9: 49–57.

Eccles, J. (1985) 'Sex Differences in Achievement Patterns', in R. A. Dienstbier and T. B. Sonderegger (eds), *Nebraska Symposium on Motivation, 1984*. Lincoln, NE: University of Nebraska Press. pp 97–132.

Elkind, D. (1967) 'Egocentrism in Adolescence', *Child Development*, 38: 1025–34.

Emler, N. P. (1987) 'Socio-Moral Development from the Perspective of Social Representations', *Journal for the Theory of Social Behaviour*, 17: 371–88.

Erikson, E. (1968) *Identity, Youth and Crisis*. London: Faber & Faber.

Fagot, B. I. (1979) 'Play Styles in Early Childhood: Continuity and Change as a Function of Sex'. Paper presented at the meeting of the International Society for the Study of Behavioural Development, Lund, Sweden, June.

Federici, F. (1975) *Wages against Housework*. Bristol: Falling Wall Press.

Fennema, E. (1980) 'Success in Maths'. Paper presented at Sex Differentiation and Schooling Conference, Churchill College, Cambridge, 2–5 January.

Firestone, S. (1970) *The Dialectic of Sex: The Case for Feminist Revolution*. New York: Jonathan Cape.

Ford, M. R. and Lowery, C. R. (1986) 'Gender Differences in Moral Reasoning: A Comparison of the Use of Justice and Care Orientations', *Journal of Personality and Social Psychology*, 50: 777–83.

Gilligan, C. (1982) *In a Different Voice: Psychological Theory and Women's Development*. Cambridge, MA: Harvard University Press.

Hacker, H. (1951) 'Women as a Minority Group', *Social Forces*, 30: 60–9.

Hart, D. and Damon, W. (1985) 'Contrasts between Understanding Self and Understanding Others', in R. L. Leahy (ed.), *The Psychology of the Self*. New York: Academic Press. pp. 151–78.

Hendry, L. B. (1983) *Growing Up and Going Out: Adolescents and Leisure*. Aberdeen: Aberdeen University Press.

Hesse-Biber, S. (1985) 'Male and Female Students' Perceptions of their Academic Environment and Future Career Plans: Implications for Higher Education', *Human Relations*, 38: 91–105.

Hewstone, M. R. C. and Brown, R. J. (eds), (1986) *Contact and Conflict in Intergroup Encounters*. Oxford: Basil Blackwell.

Hogg, M. A. and Abrams, D. (1988), *Social Identifications: A Social Psychology of Intergroup Relations and Group Processes*. London: Routledge.

Hogg, M. A. and Turner, J. C. (1987) 'Intergroup Behaviour, Self-stereotyping and the Salience of Social Categories', *British Journal of Social Psychology*, 26: 325–40.

Honess, T. (1985) 'Situated Identities'. Paper presented at the Annual Conference of the British Psychological Society, April.

Huici, C. (1984) 'The Individual and Social Functions of Sex Role Stereotypes', in H. Tajfel (ed.), *The Social Dimension*, vol. 2. Cambridge: Cambridge University Press.

Huston, T. L. and Ashmore, R. D. (1986) 'Women and Men in Personal Relationships', in R. D. Ashmore and F. K. Del Boca (eds) *The Social Psychology of Female–Male Relations: A Critical Analysis of Central Concepts.* New York: Academic Press. pp. 167–210.

Johnson, F. L. and Aries, E. J. (1983) 'Conversational Patterns among Same-sex Peers of Late-adolescent Close Friends', *Journal of Genetic Psychology*, 141: 225–38.

Kahn, V. S. (1976) 'Purdah in the British Situation', in D. L. Barker and S. Allen (eds), *Dependence and Exploitation in Work and Marriage.* Harlow, Essex: Longman.

Kalmuss, C., Gurin, P. and Townsend, A. (1981) 'Feminist and Sympathetic Feminist Consciousness', *European Journal of Social Psychology*, 11: 131–47.

Kanous, L. E., Daugherty, R. A. and Cohn, T. S. (1962) 'Relation between Heterosexual Friendship Choices and Socioeconomic Level', *Child Development*, 33: 251–5.

Katz, P. A. (1979) 'The Development of Female Identity', *Sex Roles*, 5: 155–78.

Katz, P. A. (1986) 'Gender Identity: Development and Consequences', in R. D. Ashmore and F. K. Del Boca (eds), *The Social Psychology of Female–Male Relations: A Critical Analysis of Central Concepts.* New York: Academic Press. pp. 21–68.

Katz, P. A. and Rank, S. A. (1981) 'Gender Constancy and Sibling Status'. Paper presented at the meeting of the Society for Research in Child Development, Boston, April.

Kenrick, D. T. (1987) 'Gender, Genes and the Social Environment: A Biosocial Interactionist Perspective', in P. Shaver and C. Hendrick (eds), *Sex and Gender: Review of Personality and Social Psychology*, vol. 7. Beverly Hills, CA: Sage. pp. 14–43.

King, R. (1987) 'Sex and Social Class Inequalities in Education: A Re-examination', *British Journal of the Sociology of Education*, 8: 287–303.

Kohlberg, L. and Ullian, D. Z. (1974) 'Stages in the Development of Psycho-sexual Concepts and Attitudes', in R. C. Friedman, R. M. Richart and R. L. Van de Wiele (eds) , *Sex Differences in Behaviour.* London: Wiley.

Leahy, R. L. (ed.) (1985) *The Development of the Self.* New York: Academic Press.

Leventhal, G. S. (1970) 'Influence of Brothers and Sisters on Sex-role Behaviour', *Journal of Personality and Social Psychology*, 16: 452–65.

Lynn, D. B. (1969) *Parental and Sex Role Identification: A Theoretical Formulation.* Berkeley: McCutchan.

Lynn, D. B. (1981) 'The Process of Learning Parental and Sex-role Identification', in L. Steinberg (ed.), *The Life Cycle: Readings in Human Development.* New York: Columbia University Press.

McGuire, W. J. and McGuire, C. V. (1982) 'Significant Others in Self-space: Sex Differences and Developmental Trends in the Social Self', in J. Suls (ed.), *Psychological Perspectives on Self.* New York: Erlbaum.

McPherson, J. M. and Smith-Lovin, L. (1986) 'Sex Segregation in Voluntary Associations', *American Sociological Review*, 51: 61–79.

Mackie, M. (1983) 'The Domestication of Self: Gender Comparisons of Self-imagery and Self-esteem', *Social Psychology Quarterly*, 46: 343–50.

Mahoney, P. (1985) *Schools for Boys?* London: Hutchinson.

Mischel, W. (1966) 'A Social-learning View of Sex Differences in Behaviour', in E. E. Maccoby (ed.), *The Development of Sex Differences.* Stanford: Stanford University Press.

Mummenday, A. and Schreiber, H. J. (1983) 'Better or Just Different? Positive Social Identity by Discrimination against or by Differentiation from Outgroups', *European Journal of Social Psychology*, 13: 389–98.

Musgrove, F. (1964) *Youth and Social Order.* London: Routledge & Kegan Paul.

Newson, J. and Newson, E. (1986) 'Family and Sex Roles in Middle Childhood', in D. J. Hargreaves and A. McColley (eds), *The Psychology of Sex Roles*. London: Harper and Row. pp. 142–58.

Oakes, P. J. (1983) 'Factors Determining the Salience of Group Membership in Social Perception.' Unpublished doctoral thesis, University of Bristol.

Parsons, T. and Bales, R. F. (eds) (1955) *Family, Socialization and Interaction*. Glencoe, IL: Free Press.

Rosenberg, M. (1985) 'Self-concept and Psychological Well-being in Adolescence', in R. L. Leahy (ed.), *The Development of the Self*. New York: Academic Press.

Sarah, E., Scott, M. and Spender, D. (1980) 'The Education of Feminists: The Case for Single Sex Schools', in D. Spender and E. Sarah (eds), *Learning to Lose: Sexism and Education*. London: Women's Press.

Schofield, J. W. (1981) 'Complementary and Conflicting Identities: Images and Interaction in an Inter-racial School', in S. R. Asher and J. M. Gottman (eds), *The Development of Children's Friendships*. Cambridge: Cambridge University Press. pp. 53–90.

Shaw, J. (1976) 'Finishing School: Some Implications of Sex Segregated Education', in D. L. Barker and S. Allen (eds), *Sexual Divisions and Society: Process and Change.*. London: Tavistock.

Sherif, C. W. (1982) 'Needed Concepts in the Study of Gender Identity', *Psychology of Women Quarterly*, 6: 375–98.

Sherif, C. W. (1984) 'Co-ordinating the Sociological and Psychological in Adolescent Interactions', in W. Doise and A. Palmonari (eds), *Social Interaction in Individual Development*. Cambridge: Cambridge University Press.

Sherif, M. (1966) *In Common Predicament: Social Psychology of Intergroup Conflict and Cooperation*. Boston: Houghton Mifflin.

Silbereisen, R. K., Noak, P. and Eyferth, K. (1986) 'Place for Development', in R. K. Silbereisen, K. Eyferth and G. Rudinger (eds), *Development as Action in Context: Problem Behaviour and Normal Youth Development*. Heidelberg: Springer. pp. 87–107.

Simmel, G. (1955) *Conflict: The Web of Group Affiliations*. Glencoe, IL: Free Press.

Skinner, M. and Stephenson, G. M. (1981) 'The Effects of Intergroup Comparison on the Polarization of Opinions', *Current Psychological Research*, 1: 49–59.

Spence, J. T. (1985) 'Gender Identity and Concept of Masculinity and Femininity', in R. A. Dienstbier and T. B. Sonderegger (eds), *Nebraska Symposium on Motivation*, 1984. Lincoln, NE: University of Nebraska Press. pp. 59–96.

Stephenson, G. M. (1981) 'Intergroup Bargaining and Negotiation', in J. C. Turner and H. Giles (eds), *Intergroup Behaviour*. Oxford: Basil Blackwell.

Stroebe, W. and Stroebe, M. S. (1984) 'When Love Dies: An Integration of Attraction and Bereavement Research', in H. Tajfel (ed.) *The Social Dimension*, vol. 1. Cambridge: Cambridge University Press.

Sutherland, M. B. (1981) *Sex Bias in Education*. Oxford: Basil Blackwell.

Tajfel, H. (1978) *The Social Psychology of Minorities*. London: Minority Rights Group, no. 38.

Tajfel, H. (1981) 'Social Stereotypes and Social Groups', in J. C. Turner and H. Giles (eds), *Intergroup Behaviour*. Oxford: Basil Blackwell.

Tajfel, H. and Turner, J. C. (1979) 'An Integrative Theory of Intergroup Conflict', in W. G. Austin and S. Worchel (eds), *The Social Psychology of Intergroup Relations*. Monterey, CA: Brooks-Cole.

Taylor, D. M. and McKirnan, D. J. (1984) 'A Five-Stage Model of Intergroup Relations', *British Journal of Social Psychology*, 23: 291–300.

Turner, J. C. (1975) 'Social Comparison and Social Identity: Some Prospects for Intergroup Behaviour', *European Journal of Social Psychology*, 5: 5–34.

Turner, J. C. (1984) 'Social Identification and Psychological Group Formation', in H. Tajfel (ed.), *The Social Dimension*, vol. 2. Cambridge: Cambridge University Press.

Turner, J. C. (1985) 'Social Categorization and the Self-concept: A Social Cognitive Theory of Group Behaviour', in E. J. Lawler (ed.), *Advances in Group Processes: Theory and Research*, vol. 2. Greenwich, CT: JAI Press. pp. 77–122.

Turner, J. C. and Brown, R. J. (1978) 'Social Status, Cognitive Alternatives and Intergroup Relations', in H. Tajfel (ed.), *Differentiation between Social Groups*. London: Academic Press.

Turner, J. C. and Giles, H. (1981) *Intergroup Behaviour*. Oxford: Basil Blackwell.

Wagner, D. G., Ford, R. S. and Ford, T. W. (1986) 'Can Gender Inequalities be Reduced?', *American Sociological Review*, 51: 47–61.

Weeks, J. (1986) *Sexuality*. London: Tavistock.

Whiteley, B. E., Schofield, J. W. and Snyder, H. N. (1984) 'Peer Preferences in a Desegregated School: A Round Robin Analysis', *Journal of Personality and Social Psychology*, 46: 799–810.

Williams, J. A. (1984) 'Gender and Intergroup Behaviour: Towards an Integration', *British Journal of Social Psychology*, 23: 311–16.

Williams,. J. A. and Giles, H. (1978) 'The Changing Status of Women in Society: An Intergroup Differentiation Perspective', in H. Tajfel (ed.), *Differentiation between Social Groups*. London: Academic Press.

Willis, P. (1977) *Learning to Labour*. Aldershot: Gower.

5

Social Identity in the Transition to Motherhood

Deborah Baker

Understanding social identity in the transition to motherhood involves exploring women's conceptualizations of themselves as they become members of a particular social group, 'mothers' within the contemporary social context. If social identity theory is to be used to explain this process three basic questions need to be addressed: what does this theory have to say about (1) the relationship between social identity and the social context; (2) the particular characteristics of social identity for women; and (3) appropriate methods for examining psychological group memberships within social settings?

Social Identity and the Social Context

It is my view that to look at the how mothers conceptualize their group membership and to understand how and why beliefs about group belonging may vary, we need a theoretical framework which links the way people think about themselves to what they do in particular social contexts. In many ways Tajfel's social identity theory appears to meet this need.

In his approach to the relationship between cognition and context Tajfel (1978, 1979) swam against the prevailing current of opinion in socio-cognitive psychology, which focused almost exclusively on individual interpretations of the social world, whilst ignoring its formative influence (Forgas, 1983). Reflective of an idealist epistemology, this position implies that social reality can be understood simply by looking at people's interpretations of it; no reference need be made to the objective features of the external world (Lefebvre, 1968).

Tajfel took a different stance; he suggested (Tajfel and Fraser, 1978: 303) that

> an understanding of the social context of cognition requires an analysis of the relations between the content of cognition and changes in these cognitions as they interact with changes in man [sic] and his social environment.

This is more akin to a materialist epistemology for which the actual properties of the social environment are as important as an individual's interaction in it, in determining the nature of cognition (Israel, 1972).

At one level this approach is developed in social identity theory by considering the particular properties of the social environment that have some bearing on self-conceptualization. Tajfel (1978) stressed the fact that society is made up of *groups* of individuals that differ from one another particularly in terms of the power and status they command. So in order to make sense of the social world, a person not only needs to evaluate herself in relation to other individuals, but also to structure the similarities and differences between social groups. This is achieved by means of social comparison, whereby people identify others as sharing a similar group membership to themselves (the ingroup) and differentiate this group from those who are dissimilar to themselves (the outgroup) (Tajfel and Turner, 1979). The dimensions that distinguish one social group from another are referred to as social categorizations and it is these that are internalized to create a social identity, the basis of group belonging.

The methodologies used to develop these theoretical principles in practice, however, have often severed the construction of social identity from its roots in the social context. Turner (Turner et al., 1987) gives the reason for this as being that knowledge of the social context would not contribute to an understanding of the psychological processes by which social identity is formed and maintained. In his recent development of self-categorization theory from the principles of social identity theory, he (Turner et al., 1987: 204–5) acknowledges the interdependence of the individual and society:

> individuals in their multiplicity cannot be opposed to or in reality distinguished from society: individuals are society and society is the natural form of being of human individuals . . . There is in fact a continuous reciprocal interaction and functional interdependence between the psychological processes of individuals and their activity, relations and products as society.

But he suggests (Turner and Oakes, 1986: 239) that

> The task of social psychology as part of psychology . . . is *not* to provide social explanations of behaviour . . . *nor* to provide 'psychological explanations' of, i.e. 'to psychologize 'social behaviour', but *to explain the psychological aspects of society* . . . This equates with understanding the structures and processes whereby society is psychologically represented in and mediated by individual minds. (their emphasis)

Still, as critiques of self-categorization theory (Jahoda, 1986; Reid, 1987) have pointed out, there is an inherent contradiction in a position which maintains that individuals are society, whilst at the same time compartmentalizing psychological processes and social reality and choosing to study one in preference to the other. If, as Tajfel maintained, social cognition is the product of a dynamic relationship between individual and society, then social identity should be understood by looking at the way in which it is formed (and transformed) within the social context. It is a view which is of particular relevance to an appreciation of the social identity of women.

The Social Identity of Women

Studies using Tajfel's theoretical framework to understand the meaning of womanhood have generally assumed that 'women' can be defined as a homogeneous social group; social identity is thus derived from evaluation of self as a member of the social group 'women' as distinct from the social group 'men' (for example, Williams and Giles, 1978; Condor, 1986). For women, as for members of other social groups, the need for a positive social identity is the primary motivation behind social comparison; this requires that ingroup be favourably different or positively distinct from outgroup. If this is the case, ingroup membership is associated with high status and prestige. However, if comparisons with outgroup are unfavourable, then ingroup membership comes to be associated with low status and prestige and a less positive social identity results (Tajfel and Turner, 1979). Williams and Giles (1978) assert that women do not derive a positive social identity from gender group membership since in relation to men, the dominant and higher-status group, membership of their subordinate gender group brings with it negative characteristics and inferior status.

To restore positive distinctiveness, says Turner (1982), people may leave the group physically or dissociate from it psychologically and aspire to membership of a higher-status group. Alternatively, they may develop competitive strategies that challenge or change the status relations between groups. Williams and Giles outline ways in which women have used these various means to establish a positive social identity (The Introduction to this volume provides a more detailed account of these strategies.)

The major problem with this conception of the social identity of women is, as Breakwell (1979) proposes, the assumption that 'women' constitute a homogeneous social group. She suggests that there are no static consensual definitions governing gender group membership for women and thus social identity 'as a woman' is difficult to establish. Women therefore may feel marginal to or alienated from their group, not because they see their group as lacking prestige and status when compared with men, but because they can never properly match the women they feel they are with the woman that society demands that they should be.

Another way of stating this problem is to propose that no consensus exists as to the meaning of womanhood precisely because of the varied nature of a woman's social existence. Duveen and Lloyd (1986) describing the development of 'social gender identity' found that even pre-school children recognized a multiplicity of roles for women, whereas they assigned only one to men. For instance, when children of age 3, 4, and 5 were shown photographs of men and women and asked whether these figures could occupy domestic and occupational roles, both boys and girls identified the female figures as performing both types of role whereas neither sex at any of the ages studied recognized men as performing both work and domestic roles.

So it would be more accurate to regard women as a heterogeneous social group, implying that distinct social identities are developed in relation to both work and domestic roles; so the social identity of a woman who has worked for a number of years and is committed to her career may be quite different from that of a mother who has chosen to care for her children at home.

A further implication of heterogeneity is that women may define their social identity (or identities) by comparison with women in other groups rather than with men. First-time motherhood provides fertile ground for examining such comparisons, since for most women it marks the transition from a social identity that is work-based to one founded upon the role of mother.

'Mothers' as a Social Group

Some socio-psychological studies of motherhood, whilst not explicitly concerned with social identity, have looked at self-image as a mother as it relates to former identity as a working woman. Typical of these studies are those of Oakley (1980) and Pistrang (1984), who suggest that becoming a mother for the first time precipitates a loss for personal identity, as a result of giving up work and taking on the domestic role. Underlying this view is the assumption that work is self-enhancing in both personal and status terms whereas motherhood is not; work brings financial independence, promotes emotional and intellectual development and provides opportunities for self-expression and independence of spirit; motherhood brings dependence, social isolation and loss of identity and status. Translating this into social identity terms, mothers would appear to constitute a low-status group in relation to working women, ingroup membership being associated with negative characteristics and a less positive social identity. Oakley's (1980) assumptions were confirmed in her study of 55 first-time mothers; she found that women with a strong work identity had low self-esteem as mothers and expressed little satisfaction with the mothering role; these women were more likely to be well educated, to be older and to have liberal attitudes about a woman's role in society.

Other studies have found that the more career-orientated a woman is the more she wants to return to work after the baby is born (Jimenez, 1977; Hock, 1978). This again ties in with a social identity approach; members of the low-status group 'mothers' seek to restore a positive distinctiveness by returning to work and thus moving into a higher-status group (working women).

This is all very well if we accept the assumption that mothers see their group as of low status, or indeed that relative status is the primary factor in determining positive identification with ingroup for women. There are some problems with this view; Williams and Giles' (1978) original conception of women as a low-status group carries with it the unfortunate implication that without some intergroup or interpersonal changes women do not derive positive distinctiveness from sex group membership; the ideological relationship between men and women in society is internalized by women as an almost constitutional inferiority.

Condor (1986), using empirically based methods to explore the social identity of women, has disputed this position. Analysing the results of open-ended questionnaires (n = 77), Condor found that it was quite possible for women to identify strongly with their group and derive a positive social identity from group membership. This was particularly true for traditional women who supported the sex-role status quo; they did not see status as such in terms of the differential power and wealth between men and women in society, but as something that was shared within the marital relationship.

Looking more specifically at mothers, Parry's considerable work on motherhood and employment (Warr and Parry, 1982; Parry, 1986, 1987) has similarly suggested that mothers of young children often positively evaluate their role and do not see their position as lacking in status, when compared with working women, feeling that they are involved in 'socially legitimate' work by caring for their children at home. Warr and Parry (1982: 204) found that

> many mothers make a rational choice not to do additional work outside the home. As the tasks of childcare and homemaking are often personally meaningful, commitment to the employment role may be low for mothers at this stage.

Parry (1986) has also found that mothers with pre-school children who are in paid employment do not have higher self-esteem than those who are not employed. Differences between employed and non-employed mothers on a range of mental health problems are found only exceptionally: for instance, for employed mothers who had suffered a severe life event and lacked expressive support, high levels of psychiatric symptomatology were identified.

So, given the questionable relevance of status comparisons between ingroup and outgroup to understanding the basis of positive social identity for women, and specifically mothers, what alternative explanations can be derived from social identity theory? To discover these we need look no further than the neglected metatheoretical principles of SIT. In common with other socio-cognitive theorists, Tajfel and Turner (1979) presented the individual as being an *active* participant in shaping the course of her own life; the process of social categorization is a means of organizing information about the social world so that *choices* between different courses of action can be made. The degree of choice exercised in group affiliation may thus be a powerful determinant of whether a social identity is experienced as positive. Skevington (1984) has illustrated this with regard to groups of nurses, where the degree of choice established in relation to nurse training and the range of choice available in day-to-day activity contributed towards the more positive social identity of State Registered nurses when compared with State Enrolled nurses. For women in general the choice between career and/or motherhood is a most important one and the degree of choice exercised in deciding on one or other of these courses of action is likely to effect the positivity of social identity derived from group membership.

Zajicek (1979, 1981) in her studies of pregnancy and first-time motherhood comes to just such a conclusion; she felt, like Oakley (1980), that the major change occurring for women at this time is giving up career interests in order to take up a nurturing role within the family. However, unlike Oakley , she found that this change did not give rise to major re-evaluations of self; low self-esteem as a mother was associated with not wanting the pregnancy rather than giving up work. Zajicek (1981: 54) concluded from her studies that

> Pregnancy and the birth of a first child can be regarded as a time of potential loss and gain. An old social identity must be given up, together with a certain amount of independence and an often active working career . . . If a woman values her past life and finds herself having to give it up *not because she chooses but because pregnancy 'just happened'* then she may have problems coming to terms with a new identity and any new role task. (my emphasis)

So, in Zajicek's work, choice becomes the major factor influencing positive self-image as a mother; women with unplanned pregnancies are those most likely to have lower self-esteem and less positive feelings for their babies.

In the search for alternative explanations we should also take seriously the principle that conceptions of self are developed through interactions in the social context; thus the way in which women define their group memberships can be understood by regarding the contents of social categorizations as products of varying social experience within a particular culture. The possible effects of previous work experience on self-image as a mother and satisfaction with motherhood has already been mentioned. The pattern of women's relationships with family and friends also have a bearing on motherhood experiences. It would seem that the greater the identification with or proximity to other ingroup members, such as own mother and relatives or friends with children, the more positive are feelings about 'self as mother' and the greater the satisfaction with motherhood. Bott (1957), Abernethy (1973) and Gladieux (1978) among others have examined the relationship between social network and motherhood experiences. They have discovered that some women, more often those with lower occupational and educational status, are part of 'tight knit' social networks, characterized by strong ties with their own mothers and friends who are also likely to be mothers. This network provides them with a positive image and a more traditional view of motherhood and, as a result, these women are more likely to experience pregnancy and early motherhood as fulfilling. Other women, often those with higher occupational and educational status, tend to belong to social networks characterized by 'loose knittedness' – that is, less close ties with their own mothers and friendships that are generally work-based. These women have a broader and less positive view of the role of mothers and are less likely to experience motherhood as fulfilling.

In summary, my view of social identity in the transition to motherhood is governed by the basic assumption that 'mothers' constitute a distinct social group whose identity is established in comparison with other groups of women rather than men. Positivity of social identity in the transition to motherhood is not so much dependent on status comparisons with women in other roles, but on the extent to which motherhood is a chosen activity and the strength of links with other mothers at this time.

Measuring Social Identity

To understand social identity as it is actively constructed within social contexts, a method is needed that provides a means of identifying those social categorizations that are consensually definitive of group membership and that measures the extent to which these form a positively valued aspect of self concept.

At present no such methodology exists within the framework of SIT; Brown and Williams (1984), in their review of methods used to examine the theory, conclude that whilst much empirical work has focused on various aspects of intergroup behaviour, little attention has been paid to investigating the nature of social identity and developing a quantitative measure of identification. Moreover, the general emphasis on laboratory experiments which has dominated recent developments of the theory precludes an exploration of the generation and reproduction of social identities in contemporary contexts (see the Introduction to this volume for more detail). One way of dealing with this problem is to look to other theories for alternative methodologies.

A method which does allow for examination of the way in which people both identify with, and construe themselves in relation to, others is repertory grid technique, which is based upon the premises of personal construct theory (Kelly, 1955). This theory has in common with socio-cognitive psychology the basic principle that individuals actively organize and interpret experience in order to make sense out of the world in which they live. From social experience people generate a hierarchically ordered system of bipolar constructs, which is used for predicting future experience and which is changed by validation or invalidation in the light of experience itself (Kelly, 1955).

Repertory grid technique was designed to explore this process; it consists of a list of people to compare (the elements) and a list of terms used in the process of comparison (the constructs). Standard grid technique involves the researcher repeatedly choosing three elements in different combinations from the participant's element list; the participant is then asked to describe the ways in which one of the elements resembles another and differs from the third (Ryle, 1975). All the elements are people known to the participant, who are named before the procedure begins; they can be members of the family, people in different roles, liked/disliked people and so on. As these comparisons are carried out, the researcher notes down all the descriptions of similarity and difference, which are the bipolar constructs. When a list of constructs has been exhaustively assembled by these means, the participant is asked to rate, usually on a seven-point scale, all the people in relation to all the constructs. From the grid of figures generated by this procedure it is possible to find out the extent to which an individual sees herself as similar to or distinct from others (identification), and the dimensions used to compare and contrast others with self (construction).

Wilkinson (1986), in her review of feminist research, feels that repertory grid technique is a useful way of eliciting the subjective and personal meanings of being a woman, and Breen (1975) has used it for this purpose to explore intrapsychical change in the transition to motherhood. Breen looked at women's psychological adjustment to motherhood, believing this to involve a restructuring of perceptions of self in relation to own mother and husband. A good adjustment was

evidenced by identification of self with a positively valued mother as
well as a distancing of self from husband as roles become more
differentiated in the early months of motherhood.

However, repertory grid technique can be adapted to look at shared
or consensual meanings and so has potential as a way of measuring the
social identity of first-time mothers. Firstly, it is ideally designed for
this purpose because at its basis is the process of social comparison:
evaluation of self in relation to others. Secondly, the elements can be
used to represent prototypical ingroup and outgroup members; as
Turner and Oakes (1986) and Turner et al. (1987) indicate, prototypes
embody the ideal or consensually agreed characteristics of groups and
therefore their comparison is likely to elicit the social categorizations
underlying group membership and social identity.

Kelly, although emphasizing the uniqueness of each individual's
construct system, did acknowledge that shared meanings could be
generated from experience. For instance, in the commonality corollary
of his theory he states that 'people belong to the same cultural group
not merely because they behave alike, not because they expect the same
things of others, but, because they construe their experience in the
same way' (Kelly, 1955: 94). In other words, membership of a social
group involves the use of shared dimensions of construction in
interpreting experience.

Tajfel and Wilkes (1964) have shown that, as a general principle,
those dimensions *most frequently used* to distinguish between people
are those of most salience (or subjective importance) and that
judgements along these dimensions will tend to be more polarized. In
the case of social categorization this produces the accentuation of
intragroup similarities and intergroup differences (Tajfel, 1978).
Applying this principle using repertory grid methodology means that
those constructs most frequently elicited when social groups are
compared constitute those most salient in defining group membership.
So positivity of social identity can be evaluated by assessing both the
closeness of identification between 'self', 'ideal self' and ingroup (as
represented by a prototypical member), and also the extent to which
these elements are distinguished from outgroup using the more
extreme judgements on the positive poles of salient dimensions.

It is this methodology and the ideas discussed above that I have
applied in a study of the social identity of first-time mothers (Baker,
1986).

Motherhood and Social Identity

The Study

In my study of social identity in the transition to motherhood, I
initially wanted to identify the social categorizations used by first-time

mothers to distinguish 'mothers' as a social group from 'working women'. Next I wanted to find out whether ingroup membership was positively or negatively valued, and finally I hoped to determine which aspects of women's social experience were causally linked to variations in the positivity of social identity as a mother and, hence, satisfaction with motherhood and feelings for the baby.

The women I interviewed were all first-time mothers from the Wiltshire towns of Trowbridge, Bradford on Avon and Melksham. They were interviewed on three occasions during pregnancy and early motherhood during the years 1982–3. The first interview took place in participants' own homes, eleven weeks before the baby was born. A postal questionnaire was sent to each mother one month after birth and a third interview was given, again in participants' homes, approximately sixteen weeks after birth. Each interview was about an hour long. Women participated on a voluntary basis; 68 were interviewed initially and 63 completed the full programme of interviews. Of these the first 10 formed a pilot study, leaving a total of 53 first-time mothers for the main study. The ages of these women ranged from 17 to 41, the average age for the group being 25.

Previous employment was classified using an index specially designed for women's occupations (Elias, 1981). The occupations of the women in the sample represented the whole spectrum from professional and managerial to personal service, the largest single categories being clerical/secretarial (38 per cent). The percentage of women falling into each occupational category reflected national trends, as observed in the National Training Survey (Elias and Main, 1982). Social class was not used as a measure of women's social status since for married women it is conventionally assessed on the basis of husband's occupation and thus is likely to misrepresent women's experience (for more detailed reasoning behind this exclusion, see Baker, 1986).

Levels of education also covered a wide spectrum, from university degrees to no educational qualifications; the majority of women (59 per cent) were educated up to ordinary level GCE standard, but had not continued with further education.

The Motherhood Grid
The motherhood grid was developed in the context of this study as a means of exploring the characteristic patterns of identification and construction underlying social identity as a mother. It was the central core of the interviews at 11 weeks before birth and 16 weeks after.

The choice of elements for this grid reflected the principle assumption that since becoming a mother for the first time involves the transition from the role of working, then social identity will rest on identification with the ingroup 'mothers' as distinct from the outgroup 'working women'. After piloting many options, the elements 'a good mother' and 'a career orientated woman' were chosen as prototypical members of these two groups. 'Yourself' and 'as you would like to be' were also used so that positive identification with ingroup could be evaluated as the extent of identification between self, ideal self and 'a good mother'. 'Own mother' and 'a close friend' were included as elements as well, given the potential importance of a mother's social relationships for the positivity of social identity. Finally 'not a good mother' and 'a successful woman' were used, the former to provide a comparison point by which to define the characteristics of 'a good mother' and the latter as a means of assessing the relative status of ingroup. For example, if 'a successful woman' was seen as close to other ingroup members, one could deduce that motherhood was invested with high status; on the other hand, if this element was identified with outgroup, then one would assume that working was perceived as the more prestigious activity.

These elements were compared by the triadic method mentioned earlier (p. 91) at 11 weeks before birth, to elicit a maximum of 7 bipolar constructs for each participant. These were then rated on a seven-point scale for each element and this rating procedure was repeated at 16 weeks after birth, using the same constructs and elements. This gave rise to two 8×7 grid matrices for each subject which were directly comparable over time. The contents of these grid matrices were analysed using Landfield's (1971) method of construct categorization and Slater's (1972) Ingrid grid analysis package. The form of these analyses can be briefly summarized as follows:

1. The most salient (that is, frequently used) social categorizations were identified by categorizing the constructs for the sample as a whole using the Landfield Rep Test method. Here we have 22 rating categories, each identified by name, definition and example. Landfield intended that each pole of the constructs should be taken separately and placed in as many categories as are appropriate, referring always to a provided index of fully scored descriptions. Following Topcu (1975), this procedure was modified in this study so that each construct pole was fitted into one category only. This provided a measure of salience, by counting the number of constructs falling into each category.

2. Patterns of identification were assessed by calculating the distance of self from other elements using the Ingrid program. These were calculated for the sample as a whole and for each individual, both pre- and post-partum.

3. In order to look at the way in which self and ingroup was

distinguished from outgroup, a list of constructs correlating with each element at the 5 per cent level of significance or above was compiled for each individual and for the sample as a whole.

The Interviews

In addition to these data, interview material was used to produce a substantive outline of the social context of motherhood. This included information about previous work experience (occupation, number of years worked and anticipated time before return to work), the planning of pregnancy, age, education, attitudes towards women, satisfaction with motherhood and feelings for the baby. Views were sought on working in comparison with being a mother at home, the changes in life-style motherhood brings, changing patterns of contact with and feelings about own mother and friends, and preparation for and experience of the birth itself. These data were integrated wherever possible with evidence about social identity from the motherhood grids, using a variety of methods including ANOVA and Chi-squared tests of significance.

Social Identity as a Mother

The initial point to emphasize from analyses of results is that 'mothers' were conceptualized as a distinct ingroup by the women in this study and there was a considerable degree of consensus as to the defining dimensions (or social categorizations) underlying group membership. When data from the motherhood grids were pooled for all the women in the main study ($n = 53$) at 11 weeks before birth it was clear that 'self' and 'ideal self' were most closely identified with 'a good mother'. Other elements seen as 'like me' and so as ingroup, were 'own mother' 'close friend' and 'a successful woman'. Those seen as dissimilar to self (though not as similar to each other), were 'a career orientated woman' as representing a prototypical working woman (outgroup) and 'not a good mother'.

There was no change in these patterns of identification at 16 weeks after the birth, suggesting that ingroup identification was already well established by late pregnancy.

The perceived distinctiveness of mothers in comparison with career women can be further illustrated by looking at the constructs that were most frequently used to differentiate between the elements on the grid by the sample as a whole. Table 5.1 gives some idea of the variety of characteristics used in this comparison.

The most used constructs fell into the Landfield categories of 'Tenderness' and 'Forcefulness', which accounted for 40 per cent of the total number of constructs elicited; these categories together form what I have called the *maternal dimension*, underlining those qualities

Table 5.1 *Categorization of constructs from the motherhood grids (n = 53) using Landfield's (1971) Repertory Test method*

Category name	Total number of constructs	Examples of most common constructs
Tenderness (high)	90	Unselfish, cares for children
Forcefulness (low)	75	Patient, contented
Forcefulness (high)	54	Impatient, quick-tempered
Tenderness (low)	57	Dislikes children, uncaring
Social Interaction (inactive)	48	Home centred, unsociable
Factual Description (b)	39	Uninterested in children
Social Interaction (active)	39	Sociable, friendly
Factual Description (a)	37	Interested in family
Self Sufficiency (high)	29	Copes well
Egoism	28	Selfish, single minded
Self Sufficiency (low)	28	Copes badly/not well
Emotional Arousal (b)	24	Unhappy, anxious
Status (high)	23	Successful, ambitious
Self Reference (b)	23	Different ideas to me
Self Reference (a)	21	Similar ideas to me
Organization (high)	16	Well organized, efficient
Status (low)	16	Unsuccessful, not ambitious
Organization (low)	15	Disorganized, inefficient
Closed to Alternatives	14	Intolerant, rigid
Emotional Arousal (a)	13	Happy
Intellective (high)	6	Clever
Intellective (low)	6	Not clever
Morality (high)	4	Responsible
Morality (low)	3	Irresponsible
External Appearance (a)	2	Dresses well, cares about appearance
External Appearance (b)	2	Not concerned about appearance

One modification of Landfield's original category names was the subdivision of the categories Factual Description, Emotional Arousal and Self Reference into (a) and (b). This enabled a distinction to be drawn between opposing constructs falling within each of these categories.

stereotypically associated with the mothering role. This was the major dimension used in *intergroup comparison*; in both late pregnancy and early motherhood, self, ideal self and a good mother were all described using positive 'maternal' constructs such as unselfish, caring, patient, understanding, etc., as distinct from 'a career orientated woman' who was described as not interested in children, quick-tempered, impatient, single-minded, selfish and so on.

The categories next in importance were 'Social Interaction' and 'Factual Description', which accounted for 23 per cent of the total number of constructs used and formed *the social dimension*, reflecting the social aspects of the mothering role as compared with other activities. This dimension was used for *intragroup* comparison: whilst self and own mother were described using constructs such as home centred, unsociable and reserved, ideal self and a good mother were characterized by both these constructs and also by their opposites – for instance, sociable, friendly and outgoing. Clearly there is some lack of consensus here about the social consequences of being a mother; the reasons for this will become clearer when discussing positivity of social identity in the next section.

As with patterns of identification, there was no significant change in the salience of particular construct categories for description of the elements from 11 weeks before birth to 16 weeks afterwards; in other words becoming a mother in itself did not precipitate a polarization of views leading to accentuation of ingroup similarities and outgroup differences.

This lack of change in patterns of identification and construction from late pregnancy to early motherhood confounds the view that the experience of first-time motherhood brings with it major changes in social identity. It may well be that any major shift from a work-based social identification to one based on motherhood would have been best observed in the early months of pregnancy when the psychological impact of changing roles may have been more immediate. On the other hand, changes in social identity could occur gradually over long periods rather than in just a matter of months; women may map out the parts of their lives they intend to devote to mothering and/or working so that change in social identity is fluid rather than abrupt.

That such change does occur is given some credence by the work of McCoy (1985), who looked at identity transition for women undergoing voluntary sterilization (necessarily at the end rather than the beginning of their childbearing years). He found that at this time mothers developed an increased ideal identification with working women and ascribed negative qualities to family members including own mother and close friends. Thus patterns of construing would seem to be the reverse of those identified in my own study as mothers moved towards a more work-based social identity.

Nevertheless what did clearly emerge from patterns of identification and construction in my own study was that motherhood was perceived positively, but that this had little to do with its *relative status* as an activity when compared with working. Table 5.1 shows that constructs falling into the category of 'Status' accounted for only 5 per cent of the total number of constructs used. So the mothers themselves appeared to attach little importance to relative status as a means of evaluating their role in relation to working. It is also interesting that there was a lack of consensus in characterizing the element 'a successful woman';

although this element was identified as 'like me' and therefore as ingroup, it was described using characteristics common to both ingroup and outgroup. These were positive maternal constructs such as unselfish, caring, understanding; those indicative of self-sufficiency such as confident, independent, copes well; and those suggestive of a certain toughness and intolerance such as strong minded, impatient and quick-tempered. Two interpretations are possible: it may be that some subjects identified success as a facet of mothering, others as a consequence of working; alternatively, it could be that success as such is seen in terms of possession of those characteristics important for good mothering as well as those associated with achievement at work. Whatever the interpretation, there was certainly no consensus that pursuing a career is to be successful as a woman and to be a mother is not. So while motherhood may be ideologically defined as having low status, this is not necessarily internalized by mothers as the basis for their social identity. This concurs with Condor's (1983) more general conclusion that for some women, relative status has little to do with the positivity of social identity and suggests that, as a concept, it is too limited in its ability to provide an explanation for the influence of social contextual factors on the nature of social identity.

Positive Social Identity and the Social Context
Focusing on specific aspects of a woman's experience prior to motherhood – in other words, placing motherhood in its historical context – yields more fruitful results than status comparisons. As expected, antecedent social factors were associated with variations in the positivity of social identity as a mother and, as a consequence, in satisfaction with motherhood and feelings for the baby.

Mothers with a more positive social identity were those who identified most closely with other ingroup members; such patterns of identification were accompanied by the greater salience of positive 'maternal' constructs in characterizing self and ingroup. These mothers tended to be younger women (21 to 25 years) who had worked for fewer years (less than 7), were less highly educated, and had more traditional attitudes towards the role of women in society (as measured by the Attitudes towards Women Scale of Spence et al., 1975); they anticipated returning to work when their children were relatively young (5 to 11 years) and expressed much satisfaction with motherhood. Characteristic of the experience of these mothers was a supportive social network, which provided continuity in the transition from work to motherhood. More often than not they lived near their own mothers, and also had relatives with children in the area; new friends were made during the course of confinement who shared their experiences and maintained contact in the early months of motherhood.

Decisions about returning to work were generally based on easy access to part-time work and flexible child-care arrangements within the family network.

Ms Harper's experience of first-time motherhood is illustrative of this kind of background and social identity. She was 24 and had worked as a hairdresser for six years before becoming pregnant. In late pregnancy she felt that becoming a mother was

> what I've always wanted; my job was interesting but since I've known my husband, becoming a mother has been the most important thing . . . I'm looking forward to everything . . . it's something we've talked about and we're ready for the changes . . . having a baby, that's the most important thing.

Ms Harper felt close to her own mother: 'I've always seen a lot of my mother, always been able to talk to her, especially since I've been married myself.' Her parents lived nearby and her elder sister, who had recently had her first baby, also lived in the area. After the birth of her baby, Ms Harper expressed positive feelings about motherhood:

> I enjoy everything about being a mother . . . it's made me more responsible . . . it all stems back to having to think about the baby; when you're working you only think about yourself . . . it must make you different being a mother.

She saw a lot of her own mother and sister, who both did some babysitting for her; she also retained her close friendships, and made new friends during her confinement in hospital whom she saw regularly. She anticipated returning to work part-time when her children were at primary school, though she thought she might work from home in pre-school years. She missed only the financial benefits of working.

In comparison, the oldest mothers in the sample (31 years and over), who had worked for longer (8 to 11 years and over) were likely to have a less-positive social identity; characteristically, self was seen as less similar to ideal self and a good mother and, along with other ingroup members, was described most saliently using constructs such as 'sociable', 'friendly', 'outgoing', and 'interests outside the home' rather than by 'maternal' constructs. These mothers tended to be more highly educated and to express more liberal/radical attitudes towards the role of women in society; they anticipated returning to work comparatively late (children 11 years or over) and expressed less satisfaction with motherhood. However, the explanation for this did not appear to lie in a loss of a more valued work identity, a greater career orientation or a thwarted desire to return to work in early motherhood. There was no identification with 'a career orientated woman' nor was there any indication of this element being perceived more positively than 'a good mother'. Also there was no apparent desire to hurry back to work; indeed these mothers generally wanted to delay returning to work as long as possible, expressing a dissatisfaction with their working lives and a need to do other things. Rather, the emphasis on the social aspects of the mothering role indicated the ideal of an active social life which may not have been available to them in early motherhood. These women tended to live some distance from their families and had little contact with them, so at a practical level there would be no immediate help with looking after the baby. Also friendships were mainly work-based, so that giving up work meant losing friends.

Ms Pritchard's experience is typical; she was 32 and had given up her job as a manageress six months previously, having worked for 11 years. In late pregnancy she had no clear ideas about motherhood: 'I haven't really thought about it . . . obviously I'll be more tired . . . that's the only thing I can say about it.' She enjoyed working because of the social contact, but no longer found it challenging: she felt that there was too much pressure at work and that her job no longer held any interest for her. She felt a certain freedom about being at home 'being able to be my own boss'. She had little contact with her family who lived 200 miles away, or her close friends who lived in a town some miles distant.

In early motherhood Ms Pritchard enjoyed caring for her baby, particularly 'the giving and receiving of love', but found motherhood restricting:

I don't have a lot of time to myself; everything has to be crammed into a couple of hours when he's sleeping . . . everything I want to do for myself has to be really carefully planned.

She had no contact with relatives and had made no new friends as a result of motherhood; indeed she found her contemporaries rather tedious!

You go down to the postnatal classes . . . women when they've had babies, I don't know what happens to them, everything else goes by the board . . . I don't know what they were like before, but nothing seems to interest them apart from babies.

Ms Pritchard also found it difficult to see her old friends: 'it's a bit difficult getting to see them on public transport . . . there's nowhere to feed amongst other things'. She did not, however, envisage going out to work, hoping to set up a business from home at some point the future.

Also associated with differences in the positivity of social identity as a mother was the planning decision, whether pregnancy was chosen or not. Mothers who had planned their babies had a more positive social identity. The planning of pregnancy was also associated with higher occupational status prior to motherhood and very positive feelings about the baby at 16 weeks post-partum. For instance, Ms Shaw, a computer programmer before becoming pregnant, felt that at 25 it was the right time in her life to be having a baby, so that she could be relatively young whilst her children were growing up. In early motherhood she enjoyed most aspects of child care, especially feeding, bathing and watching her baby grow and develop. Her feelings about herself as a mother at this time were positive:

> I think I'm more patient, more tolerant since I've been a mother ... you've got to give up a lot of your time for the baby, there's no choice about that ... generally I feel more confident about myself, more sociable towards people ... I've also got more space, more time than when I was working.

Mothers who had not planned their pregnancies, on the other hand, were among those most likely to have a less positive social identity. Like the oldest mothers in the sample described earlier they identified less closely with other ingroup members, who were most saliently described using 'social' rather than 'maternal' constructs. But in addition they also saw themselves as similar to rather than as distinct from outgroup; this was indicated by identification with 'a career orientated woman'. Also associated with an unplanned pregnancy was lower occupational status prior to motherhood, and ambivalent feelings about the baby at 16 weeks post-partum.

So it was mothers who had not made an active choice to become pregnant and who would have preferred to have a baby later in their lives, who were ambivalent about their group membership and compared it less positively with their experience at work.

One such mother was Ms Harris, who did not plan her baby. Prior to motherhood she was a production worker and at the age of 24 felt that she was not mature enough to be having a baby. In early motherhood she enjoyed the practical side of caring for the baby, but found it difficult to come to terms with the impact that motherhood had had on her life:

> It's a hell of a difference ... sometimes he takes over and my life's not my own any more ... I can't go out without a babysitter. Some things are good about being a mother, but it's the crying all the time ... it really gets me down.

Her feelings about herself at this time were that she was 'more tired' and that she didn't feel like herself any more. She missed being at work, largely because of the social contact, but also because of financial difficulties, and was looking for a job in the evenings so that she could get out a bit more.

Summary

My study of first-time motherhood explored social identity in relation to context. Using repertory grid methodology as a measure of social identification revealed the 'maternal' and 'social' dimensions as the major ways of defining group membership for mothers. Differences in the usage of these dimensions in characterizing ingroup were linked to the positivity of social identity, previous social experience and the experience of motherhood itself. Data from interviews further illuminated these findings, suggesting that the positivity of social identity was dependent on the continuity of social relationships in the transition to motherhood and choice of group membership, rather than the relative status of mothers as an ingroup.

Concluding Comments

The unique contribution that social identity theory can make to any socio-cognitive study is its emphasis on the important function of group identification and social categorization as ways in which people contextualize themselves within society. However, some would question the value of applying such a theory to understanding the meaning of womanhood, since it necessitates analysis of the global rather than the particular, the consensual as opposed to the personal. Feminist research, for instance, has signalled a movement towards more qualitative research methods that focus on women's personal constructions and experience (for instance, Stanley and Wise, 1983; Wilkinson, 1986). In practice, this often means that normative or stereotypic constructions are dismissed as misrepresentations of the 'truth' and women who adhere to, or express themselves by use of such beliefs are portrayed as 'lying in conformity to some social prescription or other . . . misled as to their own true nature by the process of brainwashing' (Frost, 1980: 54). Some researchers even go as far as to suggest that such women should be identified as 'fakers' (Nicholson, 1986). This leads to the inevitable contradiction whereby whilst emphasizing women-centred research which explores 'subjective interpretations of reality providing a perspective on how women see their lives' (Nicolson, 1986: 147), some women's accounts are judged to be more 'truthful' than others.

However, what social identity theory tells us is that normative or stereotypic constructions of reality are not abstract categories imposed on passive individuals, but are actively created and recreated by social comparison within particular contexts. What we can learn by exploring social identifications based on such comparisons is how women define, maintain, develop and change their social status within society.

Contextualizing social identity for women in this way means seeing it as a varied and changing aspect of self concept; in this respect I think that it is helpful to view 'women' as a heterogeneous social group rather than a homogeneous gender group; this allows for direct links to be established between the social identity of women and their social activity, through both its contemporary and its historical expression. Little work of this kind has been done, and yet there is much potential for using such a model to understand the multiplicity of social identities for women, from adolescence to old age, from work to motherhood.

Note

Pseudonyms have been used wherever data from interview material are quoted.

References

Abernethy, L. D. (1973) 'Social Network and Response to the Maternal Role', *International Journal of the Sociology of the Family*, 3: 86–92.

Baker, D. J. (1986) 'Motherhood: A Beginning'. Unpublished Ph.D thesis, University of Bath.

Bott, E. (1957) *Family and Social Network: Norms and External Relationships in Ordinary Urban Families*. London: Tavistock.

Breakwell, G. M. (1979) 'Women: Group and Identity?' *Women's Studies International Quarterly*, 2: 9–17.

Breen, D. (1975) *The Birth of the First Child: Towards an Understanding of Femininity*. London: Tavistock.

Brown, R. and Williams, J. (1984) 'Group Identification: The Same Thing to All People?' *Human Relations*, 37: 547–64.

Condor, S. (1983) 'Womanhood as an Aspect of Social Identity: Group Identification and Ideology'. Paper presented at the British Psychological Society Annual Conference, University of London, December.

Condor, S. (1986) 'Sex Role Beliefs and "Traditional" Women: Feminist and Intergroup Perspectives', in S. Wilkinson (ed.), *Feminist Social Psychology*. Milton Keynes: Open University Press.

Duveen, G. and Lloyd, B. (1986) 'The Significance of Social Identities'. *British Journal of Social Psychology*, 25: 219–30.

Elias, P. (1981) *The MRG/EOC Occupational Classification*, DP131. Manpower Research Group, University of Warwick, September.

Elias, P. and Main, B. (1982) *Women's Working Lives: Evidence from the National Training Survey*. Research report, Institute for Employment Research, University of Warwick.

Forgas, J. P. (1983) 'What is Social about Social Cognition?' *British Journal of Social Psychology*, 22: 129–44.

Frost, K. (1980) 'On the Variety of the Forms of Self Knowledge: Some Thoughts on Women's Perceptions of Themselves', in P. Salmon (ed.), *Coming to Know*. London: Routledge & Kegan Paul.

Gladieux, J. D. (1978) 'Pregnancy – the Transition to Parenthood: Satisfaction with the Pregnancy Experience as a Function of Sex Role Conceptions, Marital Relationship

104   *Deborah Baker*

and Social Network', in W. B. Miller and L. Newman (eds), *First Child and the Family Formation*. Carolina Population Center, University of North Carolina at Chapel Hill.

Hock, E. (1978) 'Working and Non-working Mothers with Infants: Perceptions of Their Careers, Their Infant's Needs and Satisfaction with Mothering', *Developmental Psychology*, 4: 37–43.

Hoffman, L. W. (1978) 'The Effect of the First Child on the Woman's Role', in W. B. Miller and L. F. Newman (eds), *First Child and the Family Formation*. Carolina Population Center, University of North Carolina at Chapel Hill.

Israel, J. (1972) 'Stipulations and Constructions in the Social Sciences', in J. Israel and H. Tajfel (eds), *The Context of Social Psychology*. London: Academic Press.

Jahoda, M. (1986) 'Small Selves in Small Groups', *British Journal of Social Psychology*, 25: 253–4.

Jimenez, M. H. (1977) 'Relationships Between Job Orientation in Women and Adjustment to the First Pregnancy and Postpartum Period'. Unpublished Doctoral Dissertation, North Western University, Illinois.

Kelly, G. A. (1955) *The Psychology of Personal Constructs*, vols I and II. New York: W. W. Norton & Co.

Landfield, A. W. (1971) *Personal Construct Systems in Psychotherapy*. Chicago: Rand-McNally.

Lefebvre, H. (1968) *Dialectical Materialism*. London: Jonathan Cape.

McCoy, D. (1985) 'Voluntary Surgical Sterilization as Identity Transition'. Paper presented to the BPS Social Psychology Section Annual Conference, Cambridge, 17–19 September.

Nicolson, P. (1986) 'Developing a Feminist Approach to Depression following Childbirth', in S. Wilkinson (ed.), *Feminist Social Psychology*. Milton Keynes: Open University Press.

Oakley, A. (1980) *Women Confined*. Oxford: Martin Robertson.

Parry, G. (1986) 'Paid Employment, Life Events, Social Support and Mental Health in Working Class Mothers', *Journal of Health and Social Behaviour*, 27: 193–208.

Parry, G. (1987) 'Sex Role Beliefs, Work Attitudes and Mental Health in Employed and Non-Employed Mothers', *British Journal of Social Psychology*, 26: 47–58.

Pistrang, N. (1984) 'Women's Work Involvement and Experience of New Motherhood', *Journal of Marriage and the Family*, May: 433–47.

Reid, F. (1987) Book Review, *British Journal of Social Psychology*, 26: 347–8.

Ryle, A. (1975) *Frames and Cages*. Sussex University Press.

Skevington, S. M. (1984) 'Choice, Status and Ingroup Conflict in the Work of Trained Nursing Groups', *Ergonomics*, 27(5): 565–76.

Slater, P. (1972) 'Notes on Ingrid'. Unpublished manuscript, Institute of Psychiatry, London.

Spence, J. T., Helmreich, R. and Stapp, J. (1975) 'Ratings of Self and Peers on Sex Role Attributes and their Relation to Self Esteem and Conceptions of Masculinity and Femininity', *Journal of Personality and Social Psychology*, 32: 29–39.

Stanley, L. and Wise, S. (1983) *Breaking Out: Feminist Consciousness and Feminist Research*. London: Routledge & Kegan Paul.

Tajfel, H. (ed.) (1978) *Differentiation between Social Groups: Studies in the Social Psychology of Intergroup Relations*. London: Academic Press.

Tajfel, H. (1979) 'Individuals and Groups in Social Psychology', *British Journal of Social Psychology*, 18: 183–90.

Tajfel, H. and Fraser C. (eds) (1978) *Introductory Social Psychology*. Harmondsworth: Penguin.

Tajfel, H. and Turner, J. (1979) 'An Integrative Theory of Intergroup Conflict', in W. H. Austin and S. Worchel (eds), *The Social Psychology of Intergroup Relations*. Monterey, CA: Brooks-Cole.

Tajfel, H. and Wilkes, A. L. (1964) 'Salience of Attributes and Commitment to Extreme Judgements in the Perception of People', *British Journal of Social and Clinical Psychology*. 3: 40–9.

Topcu, S. (1975) 'Psychological Concomitants of Aggressive Feelings and Behaviour'. Unpublished Ph.D. Thesis, London University.

Turner, J. C. (1982) 'Towards a Cognitive Redefinition of the Social Group', in H. Tajfel (ed.), *Social Identity and Intergroup Relations*. Cambridge: Cambridge University Press.

Turner, J. C. and Oakes, P. J. (1986) 'The Significance of the Social Identity Concept for Social Psychology with regard to Individualism, Interactionism and Social Influence', *British Journal of Social Psychology*, 25: 237–52.

Turner, J. C., Hogg, M. A., Oakes, P. J., Reicher, S. and Wetherell, M. (1987) *Rediscovering the Social Group: A Self-Categorization Theory*. Oxford: Basil Blackwell.

Warr, P. B. and Parry, G. (1982) 'Paid Employment and Women's Psychological Well Being', *Psychological Bulletin*, 91: 498–516.

Wilkinson, S. (ed.) (1986) *Feminist Social Psychology*. Milton Keynes: Open University Press.

Williams, J. A. and Giles, H. (1978) 'The Changing Status of Women in Society: An Intergroup Perspective', in H. Tajfel (ed.), *Differentiation between Social Groups: Studies in the Social Psychology of Intergroup Relations*. London: Academic Press.

Zajicek, E. (1979) 'Self Perceptions during Pregnancy and Early Motherhood', in O. Harnett, G. Boden, and M. Fuller (eds), *Sex Role Stereotyping*. London: Tavistock.

Zajicek, E. (1981) 'The Experience of Being Pregnant', in S. Wolkind and E. Zajicek, *Pregnancy: A Psychological and Social Study*. London: Academic Press.

6

Talking about Career and Gender Identities: A Discourse Analysis Perspective

Harriette Marshall and Margaret Wetherell

A woman starting as a laywer, does she see herself – it doesn't quite sound right – but, does she see herself as a woman or does she see herself as a lawyer? Does she see herself as a woman in a man's profession or does she see herself differently? Any woman coming into law will be faced with these questions of identity.

This chapter is focused on a set of accounts given by a group of women and men students just embarking on their careers as middle-class professionals. The group we studied were training as lawyers and were about to become solicitors and advocates within the Scottish legal system. We want to examine how these particular women and men construct their identity and their image of themselves in relation to their gender, as they talk about the process of becoming a lawyer and the wider roles of women and men.

Our interest lies in the *representation* of identity as opposed to the psychological process hypothesized to underlie social categorization and social identity formation. Furthermore, we will focus on representations as they appear in discourse, in what is actually said. How do people talk about this aspect of their lives? How do they make sense of themselves in relation to their jobs and their gender? What, in other words, is the common sense about self and social identity?

This area of discursive representation is one that has received little empirical attention in social identity research, although hypotheses about the nature of identity representation abound in social identity theory (Tajfel, 1982; Tajfel and Turner, 1979; Turner and Giles, 1981; Turner et al., 1987). A distinction is often made, for example, between social and personal identities as two different types of self-representation, or between contrasting levels of self-categorization. It is argued that when a group or social identity is salient, individuals begin to think about themselves and others in terms of attributes which are collectively shared and which define that group, and, as a result, individual differences and the traits that mark out one's personal unique and individual identity become less prominent in the individual's self-conception. Thus, for instance, when a woman categorizes herself as feminist what becomes dominant in her self-concept are the attitudes, traits, norms and values shared with other feminists rather than the idiosyncrasies of her individual temperament and personality. In effect, social identity theorists suggest that individuals become *depersonalized* as they begin to attribute their stereotypic representation of the group category to themselves, transforming action and perception. This attribution or self-representation is studied, however, as an internal cognitive process, and social identity theory offers, not a blow-by-blow account of the relevant introspections, but a broad predictive analytic scheme.

Because of the level at which representation is located in social identity theory, with this emphasis on internally organized cognitive or mental events, we found that it was extremely difficult to use this model to analyse the nitty-gritty of everyday talk and interaction. It is not clear whether we could expect people to understand and communicate these cognitive processes. What traces of these representations might emerge in what people say about their identities and group memberships? If some other mental process was described in an interview could we say that social identity theory was disconfirmed? What relationship will hold, in general, between the process of identity negotiation as it is described in social identity theory and ordinary talk and conversation? No translation rules are offered or indeed any speculation about the interplay between social identity processes and the substance of daily life as it emerges from conversation and talk.

In common with other social psychological theories, social identity theory lacks an elaborated model of language and discourse. We hope to demonstrate that this hampers and unduly confines the study of identity representation. Indeed, a very different concept of representation emerges if one takes discourse seriously as an object of study, and begins with language (Litton and Potter, 1985; McKinlay et al., forthcoming; Potter and Litton, 1985). One of the aims of this chapter is to illustrate this discursive approach to identity representation and outline some of the fundamentals of language practices which must be taken into account in any analysis.

Social psychology is not only generally reticent about perspectives on natural language use, it also lacks tools for this kind of investigation. How does the researcher work with language data and transcripts of interviews? For our study we made use of discourse analysis, an approach developed in other contexts, as our guiding methodological and theoretical model (Gilbert and Mulkay, 1984; Potter and Mulkay, 1985; Potter and Wetherell, 1987; Wetherell, 1986; Wetherell and Potter, 1988; Wetherell and Potter, forthcoming; see also Coupland et al., 1988; Coupland et al., in press).

Discourse Analysis: Theory and Methodology

Discourse analysis, theory and methodology, has been described in detail elsewhere (Potter and Wetherell, 1987). A number of definitions could be given but, broadly speaking, discourse analysis covers the investigation of all type of written texts and spoken interaction, with particular emphasis on the functions served by language and the implications of particular linguistic constructions. Here, we simply need to pick out a few overarching principles. Our discussion of these will indicate the general procedures we adopted for the analysis of the set of accounts collected from the female and male law students. The second aim of this presentation is to begin to indicate the distinctive differences between the linguistic and the cognitive focus on identity.

Language: Ephemeral or Central?
One of the reasons why social psychology as a whole has neglected discourse and social identity theory has overlooked the *linguistic* practices involved in identity representation lies in the prevalence in the discipline of a particular view of language. According to this view language is taken to be the mere tool or medium of communication.

The interesting entities, social psychologically speaking, are thought to be the two or more people communicating, their mental states and their social environment while language or the flow of words between simply acts as the connecting channel. This channel may, on occasion, transmit extra noise but on the whole provides a faithful rendition of messages which originate elsewhere.

If we return to the 'medium' metaphor, language as a medium is seen as relatively colourless, odourless, and unintrusive. For this reason it is not of interest as an object of study, except around the edges where it begins to take on additional features, conveying the extra noise of personalized accents, unintended clues to deception, or intimations of mental states best repressed, for instance.

The socio-psychological research which has been conducted on language has tended to focus on these additional aspects which, crucially, are taken as peripheral to the main thrust of communication, although they may also have their own important and subtle effects on social interaction (Giles, 1977; Giles and St Clair, 1979). Accents shared in common, for example, might increase a sense of group solidarity or increase the chances of accommodating and cooperative interaction.

In contrast to this emphasis, discourse analysis makes language a site in itself. It is not the conveyor of social life, it is an essential constructive feature. Language is not a medium which neutrally transmits and reflects processes taking place elsewhere; it is vitally constitutive of social and psychological processes. Thus discourse is not accidental or incidental to social psychological analysis. It is the very place where the researcher should work.

The events which happen at this site include the construction and negotiation of mental states, the creation of participants as certain types of being or identities, and the production of social realities. Cognitive representations are not only 'internally' organized, they are additionally 'externally' organized in discourse as participants communicate and construct a version of their psychological state. The very meaning of utterances depends on a system of oppositions and differences within language.

In general, discourse analysis takes off from wider developments in linguistic theory, literary theory and sociology: semiotics (the analysis of signs and the relations between signs), pragmatics (the rules underlying the combination of signs), ethnomethodology (the methods used to make sense of social life) and so on, which have stressed the action-orientation of discourse, and its constructive nature, and which· have framed language as a complex material social practice in its own right, as an important and effective constituent of social life in itself.

In summary, then, the first general point is that we will not treat our interview data as a pointer to some other site: to underlying determining cognitions, for example, or to behaviour or physical events. We will not treat the language as an indicator or marker of processes taking place elsewhere; we will focus on the discourse itself.

Language, Power and Ideology

If language is taken as a complex social practice in its own right then we become immediately concerned with power and ideology (Thompson, 1984). Some constructions of the world or discourses become so powerful, for example, that their constructive dimension becomes obscured. They appear as common sense, as what is natural and taken for granted. The construction of 'race', for instance, as a particular biological and social categorization, is a good example of this process (Reicher, 1986). It is through the deconstruction of these, by taking apart and making clear just how certain ideologies have filtered into our notions of common sense and circulate in everyday conversations, that other alternative and less oppressive discourses might emerge (Coward, 1984; Parker, 1989).

If the analyst is attentive to the interplay between ideology and discourse, then with any body of linguistic data, questions arise about the implications of one type of construction versus another. The analyst attempts to denaturalize the text, not taking it for granted or seeing it as a simple reflection of reality, but asking why this particular construction has appeared in this context and what ends it achieves.

This questioning and denaturalizing outlook is our second guiding principle.

Discursive Variability and Inconsistency

Because language is action-orientated, tuned to attaining many different purposes and goals from apologies to accusations, for example, and from explanations to disclaimers, people's discourse is commonly highly variable and inconsistent over time. To bring off an apology, for instance, it may be more persuasive to characterize one's actions and intentions in one way, but to successfully accuse someone else of wrongdoing may involve a different construction.

We are not suggesting that this type of transition would mark out a dishonest or machiavellian person, and that thus we are all dishonest in social life. Rather, the casting and recasting of events or the creation of different versions is endemic in natural discourse. It is a pervasive and unavoidable feature of social life.

What are the implications of the burgeoning of versions for analysis? How do we deal with multi-accounts of events, motives and so on, with manifold descriptions of a given cognitive state varying substantially in different discursive contexts? One route is to reify one version as the 'truth' and other versions as contingent, ironical or deceptive. With this procedure a coherent picture of the individual and their real psychological determinations can be maintained.

As we have argued elsewhere (Potter and Wetherell, 1987, Chapter 4), the analytic grounds for these distinctions between real and other versions are frequently extremely problematic. The procedure we prefer is to give up the attempt to make the individual consistent, or to produce one belief or attitude, and the right account of a mental state. This involves the radical step in socio-psychological analysis of relinquishing the individual as our main unit of social analysis and accepting individual fragmentation, diversity, incoherence and flexibility. Some of this diversity will become apparent as we examine our data.

Units of Discourse Analysis

If the individual and their motives, cognitive processes, attitudes and so on lose their centrality, on what do we base our analysis? There are many important aspects to investigate from the way a rhetorical strategy functions to the meshing of turns in a conversation. Given that we are concerned here with ways of making sense of the self and identity, our focus will be more on the content of what is said.

In particular we will be searching for regularities in the broad interpretative resources individuals draw on as they try to answer the interviewer's questions and construct a story about themselves and their careers. We will not expect individuals to be consistent in their use of these resources. Thus someone might draw on both essentialist and non-essentialist models of gender, for example, in the course of the interview as the purpose and context of their discourse changes. They might argue that women and men are different in fundamental and intrinsic ways, that women are more emotionally inclined, for instance, and then also argue that there are no important or crucial differences between women and men. The interpretative resource is our unit of analysis in this case, and we are interested in the ideological implications, the possibilities and constraints, of one construction or version of self versus another. A detailed description of the stages involved in the analysis of these interpretative resources or repertoires can be found in Potter and Wetherell, 1987 (Chapter 7) and Wetherell and Potter, 1988.

The four points just described set the terms of reference for our analysis. Before going on to describe the regularities in ways of making sense of self and career evident in the interviews, some background to the collection of the interview material is required.

Background to the Study

This study formed part of a larger project investigating gender, identity constructions and speech styles which used both Q Sort techniques and interview procedures (Marshall, 1986). We will concentrate here on the interview material alone and on identity construction, rather than the material on speech styles. It should be noted that our aim is to use this material to introduce some general and more theoretical points about the representation of identity. We will not present a systematic and exhaustive analysis of this aspect of the interviews.

Interviews with 23 women and 7 men were selected randomly for our analysis from the larger collection of interview material. Respondents were volunteers who responded to a request in a jurisprudence lecture and were all law students at Edinburgh University. They were told that the purpose of the research was to investigate various aspects of their personal and social identity, or their ideas about themselves and their work. The majority of those interviewed were in the third and fourth years of their law degrees and thus in the later stages of their training. This sample came predominantly from self-defined middle-class backgrounds and their ages range from 20 to 40, but most were in their twenties. The group included several women who were mature students employed in other types of jobs prior to their law training.

All interviews were conducted on a one-to-one basis in the Psychology Department of the University of Edinburgh. The interview style was informal and conversational but covered the same topics for all participants. The schedule used is reproduced in the Appendix. Transcription stressed readability for content rather than the detailed reproduction of speech features such as intonations and overlaps. Material omitted in the extracts below is indicated by . . . and pauses by (.).

Our analysis concerned two broad topics in the representation of identity. First we will look at the general resources used by both women and men to make sense of personal self and professional/ occupational identity, and this will set the scene for a later discussion of the construction of gendered social identities.

Becoming a Lawyer: Traits, Roles and the Tensions

This section focuses on responses to questions about the person's sense of themselves as a lawyer and their view of the characteristics required for solicitors and advocates (questions 7 to 13 in the interview schedule).

Much of this discourse will sound extremely familiar. As we noted we are interested in forms of common sense. Despite this, or rather for this reason, it is fascinating, particularly for the social identity theorists. How do people construct their sense of self in different contexts in relation to their occupations? How do they relate personal self to occupational characteristics? In one sense we know the answers already as we too are enmeshed in this everyday discourse and produce it ad nauseam in our own daily lives; but to develop a body of knowledge for a critical social scientific assessment and as part of our task of denaturalizing what is taken for granted, the threads need to be laid out in a more painstaking fashion.

Personal Selves: The Trait/Type Interpretative Resource
In common with other everyday discussions of the self (Potter et al., 1984; Wetherell et al., 1986; Wetherell and Potter, 1989) a trait/type repertoire of the person completely dominated respondents' general references to themselves. These references assumed a fixed personality distinguished by a set of characteristics: abilities, preferences, habits, traits and temperaments. These characteristics, which are used to explain and justify behaviour, were represented as relatively constant over time. The individual thus presents an enduring personality allowing fixed benchmarks for self-definition, 'I am the type of person who . . .' The series of extracts which follows indicates the tenor of this repertoire.

> Female 12: 'I'm not really a very showy person.'
>
> Female 11: I am fairly extrovert in social life but I do like things to be fairly routine so I know what is going on around me.'

Female 9: 'I'd be too sympathetic, always wanting to help the underdog.'

Female 8: 'I think of myself as (.) oh, efficiency. I think of myself as someone who is very much in control of the work that they are doing, someone who can organize themselves and organize others . . .'

Female 16: 'I'm not outgoing enough. You have to be very confident and . . . everything just on top of your head which I haven't got.'

Female 13: 'I'm the sort of person that if I don't like a subject when I start off I think I don't like it and that's the end of it, it's doomed from there.'

Female 2: 'I'm not a waffler, I like things with a right answer and a wrong answer.'

Here we find a strong sense of personal self as an idiosyncratic human being with distinct and distinguishing traits. Although this is an extremely commonplace repertoire in Western societies, it is not inevitable that one should describe self in this way. Novels, for example, are full of alternative methods for making sense of oneself in romantic and humanistic terms: for example, as an authentic or true self with various fronts or masks, or as a self with hidden depths and unconscious motives (cf. Gergen and Davis, 1985; Harré, 1983; Shotter, 1984; and Potter and Wetherell, 1987, Chapter 5, for general discussions of the social construction of self and the possibilities available in discourse for self-description).

It is important, too, to appreciate the implications of this method of self-construction. What is ruled out in this version? In particular it is a highly individualistic method of making sense. The individual is not a social being in this model but a personal being, and social influence must thus be extraneous. The trait model of self encourages a particularly asocial model of oneself, others and the social world – asocial because the part played by the social context in moulding the self is down-played.

Images of Lawyers

The respondents were equally able to provide an image or set of characteristics for their profession. Most described in great detail the traits they thought a lawyer should possess, frequently distinguishing between the requirements for advocates and solicitors.

Female 15: 'You've got to be hardworking and able to communicate with people properly, otherwise clients won't know what you are going on about . . . A lawyer has to listen carefully, I don't think it's so much a question of being articulate because if the person you're dealing with is not articulate it is like putting a barrier up.'

Female 14: 'Solicitor? Compromise, probably, gets on with people, relate to people, ability to get on with people which I think must be difficult after years of theory – actually getting on with people's problems . . . Practical, down-to-earth and considers the minimum of analytical technique, mentally seeing what the options are, having that much knowledge, and being able to isolate the options and present them and advise them what is going to come up.'

Male 4: 'To make it as a lawyer you have to be someone who is methodical and knows their stuff. Someone who is going to work steadily and who wants to achieve.'

Female 17: 'As an advocate you have to be forceful and straight to the point.'

Female 11: 'Well lawyers shouldn't be gossips, listens carefully, that's important, especially for an advocate in court, opinionated they shouldn't be . . .'

Although the main focus in the rest of this section will be on the relationship articulated between personal self and career characteristics defined in these ways, it is worth making a few points first about the type of description put forward for occupational characteristics.

As we have noted, none of our respondents have any difficulty in generating some trait style image for their profession. The interview question was generally interpreted by the respondents as an entirely reasonable and sensible request. A very few, however, counterposed the generalizing and categorizing discourse required with the contrasting style of discourse which stresses exceptions, individual difference, particularizations, and the impossibility of making generalizations (cf. Billig, 1985; Condor, 1987). For instance,

Female 11: 'I don't think you can answer that. I think the successful advocate is going to be totally different from the successful legal aid solicitor who's different from whatever and obviously again even with a solicitor he can sit in a big, plushy room and deal with his big, plushy clients, so, do you want the ideal lawyer?'

But even in these cases a set of characteristics or image was still produced at other points in the interview (see the previous comments of Female 11).

The second point to note is that although the image which emerged from these descriptions had some shared features across the respondents in the sense that there seemed agreement about the agenda or the rough domains from which traits should be selected (relations with people, speaking style, working style), one could not conclude that there was a collectively shared stereotypic representation, image or consensus about the desirable traits. The collective image was fragmented and inchoate, which is what one would expect if images are being constantly constructed and reconstructed for different pragmatic ends.

Some of the obvious inconsistencies across respondents are illustrated below.

Female 12: 'I don't think they have to be straight to the point.'

Female 9: 'I don't think it helps to be too sympathetic, you've got to forget other people's problems . . . but underneath be quite ruthless.'

Female 15: 'I don't think its so much a question of being articulate.'

Female 1: 'You have to be able to detach yourself from the situation as a lawyer.'

Female 13: 'I suppose in a way you should have a good memory, but I don't think that is vital.'

Female 4: 'I think you need . . . to explain what you mean very precisely.'

Male 2: 'Someone who was sympathetic to them and try to identify with them.'

Female 3: 'For example you have to have clear expression.'

Female 18: 'You need to be a person who shows concern.'

Female 4: 'You need to have a retentive memory . . . some of them pluck cases out of the air, really obscure things.'

Possibly, if questioned, interviewees could explain away any seeming inconsistencies in these ideas about how a lawyer should behave; equally they could be the basis for dispute between interlocutors concerning the proper way a lawyer should act.

Counterposing Versions of Self and Career: The Tension Account

We have seen that these respondents present a strongly individualistic trait/type repertoire of personal self and that they equally frame their occupational identity as a set of trait-like characteristics. This pairing produces a particular kind of account which articulates a possible tension between self and group identity in the shortfall or space between oneself and being a lawyer.

Female 12: 'If I was an advocate it would be a role I was adopting as I'm not really a very strong person and I think an advocate is going to be the centre of attention whether or not he likes it. I'm not one for standing up and everything depending on me in the centre of the stage. It might put me off. There would be parts of that I would find difficult but obviously I'd have to assert myself.'

Female 19: 'You must be a good communicator and choose your words carefully which I don't think I'd be very good at. I think I'll have trouble choosing words carefully and I'll have to try and be a bit more tactful. You can't be straight with people, you have to be a bit more diplomatic and answer their questions. I tend to be too direct.'

Male 5: 'To be a good lawyer you must be a person who listens carefully. I don't know about being logical, I'm not a very logical person. I think you need to sparkle in certain ways and get trust and they feel they can relate to you, that is most important. If you haven't got that you are sunk that is why so many don't make it.'

Male 2: 'I suppose the latter is very much adopting a lawyer's way of doing things rather than being yourself, so I'd probably be myself at the beginning, I'd like to think that I'd be myself, it's not nice imagining being a hard-nosed but maybe you'd get it knocked out of you in a few months.'

In all these extracts and indeed in about 80 per cent of the interviews a distinction is drawn and thus a tension created between the self and the profession. The personal self is not at all coexistent with occupational/professional identity. There is a space between them which needs to be bridged.

Thus Male 5, for example, describes the characteristics of a good laywer and then ruminates on his own match with these. The respondents are projecting forwards, comparing their constructed image of their occupation with their present self. A tension account seems particularly suited to the theory of a fixed personal self and the delineation of a relatively rigid set of traits for one's professional identity.

We are not suggesting that respondents would always describe themselves and their careers in this way or that one type of description will be closer to the 'truth' than others. Discourse serves so many pragmatic functions and so many different types of 'truth' are constructed as those functions change that, from our stand-point, as we have already noted, it is particularly misleading to approach language as simply either accurately or inaccurately reflecting reality.

We would predict that there would be many contexts when respondents will develop quite alternative repertoires – down-playing, for instance, the special attributes required to be a lawyer, and presenting a model of self where there is no tension, which is not at all fixed as a type but is, say, entirely flexible and responsive to the situation (a situationist or behaviourist type of repertoire, perhaps, in the terminology of psychological personality theories).

Trait interpretative repertoires and tension accounts are particularly suited to the discursive demand set up by the interview questions to tell a story or narrative about oneself in relation to career choice, and the requirement to explain oneself coherently while avoiding any imputation of arrogance: that is, of arrogating desirable characteristics to oneself. Clearly this discursive context is recurrent in daily life, but there are other contexts (involving justifying oneself, for example, or blaming others, or persuading others of one's fitness for a post) that are likely to foster other repertoires.

When we examined these stories of tension in further detail it became clear that there were three rather different ways of making sense of the relation between personal self and occupation.

Right Types and Wrong Types

In this first version of the relation between personal self and the representation of the lawyer it is simply the case that either you are the right type for law or you are not. The self, that is, is so fixed there is no likelihood of successfully taking on the professional identity unless your personal self happens to coincide more or less completely with the fixed characteristics demanded of lawyers. According to this use of the trait/type repertoire, selves cannot be moulded through training and, similarly, the occupation is unlikely to be changed by the characteristics of the incumbent.

> Female 5: 'It depends what sort of person you are and whether you fit in to what the job requires. I think it is either something you are or you aren't. I'm not sure there is anything you can do to change yourself.'

> Female 7: 'If you want to be a lawyer you have to be willing to study and slog. I think it depends what sort of brain you've got, if you enjoy that sort of thing. I know a lot of my friends do and have that ability.'

> Female 8: 'I think some of those things come naturally to me and some don't.'

> Female 8: 'Well I think there are obviously ones who have innate spark, who have the right way of thinking about things, who can amass knowledge and detail and keep it there in their heads.'

> Female 4: 'It's very difficult because some people are good at exams and not good lawyers. Whereas I would say I'd probably be a good lawyer, although I'm not so good at exams.'

> Female 3: 'I would definitely not be able to be an advocate, I couldn't do that – stand up in court and be so sure that I was right, I couldn't do that. I think for some people it could be learnt but not for me.'

In this theory of personal self and career self the emphasis is on the unchanging nature of personal self – either you are naturally the right type of person with the right type of brain, the right skills and preferences, or your type prevents you from acting out the role. Personal selves are prior and set the limits for social selves. Thus, according to this model, the self cannot be flexibly transformed by group membership; the individual is not an actor, capable of taking up different personae and acting through different masks.

What functions does this method of making sense serve? It seems to achieve one very important function at least. It provides a rationalization for failure and explains ambivalence or the rejection of particular career paths. If one is a certain type, that type cannot be altered and if it happens to be a type not suited to law then it becomes reasonable and accountable to fail to become a lawyer, to fail an exam, to develop an interest in another career, or to wish to become a solicitor rather than an advocate. If the alternative view is developed that personal self can be easily moulded or changed through training or experience of an occupation then how is it possible to account for a failure to successfully embrace an occupation without discrediting one's self?

This functional use of the trait/type repertoire emerges clearly in the last two extracts above, and in those below where more context has been given.

> Female 5: 'I'm doing law for purely practical reasons, I've got no life-long ambition to become a lawyer and change the course of the world. I want to get a job at the end and as such how I see myself as a lawyer doesn't mean much to me . . . But if some super teaching job came along I'd be happy to do that. It's not the whole of my life to be a lawyer. It seems most profitable at the moment. [Several pages omitted] I'm not interested in going to the bar. I haven't got the temperament for it, and I don't have the interest for it . . . I don't think it's a case of you matching up to certain characteristics as what sort of person you are and whether you fit in to what the job requires. I mean you can't wake up one morning and say "right I'm going to be more determined than I was yesterday". I think it is something that you are or you aren't. And it is a question of wanting to find out whether you have the determination. I'm not sure there is anything you can do to change it. Other characteristics can be improved slightly. I think basically you have it or you haven't.'

> Female 9: 'When I started law I thought it would be boring. Two of my brothers do law. I think it is a struggle at the moment. I think everyone finds it a struggle. There's an awful lot of work, you don't feel you're getting anywhere, battling away against the tide of technical bits. I think I'm doing averagely but I'm not doing the work that's needed to do very well. I just won't fit into the mould.'

Reshaping the Self

The second method for conceptualizing the tension between personal self and occupational self equally begins from trait/type theory – with the notion of personality structured by fixed traits – but, in contrast, this personality is seen as being reshaped so that either a new fixed form emerges or a new self comes to overlay the underlying essential self. Reshaping can occur through personal efforts, training, experience, and the simple assumption of roles. As one becomes a lawyer, personal self is changed and one becomes a new type of person. In the terminology of psychological theory this could be described as trait theory supplemented with a role model. In fact the concept of role is frequently articulated to frame this resolution of the tension seen between self and professional identity.

> Female 7: 'In international law, you have – I don't think there is much room for shyness, you'd have to be forceful and I'm quite shy . . . I would have found that difficult but I might have learnt over the years whereas at the beginning it was really difficult. It is like learning a new way of speaking.'

> Female 8: 'I think, I'm very used to adopting a role actually because

certainly to teach someone you do . . . I don't think it is something that can be learnt deliberately, it's something that grows on you. I think you develop an artificial way of dealing with customers, people on railways stations asking questions, it is just something you do. I'm sure I've changed from when I started teaching in the way I treat different people.'

Female 5: 'I personally wouldn't find it [dealing with clients] difficult, I wouldn't find it so difficult now as a few years ago because I've taught and I've taught a modern language and a teacher who stands up in front of a class, the chances are that at the end of the lesson the students will go out having no clue what the lesson was about. Therefore as a teacher you have to be constantly stopping, saying now did they understand that, should I go over it again . . . A few years ago I'd have found that more of a problem.'

Male 2: 'I think for me it would be a role that certainly at first I'd have to adopt, possibly I'd get used to it and it would become part of myself.'

A fundamentally different conception of self emerges here. The self is a type but it is a type that can be changed. It is not a question of *being* the right type for law, one *becomes* the right type over time.

The Real Self Shines Through
Finally, in this section on the relation between personal self and images of the law, it is worth noting a third method of conceptualizing the tension between self and career. This method was much less prevalent. It develops a humanistic voice which in turn develops the idea of authenticity. Role-playing or taking on the characteristics of an occupation is seen as inauthentic. The preferred option is to simply 'be yourself' in the job and let your real self shine through.

Male 2: 'I think I'd like to relate to them [clients] on a very personal level, rather than put on a legal frame of mind, rabbiting away over their heads, as far as possible try and identify with their situations. [Several pages later] It wouldn't be so much a role that I'd adopt, I'd try not to adopt a role, in some sense I'd just try and be myself . . . I'd like to think that I'd be myself.'

Male 3: 'I'd like to be honest, I'm not sure I can project honesty, well something like honesty. I think if you are honest it comes through, if you're genuine.'

Female 15: 'I wouldn't like to pretend I wasn't someone that I am, I'm looking for respect by other people just as a human being.'

In this repertoire occupational characteristics tend to be portrayed as an undesirable barrier between oneself and others. It is dangerous to become too professional, with its attendant risk of losing personal integrity. Whereas in the strong trait/type model occupational characteristics are simply attainable or not attainable and in the more role-based version they are seen as invoking a positive transformation, here they impede and contaminate the self.

It is clear from the pattern of extracts above that these methods for conceptualizing the tension between personal and occupational self were not mutually exclusive. Typically, respondents drew upon two or three at different stages in the interview and even within a response to one question. No contradiction seemed to be perceived between the notion of self as either the right type or the wrong type, the self as being transformed through the adoption of a professional identity and the notion of an authentic self that may be dissonant with professional traits. That is, in discursive terms respondents did not generally orientate to these differences as inconsistencies for which they should account.

As psychologists we can understand these repertoires (traits, roles, and humanistic selves) as coming from different theoretical traditions and thus as problematically related. Whereas the clear impression gained from the interviews is that in everyday lay discourse these are not necessarily competing perspectives. Which perspective one adopts, however, at any given moment sets clear limits on the other possibilities which can be articulated. These methods of self-presentation have obvious consequences for what one can do with oneself, and for what can be easily explained and made legitimate.

Gender, Law and the Self

What happens if gender is now added to this equation? What are the predominant ways among our sample of representing gender, self and the law, and what contradictions and inconsistencies surrounded the construction of a professional identity for women as opposed to a professional identity for self?

Our summary of the main voices emerging makes depressing reading. Essentialist models of gender were commonplace and a negative value was frequently accorded to women.

Gender Similarity and Difference

Two contradictory notions emerged in general references to gender: that women and men are essentially different in traits, outlook and abilities; and that gender makes no difference, and women and men are basically similar.

> Female 20: 'There are some boys that actually, I would say they are better than the girls, they're more ambitious in a way. I think there's a certain determination for them to get on, to do terribly well.'
>
> Female 10: 'I don't know any women at all, female solicitors. I don't know. I don't think there would be that much difference.'
>
> Female 21: 'Well, it tends to be the girls that are less competitive anyway, not necessarily, but on the whole.'

Female 9: 'I don't think it makes much difference because there are more females doing it than males.'

Male 6: 'From past statistics women tend to be more compassionate, particularly with divorce which men are traditionally insensitive about.'

Female 5: 'I don't see any difference. There's no suggestion that its something women can't do or achieve.'

It is very important to stress that there are not two different camps of people here: one set who believe in difference and one which believes in similarity. Those interviewed drew freely on *both* notions. Most respondents developed an essentialist model of gender and many also argued that men and women were the same in outlook and abilities. This kind of variability, as we have noted, is commonplace in natural discourse. Both repertoires are very useful in different contexts for achieving a variety of goals.

Again, as with respondents' images of lawyers, the general picture of women and men which emerged was to some extent inconsistent and fragmented. Thus, women were described variously as less competitive and less career-minded, and also as more career-orientated and more ambitious. Men were described as more concerned with petty issues, as fiddling around, and as being more forceful and to the point.

Women and Men as Lawyers

The general effect of the stress on essential differences which dominated the discussions of women and the law was to push discussions of gender and the law in one direction only. (The gender similarity interpretative resource was more comon when respondents considered other people's reactions to their career choice.) Effectively, the relation between women and occupational identity became problematized, whereas the relation between men and occupational identity became normalized.

For women, another form of tension was constructed in addition to the discourse of tension between personal self and occupational self described earlier. Women and lawyers were portrayed as dissonant, the identity relationship became a site of struggle but, in contrast, the masculine and the law became synonymous, with the masculine personality portrayed as identical with the legal personality.

There were two contrasting ways in which this theme was played out and we shall deal with these separately.

Femininity as a Lack

In this version, women were constructed as lacking in relation to the characteristics required for the professional identity. Part of the process of becoming a lawyer, therefore, for a woman, is learning to overcome feminine traits.

Female 3: 'I think women find it harder to disassociate themselves from the problems. Men maybe can take a more objective look at it. But I'd hope that a woman could disassociate herself from a case otherwise it's a bad thing if you're getting involved with a problem and you can't look at it objectively, you're less likely to find the solution to it. So it's better you learn to stand back to look at it.'

Male 7: 'I'm all for equal opportunities. No I'm not sexist. I think I'd feel safe with a male lawyer. I think because of the press as well, you don't expect a women lawyer to be as competent, you don't expect it. Some of the girls doing law are amongst the most moronic, they just keep their noses in their books and copy them out to their hearts content each day. They don't even do well. Girls just worry too much, more than the men do. Some girls usually the first class ones do work harder than the boys, but some of them just don't get the results.'

Female 22: 'I don't know whether its just me, but I feel the boys in our year are more confident – they are going to get there. I think the girls are slightly less, they're certainly quieter. I know there are exceptions to the rule but, I don't know, later on, I don't know if one is better than the other but possibly boys have got what it takes to make it.'

Thus, women must become most dispassionate, more confident and less tied to their books. They must change these essential aspects of femininity if they are to become successful lawyers. It is clear that masculine characteristics are not in tension with occupational identity in this way. Indeed women must become more like men to become successful lawyers.

Femininity Changes the Law
In contrast to this definition of women as lacking in relation to the law, the second version constructs women as positive agents of change. Feminine characteristics are portrayed as good for law. Women lawyers will change the dominant style.

Female 23: 'I think more women going into law is important, as much as that they are interested in different areas of law than men, as of improving the quality. I think it does improve the quality of the profession. Perhaps areas like family law, even law concerned with property, women just have a very different viewpoint, or are prepared to argue more.'

Male 6: 'From past statistics women tend to be more compassionate, particularly with divorce which men are traditionally insensitive about. So I think women might make an impression which will help make law more accessible because they do tend to see what is important for the client better than men do, so that might bring change.'

Female 4: 'Having more women going into law makes for a difference and it's quite good. Even though there's the same amount of women as men starting law now, I think its still thought of as a man's job, into a man's world, and they'll act differently in that world.'

It is still the case here that gender and occupational identity are full of conflict and a site of struggle for women. The characteristics of the lawyer are still the characteristics of the male, feminine characteristics are still orthogonal, and women and men are still seen as possessing these traits in a fixed or essentialist way. However, this time, it is the law, the masculine, which is lacking and conservative, and the feminine is the desirable direction for change.

If the relationship between gender and identity and professional identity is constructed as problematic for women, how do they articulate other possible identities?

Housewives and Career Women

In general, the female respondents interviewed placed a high value on the professional masculine-defined identity which they saw themselves as engaging with or striving to emulate. With very few exceptions a strong negative contrast was drawn between this desirable identity and other identities unambiguously defined as feminine.

> Female 19: 'My career is really quite important to me. If I had to choose between a family and a career it would be difficult. There is no way after going through all this education and training that I'm going to get married and have kids.'

> Female 3: 'I rate my career pretty highly, I wouldn't say as high as other people. I'd quite like to get married and have children. Again I'd hate to be a housewife, it'd be boring. I'd probably be disappointed if I reached thirty and hadn't got married.'

> Female 4: 'I value my career quite highly. This is difficult. The only thing would be if I had children, but my mother has this thing, she believes strongly that if you have children it's important that you're always there if they need you and that when they come in from school you're there. I agree with her. I don't know if that's because she's always taught us that or whether I actually think that myself but at the same time I would hate to just to be getting to the things I wanted to do and then have to give it all up.'

In these extracts the respondents are discussing the major conflict for women, as it has been constructed in this society, between child-rearing, marriage, family and career. One of the clear elements in the framing of this conflict is the negative value placed on being 'just a housewife' and 'giving it all up' (cf. Wetherell et al., 1986). This obviously feminine-defined role or expectation is used as a standard of comparison, a base, against which professional identity emerges as the winner.

The combination of the different repertoires we have identified – essential gender differences, gender similarity, femininity as lack, femininity changing law, just a housewife – produces a range of different effects and strategies. It would be very difficult to attribute a particular coherent intergroup strategy to each respondent and thus label them in Tajfellian terms, for instance, as adopting a social mobility perspective or a social change belief structure (Williams and Giles, 1978). In common with the pattern found by Susan Condor (1986), we found many inconsistencies and contradictions across domains with, for example, respondents insisting that women and men were no different as lawyers and that feminine-identified characteristics would change the law. Equally, respondents held that being a housewife was a highly positive contribution to society and a substandard choice for a career, and feminine-defined qualities were negative and also highly desirable (cf. Wetherell et al., 1986).

However, most female respondents combined, among other things, the identification of the law with the masculine (as described above), an essentialist type of view of gender characteristics and comparison of their professional 'masculine' identity with a negatively defined base or standard identity concerned with child-rearing and a lack of a career which was unproblematically defined as the 'feminine' realm. The result of this combination is a powerful ideology which marginalizes women and contributes to oppression.

Women, through these constructions, are fixed into a certain place, with a certain set of characteristics, and this place is put at a distance from the site of perceived prestige, power and interest. A general discourse is developed which understands structural inequalities in terms of sets of essential sex-linked characteristics tied to a system of values in which identities defined as masculine are prioritized. The only site where women or the feminine are unproblematically seen to belong is within the family, a position which is simultaneously devalued. The identity task, therefore, for most of our female respondents was to mark out a difference between themselves and the area constructed as the feminine by default.

As we saw in the previous section, when discussing personal self and career identity, male and female respondents articulated the issues in the same general way, developing a version of themselves and their career which set up a tension between personal self and their stereotype of the lawyer. This tension was then either resolved or unresolved, depending on how the individual further constructed their task. Gender very rarely featured in the self-analysis found in this part of the interview. It is even more interesting, therefore, that when gender does come to be mentioned another layer of tension emerges for women which is not spontaneously articulated in other contexts. This point reinforces the claim that the study of ideology and discourse is in essence a study of the choice of versions and the context of that choice. Fortunately, if there are multiple versions available of self and identity, there is also the possibility of social change and the renegotiation of the nature of self.

Conclusions

Our analysis has attempted to show in a preliminary and non-systematic way some of the methods available to ordinary people for making sense of themselves as they think about gender and career. Through spelling these methods out in detail we have tried to make them strange so that they might no longer be taken for granted but can be seen as constructions which could serve particular purposes, often maintaining the existing pattern of social relations. Thus we hope to denaturalize this aspect of common sense, opening up 'mere talk' for critical investigation so that some of the implications of different versions of self can be questioned.

We have made several assumptions in the process. First, that it is meaningful and useful to study everyday discourse. We have treated language as a practice or activity in its own right and, indeed, as a central arena for the reproduction of social structures. Second, we have assumed that there is no one 'true' representation of self and identity. At any given moment there will be varying possibilities for self-construction; the individual is thus fragmented as a result. And, finally, we suggested that variations in self-representation will have different consequences and ideological implications. We noted that the particular routes favoured within the sample we studied encourage, among other things, the continued oppression of women.

Implicitly, a contrast has been developed with the approach to representation found in social identity theory. The social identity theory approach assumes that one 'true' representative process can be hypothesized and discovered by the analyst. It is assumed that self-conception, for example, can be divided into processes of personal and social identity, or zones of self-categorization and that this is the real nature of self-representation. The discourse analyst assumes there is no one true representative process and that individuals will represent themselves in discussion in varying, even inconsistent, ways. The concept of a definitive cognitive process which determines identity representation is very different from the notion that identities are actively negotiated and transformed in discourse and further that language is the area where strategic construction and reconstruction of self occurs.

Because discourse analysis and social identity theory have such fundamentally different frames of reference and approaches to doing social science, it is of little value to set them up as competing theories in relation to these data. However, we can note some points of overlap and mutual incomprehension.

Our sample at several points adopted interpretative resources which are highly commensurate with social identity theory. One can find, for instance, voices which adopt the distinction between a personal identity, defined by traits, and a social identity, defined stereotypically. Some of the sample also talked about the transformation and reshaping of personal identity as a social or occupational identity is assumed. Clearly social identity theory tunes into one strand in this sample's common sense. Of course, other constructions deviate from this line: the insistence, for example, that personal type is so fixed that one cannot be transformed by career identity – one is either the right type of the wrong type. Similarly, social identity theorists would not encourage talk about real selves which shine through social identities. The humanistic language of authenticity and true selves behind social masks is not part of social identity theory.

In addition, although the sample could generate images of lawyers which seemed stereotypical in the sense that they were generalizations, these stereotypes were fragmented across the sample, and even within the same interview a person would develop contradictory pictures of the requirements for law as they made different assessments of their own characteristics. If individuals attribute an ingroup stereotype to self when social identity is salient then it is a variable, inconsistent and highly negotiable image of the group.

Finally, discourse analysts and social identity theorists share an interest in the strategic use of identity in broader intergroup relations. Social identity is primarily concerned with understanding how identity contributes to intergroup conflict. Similarly, discourse analysts study how linguistic representations can be used ideologically by majority groups to justify oppressive and exploitative treatment of minority groups. However, the focus is very different. Social identity theorists, using the individual as their unit of analysis, locate intergroup strategies as the coherent choice of group members; individuals may adopt a social mobility belief structure, for instance, and decide that their best strategy is to attempt to pass from a low-status to a high-status group. Alternatively, individuals might choose to fight within their group for social and revolutionary change. Discourse analysts do not expect consistency or a coherent belief structure; intergroup strategy is as variable as the versions of events and motives. It could be seen as consistent within one interpretative repertoire but may well be flexible and contradictory at the individual level.

One of the strengths of social identity theory is that, unlike other social psychological approaches, it investigates how social phenomena come to structure individual consciousness and thus how the individual is a product of society (Turner and Oakes, 1986). We would hope to continue with this task through discourse analysis. The general aim is to develop social psychological methods and theories of language so that the substance of everyday life can be investigated directly. We hope that this chapter might have gone some way to indicating why language and discourse are vital to the study of ideology, identity and self-construction.

Appendix

Interview Format

1 How did you decide that you wanted to be a lawyer?
2 Is it as you imagined?
3 How well do you think you are doing?
4 How do you evaluate how well you are doing?
5 What area in law particularly interests you?
6 How do you envisage using your law training?
7 How do you see yourself as a lawyer?
8 How would you describe a good lawyer?
9 How would you like to be seen as a lawyer?
10 If you imagine yourself interacting with a client, what do you think is the best way for you to speak?
11 Is this how you would normally interact?
12 Are there other ways for a lawyer to interact with a client?
13 Do you consider these other forms of interaction to be appropriate in law? Why?
14 Would you like to see law change in any way?
15 Do you think that more women going into law will bring about change? In what ways?
16 Do you think women and men lawyers are essentially different or similar?
17 How important is your career to you?
18 What other things are important to you?
19 How do these other things fit in with your work?
20 What other plans or hopes do you have for the future?
21 Do you have any questions you would like to ask me?

References

Billig, M. (1985) 'Prejudice, Categorization and Particularization: From a Perceptual to a Rhetorical Approach', *European Journal of Social Psychology*, 15: 79–103.

Condor, S. (1986) 'Sex-Role Beliefs and "Traditional" Women: Feminist and Intergroup Perspectives', in S. Wilkinson (ed.), *Feminist Social Psychology*. Milton Keynes: Open University Press.

Condor, S. (1987) 'Gender Categorization and Particularization'. Paper presented at the Social Identity Conference, University of Exeter.

Coupland, J., Coupland, N., Giles, H. and Wiemann, J. (1988). 'My Life in Your Hands: Processes of Self-Disclosure in Intergenerational Talk', in N. Coupland (ed.), *Styles of Discourse*. London: Croom-Helm.

Coupland, N., Coupland, J., Giles, H. and Henwood, K. (in press) 'Accommodating the Elderly: Invoking and Extending a Theory', *Language and Society*.

Coward, R. (1984) *Female Desire*. London: Paladin.

Gergen, K. J. and Davis, K. E. (eds) (1985) *The Social Construction of the Person*. New York: Springer Verlag.

Gilbert, N. and Mulkay, M. (1984) *Opening Pandora's Box: A Sociological Analysis of Scientists' Discourse*. Cambridge: Cambridge University Press.

Giles, H. (ed.) (1977) *Language, Ethnicity and Intergroup Relations*. London: Academic Press.

Giles, H. and St Clair, R. N. (1979) *Language and Social Psychology*. Oxford: Basil Blackwell.

Harré, R. (1983) *Personal Being*. Oxford: Basil Blackwell.

Litton, I. and Potter, J. (1985) 'Social Representations in the Ordinary Explanation of a "Riot"', *European Journal of Social Psychology*, 15, 371–88.

McKinlay, A., Potter, J. and Wetherell, M. (forthcoming) 'Pictures in the Head or Versions in the Talk', in G. Breakwell and D. Canter (eds), *Social Representations: Research Perspectives*. Oxford: Oxford University Press.

Marshall, H. (1986) 'Gender Identity and Speech'. Unpublished Ph.D. thesis, University of Edinburgh.

Parker, I. (1989) 'Discourse and Power', in J. Shotter and K. Gergen (eds), *Texts of Identity*. London: Sage.

Potter, J. and Litton, I. (1985) 'Some Problems Underlying the Theory of Social Representations', *British Journal of Social Psychology*, 24: 81–90.

Potter, J. and Mulkay, M. (1985) 'Scientists' Interview Talk: Interviews as a Technique for Revealing Participants' Interpretative Practices', in M. Brenner, J. Brown and D. Canter (eds), *The Research Interview: Uses and Approaches*. London: Academic Press.

Potter, J. and Wetherell, M. (1987) *Discourse and Social Psychology: Beyond Attitudes and Behaviour*. London: Sage.

Potter, J., Stringer, P. and Wetherell, M. (1984) *Social Texts and Context: Literature and Social Psychology*. London: Routledge & Kegan Paul.

Reicher, S. (1986) ' "Race" in Psychology'. Paper presented at the BPS Social Psychology Section Conference, University of Sussex.

Shotter, J. (1984) *Social Accountability and Selfhood*. Oxford: Basil Blackwell.

Tajfel, H. (1982) *Human Groups and Social Categories*. Cambridge: Cambridge University Press.

Tajfel, H. and Turner, J. (1979) 'An Integrative Theory of Intergroup Conflict', in W. Austin and S. Worchel (eds), *The Social Psychology of Intergroup Relations*. Monterey, CA: Brooks-Cole.

Thompson, J. (1984) *Studies in the Theory of Ideology*. Cambridge: Polity.

Turner, J. and Giles, H. (eds) (1981) *Intergroup Behaviour*. Oxford: Basil Blackwell.

Turner, J. and Oakes, P. (1986) 'The Significance of the Social Identity Concept for Social Psychology with Regard to Individualism, Interactionism and Social Influence', *British Journal of Social Psychology*, 25: 237–52.

Turner, J., Hogg, M., Oakes, P., Reicher, S., and Wetherell, M. (1987) *Rediscovering the Social Group: A Self-Categorization Theory*. Oxford: Basil Blackwell.

Wetherell, M. (1986) 'Linguistic Repertoires and Literary Criticism: New Directions for a Social Psychology of Gender', in S. Wilkinson (ed.), *Feminist Social Psychology*. Milton Keynes: Open University Press.

Wetherell, M. and Potter, J. (1988) 'Discourse Analysis and the Identification of Interpretative Repertoires', in C. Antaki (ed.), *Analysing Everyday Explanation: A Case Book*. London: Sage.

Wetherell, M. and Potter, J. (1989) 'Narrative Characters and Accounting for Violence', in J. Shotter and K. Gergen (eds), *Texts of Identity*. London: Sage.

Wetherell, M. and Potter, J. (forthcoming) *Mapping the Language of Racism: Discourse and the Legitimation of Exploitation*.

Wetherell, M., Stiven, H. and Potter, J. (1986) 'Unequal Egalitarianism: A Preliminary Study of Discourses Concerning Gender and Employment Opportunities', *British Journal of Social Psychology*, 26: 59–71.

Williams, J. and Giles, H. (1978) 'The Changing Status of Women in Society: An Intergroup Perspective', in H. Tajfel (ed.), *Differentiation between Social Groups*. London: Academic Press.

7

When is Gender a Handicap? Towards Conceptualizing the Socially Constructed Disadvantages experienced by Women

Lindsay St Claire

The *Oxford English Dictionary* describes 'handicap' as a word of obscure history. It originated in the phrase 'hand-in-the-cap' – the name of a seventeenth-century game in which players put their stake money into a cap while they made chance draws for it. The principle was extended to horse-racing and a 'handicap race' was one in which extra weights were allotted to horses by chance, although the term was also used to describe a race in which a 'handicapper' would attempt to even the odds by calculating the extra weights for the best horses to carry. By the end of the nineteenth century, however, 'handicap' had acquired a more general meaning: namely, to place anyone at a disadvantage by imposing an 'undue weight' upon them.

Two important points are drawn from this brief sketch to form the keystone of the proposed approach. First, handicap is *undue* – hence it is a disadvantage imposed by human choices, and not by objective physical reality. Second, it follows that handicap might be unfair, but it is not inevitable. Clearly, it is these two points that identify handicap as an area for social psychological study.

Most women know intuitively what it is to be handicapped by their gender – from trivial everyday disadvantages imposed by sexist assumptions, to life-threatening examples when the diagnosis of disease might be 'overshadowed' (see Reiss and Szyszko, 1983) by the belief that the patient is an hysterical woman. In order to contribute to the understanding, and hence, alleviation, of such problems, my purpose in this chapter is to offer a new conceptual approach, in which a 'handicap' is defined as a socially constructed disadvantage which limits, prevents, or devalues a given outcome in the handicapped person's life. This is contrasted with limitation that is caused by an objective physical, mental or behavioural problem. Thus, a woman is handicapped by her gender when beliefs about her sex, and not her sex *per se*, account for limited opportunities and performances. Overall, what is new about this approach is its theoretical underpinnings; these permit conceptual and operational distinctions between socially constructed and objective disadvantage, as well as an insight into the multidimensional nature of the social psychological pathways through which handicap might be generated, imposed on – and indeed internalized and hence self-generated by – the handicapped person.

This new approach to handicap is based on social identity theory (for example, Tajfel and Turner, 1979), but within it, three dimensions are delineated which draw on the theories of social representations (Moscovici, 1981, 1984), social cognition (Tajfel, 1972, 1981; Fiske and Taylor, 1984), and referent informational influence (Turner, 1982; Turner et al., 1987) respectively. At a deeper level, however, its roots reach into two other theoretical worlds, namely those of medical rehabilitation (Wood and Badley, 1980) and of labelling the mentally retarded (Mercer, 1973). Although still in its infancy, the new social psychological approach is presented here in the hope that it will

1 provide an heuristic aid to conceptualizing handicap in general, which will help towards identifying the social psychological, and hence potentially changeable, nature of many pathways that result in disadvantages for women and other minority groups;
2 provide a taxonomy in which to classify and relate existing research; and
3 stimulate new hypotheses and insights.

The plan of this chapter is, therefore, to describe the proposed social psychological approach to handicap together with its conceptual background and then to show how it can be applied to organize and further the understanding of women's issues.

A Social Psychological Approach to Handicap

Overview

The proposed approach begins by describing three conceptually distinct ways in which an individual might be disadvantaged or 'subnormal'. First, an individual might have something intrinsically wrong with them. This is captured by the term *impairment* which is seen as being underpinned by a medical model and therefore refers to organic pathology. From this point of view, 'normal' is a residual category which consists of those who are free from pathology. Second, an individual might be unable to do something. This is captured by the term *'subnormal' behaviour* which is seen as being underpinned by a statistical model and therefore refers to sub-average performance on distributions of relevant characteristics. From this point of view, 'normal' refers to the acceptable range, such as plus or minus one standard deviation around the mean of a Gaussian distribution. Finally, an individual might fail to fulfil a given role. *Role failure* is seen as being underpinned by Mercer's (1973) social model in which 'normal' refers to behaviour which adequately fulfils a given role. It is this last sense which is most relevant to the notion of handicap or socially constructed disadvantage, because the aetiology of role failure can be entirely social. However, handicap can also overlay, interact with and on occasions cause impairments and 'subnormal' behaviour. Before articulating and applying the proposed model to women's issues, however, it is appropriate to evaluate its usefulness through a discussion of its theoretical antecedents.

Theoretical Background

The point of departure for the proposed model was a series of papers by Philip Wood and Elizabeth Badley, setting out a three-tier model of disablement (for example, 1978a, b, c, 1980). Essentially, they defined a disabled person as someone who suffers from some boaily complaint or pathology that interferes with their customary behaviour, as a result of which they are considered unusual. Hence, their model begins with *impairment(s)* which refer to the 'intrinsic situation' (Wood and Badley, 1978b) and which are defined as abnormalities of body structure, appearance or system function (including mental systems). Clearly, impairments represent deviations from biological norms. Second, *disabilities* are the expressions of impairment(s) in everyday activities like physical, psychological or social tasks, skills and behaviours. Thus, disabilities must refer to deviations from performance norms. Third and finally, Wood and Badley (1980: 16) define *handicap* as a 'disadvantage for a given individual, resulting from an impairment or disability that limits or prevents fulfillment of a role that is normal for that individual'. Because roles are socially constructed, it follows that handicap is a social phenomenon.

A useful example to clarify Wood and Badley's model is a facial scar – an impairment that might cause no disability, but which might well cause a range of handicaps. The social nature of handicap is highlighted, according to Wood and Badley, since the range of disadvantages actually generated depends on many factors, particularly on which role the scarred person is currently attempting to fill.

There are two main differences between the proposed approach and that of Wood and Badley. First, the concepts of handicap are entirely different. It will be remembered that Wood and Badley (1980: 16) defined 'handicap' as a 'disadvantage for a given individual, resulting from an impairment or disability that limits or prevents fulfillment of a role that is normal for that individual'. This definition is unclear in several ways. First, although the social nature of handicap is highlighted, it is nevertheless caused by physical impairment. Second, it is not clear what is meant by 'normal' because roles are normal by definition, since they are defined as the (normal) behaviours associated with given social statuses (see Mercer, 1973). Third, it is not clear what is meant by 'role'. Wood and Badley (1978c) identify 5 basic survival roles including (1) effective independent existence regarding immediate physical needs like feeding, hygiene and daily living; (2) being able to move around effectively, (3) occupying work and leisure time in customary and appropriate ways; (4) participating in and maintaining social relations; and (5) maintaining social and economic independence, including supporting others (which, it is worth noting, seems to exclude many women and children from the discussion). This notion of role seems problematic in that the five survival roles seem so broad that they do not relate convincingly to any labellable social status(es), unless it is 'average adult male'!

Within the present model, behaviours that inadequately fulfil roles are simply labelled 'role failures', and a traditional definition of role as behaviour that is associated with a social status is maintained. This definition has the advantage of being clear and direct. 'Handicap' is defined as a socially constructed disadvantage which limits, prevents or devalues a given outcome in the handicapped person's life. This definition accords with dictionary and indeed, intuitive meanings. Furthermore, it is clear, operationalizable and heuristic, as I hope to demonstrate in the following pages.

The second and still more fundamental difference between Wood and Badley's and the present approach concerns the underlying assumptions: Wood and Badley's model is firmly grounded in an objective, medical tradition, since the ultimate cause of disabilities and role failures (labelled 'handicap' in their model) is always some underlying impairment. Thus, although initially promising, in that it acknowledges that individuals may have problems in social as well as physical and behavioural spheres, their approach does not help us understand how a woman can be handicapped by her gender because within their model, a person who is disadvantaged in the social sphere necessarily has something wrong with them. Put another way, in order to understand how women are handicapped by their gender, it is necessary to construct a model in which the aetiology of handicap can be entirely social, and this requirement is not met by Wood and Badley's model.

However, in addition to not fitting present requirements, Wood and Badley's model may be criticized on logical grounds. The theoretical reasoning behind this criticism derives from the work of Jane Mercer (1973, 1977) in the field of mental retardation. Essentially, Mercer points out that 'normal' may be defined in (at least) three ways: a residual category which consists of those who are free from pathology (medical model); an acceptable deviation around the mean of Gaussian distribution (statistical model); or behaviour that fulfils adequately a given role (social model). Mercer continues that to attribute disabilities (which are deviations from performance norms) to the underlying presence of an impairment (which is a deviation from a biological norm) is to confuse statistical and medical models and is logically unjustifiable. The conclusion is best clarified in her own words (Mercer, 1973: 6) which focus on the way in which low IQ scores are interpreted.

> IQ, which is not a biological manifestation but is a behavioural score based on responses to a series of questions, becomes conceptually transposed into a pathological sign carrying all the implications of the pathological model. Statistical abnormality is equated with biological pathology without any evidence based on functional analysis that this statistical sign is related to the biology of the organism or that it has any functional relationship to system maintenance.

Clearly, to assume that impairment necessarily 'drives' disability and role failures 'handicap' is to commit this logical error.

The proposed approach avoids this problem by incorporating Mercer's approach and relating 'impairment', 'subnormal behaviour' and 'role failures' to distinct underlying models of normal. So instead of being contingent on impairment, each level may be approached as a phenomenon in its own right. This step instantiates a new approach, in which it is possible for the aetiology of disadvantage to be entirely social, and which is therefore useful in understanding how a woman can be handicapped by her gender. Before focusing on handicap, however, it is appropriate to make three general observations which give an overview of the whole proposed approach and the usefulness of its terminology for conceptualizing existing research.

First, to consider impairment: Archer and Lloyd (1982), point out that physical differences between men and women are frequently evaluated as female deficiencies. In the present terminology, this means that physical differences between men and women have been conceptually transposed into female impairments. This conception is unsupported by pathological evidence and clearly derives from erroneously judging women against a biological norm which is male. What masquerade as female impairments are therefore handicaps – disadvantages that spring from beliefs, not organic facts.

To turn to behaviour, a woman might show a 'subnormal' performance, say, two standard deviations below the population mean on a distribution of some characteristic. If this occurs, statistical assumptions need confirming: is the characteristic normally distributed, or is it bimodal, like the physical strength of men and women? If bimodality is the case, both the mean and our minus two standard deviation cut point designating 'subnormality' are uninterpretable. So a statement identifying most women as abnormally weak and most men as abnormally strong respectively (which might sound reasonable, or even familiar) is meaningless (see Mercer, 1973). Similarly, assuming a given characteristic *is* normally distributed, whether or not the individual in question is a member of the population from which the distribution was derived must be checked – to use a blatant example, the mechanical skills score of a girl schooled in arts would most probably be subnormal judged against a distribution of scores derived from boys tutored in mechanics. Because of the so-called 'male-as-norm principle' (see Griffin, 1986; Kruse and Wintermantel, 1987), such statistical questions are frequently overlooked, and women's performances are mistakenly labelled subnormal. Next, exponentially to compound the error, such (mis)defined 'subnormality' in performance is (mis)attributed to some underlying female impairment, thereby completing the logical confusion of statistical and medical models of 'normal' exposed by Mercer (1973) and described above.

The third general observation concerns role failures. To reiterate, the proposed approach is very different to that of Wood and Badley (1978a, b, c, 1980), who envisaged 'handicap' as role failures ultimately underpinned by impairments. Within their approach, the contribution of social psychological factors is limited to the construction of the roles – shifting the goal posts as it were – and when failure does occur, it is attributed to underlying impairment. In the present approach, handicap refers to limitations that are social psychologically constructed – that is, precisely to those role failures that *cannot* be directly attributed to objective physical factors. So the present approach might provide a useful working vocabulary for researchers like Nicolson (1986), for example, who notes that depression following childbirth is traditionally attributed to abnormalities in women's hormones (that is, impairments), whereas she discovered that factors like the violation of expectancies about motherhood, perceived failure as a mother, or conflict between roles such as career woman and mother were to blame. In that such role expectations are social psychological constructions, the aetiology of depression, was top-down, driven by handicap, rather than bottom-up, driven by impairment as traditionally assumed.

To summarize, this overview has attempted to distinguish between and note the usefulness of the terms 'impairment', 'subnormal behaviour', 'role failures' and 'handicap' when applied to feminist issues. The argument is that three factors, namely physical differences between men and women, inadequacies in women's performances, and women's failures to fulfil roles are frequently (mis)attributed to unchangeable biological givens like women's sex or 'impairments' thought to reside therein. These misattributions are *beliefs* that are disadvantageous to women. Hence, they are instances of handicap and relevant questions concern the ways in which such expectations are created, imposed and conformed to. These questions correspond to the three areas of social psychological theory and research that form the substance of the proposed model of handicap which is articulated and illustrated in more detail below.

A Social Identity Model of Handicap

The Normative Level: Handicap 1

Within the proposed social identity approach, handicap was defined as a social psychologically constructed disadvantage which limits, prevents or devalues a given outcome in the handicapped person's life. Articulation of the approach begins with a consideration of the repertoire of roles that exist within a given society. For convenience, considerations at this level will be labelled 'Handicap 1' which is the starting point of the model, since it forms the fountain-head of biased cognitive appraisals and self-expectations that are disadvantageous to women.

For present purposes, this repertoire of roles is taken as equivalent to the potential (and actual) social identifications available to society members, and it is this conceptual link that gives the approach its foundation in social identity theory. To explain, the term 'role' in the present context refers to the behaviour associated with a particular social status within a society. Social status, in turn, simply refers to positions in society which people occupy by virtue of certain behaviours or unchangeable characteristics, like age or sex. Many have titles by which the occupants are known, like 'woman' or 'doctor'. This notion may be linked to Turner's (1982) definition of social identity. He used 'social identification' in two senses: as a process of self-location within a system of social categories; or as a noun, as any social categorization used by an individual in self-definition. The sum total of social identities in this latter, structural sense, he defines as 'social identity', which is internalized as an aspect of the individual's self-concept. Clearly, it follows that social statuses used in self-definition are equivalent to social identifications. Similarly, a role is equivalent to the criterial behaviours of a social identification.

The cognitive representation of the repertoire of social identifications that exist in a society remains a matter of speculation, but following Turner et al. (1987) it is reasonable to suppose it might be hierarchical, perhaps spreading like a family tree, from a global category like 'human being' through broad sex and national identifications, to occupational statuses and numerous more 'local' identifications. Perhaps cognitive economy is achieved in that features shared by lower-order identifications need only be listed at a superordinate level. Indeed, to discover the content and organization of such identifications might prove a fascinating challenge. The key question for present purposes would concern the organizing power of sex, which might conveniently be investigated by means of sentence verification tasks. Possibilities are so numerous that it is difficult to suggest just a couple of examples. For instance, consider reaction times taken to verify (1) that humans are humans, (2) that women are humans and (3) that men are humans. If reaction time for (1) is less than that for (2) and (3), which are equivalent, it might be suggested that 'human' bifurcates into the subordinate categories 'women' and 'men' (see Collins and Quillian, 1969; Roth and Frisby, 1986). If, on the other hand, reaction time for (1) is less than (3) is less than (2), it might be argued that men are represented as more typical examples of the category 'human' (see Rosch, 1973). Similarly, reaction times taken to verify statements about women's access to occupational roles might prove instructive. Indeed, if typicality ratings were to be controlled across subjects, it might be possible to correlate reaction times with individual differences in measures like feminism.

To return to the present approach, of more immediate relevance is the potential social identity available for women, which may be conceptualized as a subset of the sum total of roles which exists within a given society. Two types of question then arise. These concern (1) women's access to roles which may be achieved within a given society; and (2) the content of roles to which women are assigned by virtue of their sex. These two questions will be considered in turn.

First, women are handicapped if social psychological processes restrict their access to roles or, put another way, if social psychological processes operate to restrict their potential social identities. In this sense the proposed approach provides a useful means of representing the mismatch between limitations actually imposed by women's sex and those imposed by beliefs about gender. For example, women's roles in our society frequently exclude occupations that are seen as more complex, difficult, strenuous and demanding (Archer and Lloyd, 1982). These include the higher levels in public office, management and academic professions (Apfelbaum, 1987), and sport (Sewell, 1988). Archer and Lloyd (1982) continue that such exclusions are generally attributed to the 'commonsense' view that men and women differ fundamentally and that these differences involve objective female deficiencies (that is, impairments) and indeed, such differences and deficiencies have even been rarefied by past psychological research.

That such exclusions are frequently based on beliefs about gender and are therefore instances of handicap rather than objective, sex-related inadequacies is most clearly revealed by cross-cultural and historical variation in access to roles in spite of a 'universal constancy' in women's biology. For example, Sewell (1988) contrasts the relative access of women to the role 'athlete' in the UK, where women's sport receives little interest, acceptance or financial backing, and in the USSR, where women's and men's sport are on a par. Interestingly, Sewell goes on to note that the Russian situation was not engendered of enlightenment or political struggle. Rather, it was an offshoot of a change in the labour market. Quite simply, there was a shortfall in men after the Second World War and women were required to carry out manual jobs previously thought too strenuous for them. As Sewell continues, acceptance of women in physical occupations like mining and road-building led to acceptance in sport. A second example, this time based on historical change within Britain, concerns women's access to the role 'teacher'. Walkerdine (1986) points out that compulsory schooling was introduced at the end of the nineteenth century and that one of its aims was to instil 'good habits' into children, in order to lessen the chances of criminality, poverty and rebellion. Such regulation was achieved by overt surveillance and coercion. According to Walkerdine, it was later felt that covert surveillance based on 'love' rather than fear might be more effective in order to counteract the possibility that coerced children might harbour secret rebellious thoughts. Hence women, whose province was believed to be love, began to be recruited into the teaching profession, from which they had previously been excluded on the grounds that to educate them to the required level would damage their reproductive capacities and thereby damage the future of the race!

To summarize, it is clear that women's exclusion from roles in our society, although attributed to their inherent weakness, is frequently an instance of handicap – that, is constructed by social psychological processes, fuelled by economic or political interests and purposes. Thus existing exclusions also require careful analysis, since they may well impose an 'undue burden' on the development of woman's identity. Before continuing, it is worth making explicit that limited access to roles is assumed to be disadvantageous. Although it could be argued that women's exclusion from a few negatively valued roles, such as 'burglar', could be advantageous, the position adopted here is that such exclusion nevertheless restricts women's social identifications and is therefore a handicap.

The second type of question about the repertoire of roles in a society concerns the content of roles to which women are assigned, or to which women have unrestricted access. In this sense, women are handicapped if the content of such roles can be shown to be disadvantageous, or what is more interesting and subtle, if a woman's role which *appears* valued, and therefore which might entail advantages, on closer examination seems to have been constructed for some ulterior motive.

One approach that is useful in examining these points is the theory of social representations (Moscovici, 1981, 1984). According to Moscovici (1981: 181), a social representation is

> a set of concepts, statements and explanations originating in daily life in the course of inter-individual communications. They are the equivalent, in our society, of the myths and belief systems in traditional societies. They might even be the contemporary version of common sense.

Social representations are shared by members of a community and they serve to explain something in familiar terms, frequently by evoking a single meaningful image. Rather more interesting, they have a paradoxical dual nature (Moscovici, 1981, 1984) since they are simultaneously a *percept* – a representation of something that has been perceived – and a *concept* – a cognitive structure that determines what is perceived. There is therefore a self-fulfilling interplay between the two which merges them and leaves them indistinguishable. The result is that what began life as an idea becomes part of the social environment and is acted upon as if it were reality. Moscovici and Hewstone (1983) use the term 'ontologization' to encapsulate this phenomenon, and they note that an idea (for example an Oedipus complex) frequently becomes ontologized as an intra-individual characteristic.

The theory of social representations is useful to the present approach in two ways. First, it provides an enriching complement to the inductive aspect of social categorization (Tajfel, 1972), so the acknowledgement that beliefs about sex-typed categories are inferred from sample women is supplemented by an account of the dynamic construction of explanations and ideas about women within a community. Such beliefs about women provide the content of the roles that determine the criterial characteristics and associated values of the various social identifications that constitute women's social identity. Therefore, the theory of social representations is particularly relevant to the present approach to handicap, in suggesting a mechanism whereby social identifications that are disadvantageous to women may evolve within a community through social psychological processes, with little or no reference to objective reality – a triumph, in other words, of mind over matter.

Second, the study of social representations suggests empirical strategies to identify the content of women's roles. For example, Moscovici (1981, 1984) notes that it is sometimes possible to build a picture of a given representation, through observing and describing natural conversation and documentary evidence. The latter, as an example of 'objective culture', is of particular interest, because although initially created by individuals, it has a 'supra-individual existence' which is appropriate to the shared nature of social representations (Kruse et al., 1988).

Itzin (1986) undertook a review of media representations of women, that provides sobering evidence that the roles assigned to women are devalued. She cites surveys of pictorial representations that emphasize female sexuality, together with feature stories that represent women in terms of their sexuality, appearance and domestic relations, and finally, degrading and denigrating cartoon representations. Similarly, a number of studies have examined the social representations of women in British television and radio advertisements, and have found women to be portrayed as domestic consumers, offering no argument or authority (Livingstone and Green, 1986; Furnham and Schofield, 1986).

These results are consistent with a recent 7-month study of 72 German magazines, in which 3090 interaction sequences between men and women were analysed (Kruse et al., 1988). Overall, the picture was one of traditional clichés, with women reacting to men, especially in receiving their help and courtship behaviours. Although the woman was central in 47 per cent of interactions, this figure varied across the 4 categories of behaviour examined – from 67 per cent of interactions concerning emotional experiences to an average of only 36 per cent of the other behaviours. To summarize, empirical studies reveal representations of women to be limited in both range and content. This suggests that the potential social identity that exists for women is curtailed and hence that women are handicapped.

In addition to documenting the nature of existing social representations, Moscovici (1981, 1984) notes that it is sometimes possible to uncover the motivating factors behind the construction of a given representation. Perhaps the most revealing example is furnished by the 'mother' role which is clearly of great value in Western society. Chess and Thomas (1982) write of its 'mystique' as represented, for instance, in the image of madonna and child. Similarly, newspapers rarefy the special status of mothers by reporting their 'instinctive ability' to recognize at once their own infant or their extraordinary suffering on separation. St Claire and Osborn (1987) have noted the reflection of such values in our child-care laws. The value of 'mother' contrasted with other female roles, crudely put, seems too good to be true. If motherhood were indeed so beatifically fulfilling, it is difficult to believe women would have been permitted to keep so much of it for themselves! Badinter's (1981) fascinating analysis, which suggests that its value was socially constructed as an instrument of women's oppression, therefore comes as no surprise.

First, Badinter (1981) cites statistical evidence that the vast majority of infants were not reared by their mothers in eighteenth-century France, but were sent to baby farms, and never expected to be seen again. This she interprets as strong evidence against the existence of a biologically given 'mother-love'. Next, she argues that the Industrial Revolution and colonialization created an urgent need for population expansion, and hence for much improved child-care practices. Finally, she argues that the concept of mother-love as a biological given can be seen as a causal attribution for the resultant increased investment women were obliged to make in child care. In the terminology of social representations, the new intensive mother–infant relationship needed explanation. This was achieved in terms of existing images of love and sacrifice that ontologized over time into the intra-personal biological 'instinct' mother-love. Indeed, this ontologization is demonstrated whenever a mother who does not show such an instinct is considered impaired in some way. For example, commenting on the dilemma faced by a woman who was sold as a Yemeni bride by her British father, and who wanted to return to Britain and was obliged to leave the Yemen without her child, a recent newspaper feature reports 'Zana claims she is a "hard woman", able to leave her son Marcus behind', which implies that a 'normal' (soft?) woman would not be able to do so. Clearly, handicapping censure or guilt are likely to result.

To conclude, the representation of mother-love as a biological given as opposed to a 'gift' (Badinter, 1981) identifies women as physiologically destined for self-sacrifice and obscures not only the economic and political motivation behind existing child-care practices but also the possibility of alternatives. Analysed in these terms, the previously taken-for-granted value associated with 'mother' is unmasked as an instrument of women's oppression.

To summarize, Handicap 1 concerns that subset of the repertoire of roles that exist within a given society to which women have access. This determines women's actual and potential social identities. Women are defined as handicapped in this first sense if social psychological processes rather than their sex *per se* restrict their access to roles – if the content of those roles to which women have unrestricted access is disadvantageous, or if the value of a role, like gold in More's Utopia, seems to be a socially constructed imprisoning chain. Handicap 1 was defined as primary, because it provides the basic information which influences evaluations of women's performances and which provide women with normative expectations to which to conform. In other words, Handicap 1 concerns the construction of the prophecy. Handicaps 2 and 3 concern the social psychological pathways by which it is fulfilled.

The Social Cognitive Level: Handicap 2
Within the present social identity approach, handicap refers to a socially constructed disadvantage which limits, prevents or devalues a given outcome in a handicapped person's life. At the most fundamental level, Handicap 1 concerns the normative expectations that construct the content of sex-typed social categories, and hence women's social identities. Handicap 2 focuses on the way in which perceivers' beliefs can provide a vehicle for such expectations. Its essence is captured by Apfelbaum (1987) when she writes: 'No matter what she [a woman leader] does, how competent she is, even if she acts like a surrogate man, her gender identification interferes with the evaluation of her activities'. To be more precise, a woman is handicapped by her gender in this second sense whenever an observer's representation of 'women' (or some other relevant sex-typed social identification) leads to a (negative) biased appraisal of her behaviour.

The deductive aspect of social categorization (for example, Tajfel and Wilkes, 1963; Tajfel, 1972, 1981) is the cognitive mechanism through which the normative expectations associated with a given social identification are understood to shape the perception of individual women's behaviours. Thus a perceiver's beliefs about 'women' will be assigned to a given individual, whenever she is so categorized.

Many authors concur as to the empirical nature of these beliefs. For instance, Williams and Best (1986) list 50 traits generally associated with women in 25 countries, including: affected, dependent, fussy, prudish, talkative and superstitious (to list every tenth item) and – particularly relevant for evaluating behaviour – unintelligent. A number of analyses were performed in order to reduce data, and compared with men, women are believed to be passive and weak; the nurturing parent yet still under the parental influence; and finally, women's psychological needs are believed to be abasement, deference, succourance, nurturance, affiliation and heterosexuality. Similarly, having reviewed myriad studies, Snyder (1984) reveals that women are assumed to be submissive, dependent, conforming, affectionate and sympathetic. Such is the nature of beliefs likely to be brought to bear in evaluating women's behaviour, and, clearly, social categorization theory predicts that the assignment of such beliefs to a woman doctor or engineer or occupant of any social status that is inconsistent with them, is likely to result in a perceived devaluation of her performance. This devaluation is defined as Handicap 2.

Interestingly, this raises the possibility of 'positive handicap', which is equivalent to Gibbons' (1981) 'patronization effect', in that the appraisal of a woman's performance in a traditional sex-typed role is likely positively to be enhanced if she is socially categorized as 'woman'. However, buttressed by an ideology that devalues women, cognitively driven biases are likely to be more influential in the negative case (see Tajfel, 1972, 1981), because biases operate in such a way as to maintain underlying value systems, which influences the type of errors that are likely to occur. So where women are less valued than men, negatively biased evaluations of, for example, a woman doctor, are more likely than positively biased evaluations of a woman nurse.

Empirical comparisons between judgements of women made under conditions designed to enhance or reduce the use of sex as a social category seem to be unavailable, which is a pity since these would furnish the most appropriate demonstration of Handicap 2. Rather, comparisons seem to be between evaluations of men and women, which are less appropriate because a baseline evaluation of the women's performances *per se* is lacking. (Within such paradigms, it is hypothesized that beliefs about 'men' and 'women' are simultaneously assigned to appropriate targets, so that the effects of male and female sex-stereotypes are observed together.) Perhaps comparisons between women as individuals and women as women are rare because sex is spontaneously used in processing social information. Hence one cannot simply be a human being in our society but must be male or female (Taylor et al., 1978; Duveen and Lloyd, 1986). If this is indeed the case, it might be argued that women are continuously handicapped!

Such an exaggeration might, in actuality, be near the truth since biased interpretations of women's performances are so widespread that they have even been identified in the evaluation of experimental data (Kruse and Wintermantel, 1987). Furthermore, they are not only manifest in 'on-line' evaluations, but also occur in selective recall and reinterpretation of previously acquired information (Snyder, 1981, 1984). Similarly, social representations have been identified as a basis for causal attributions (Moscovici and Hewstone, 1983). In this way, beliefs about women and men, mediated by social categorization, can be understood to account for the handicapping attribution of women's success to luck and men's to skill (Deaux and Emswiller, 1974; Morant, 1988).

Handicap 2 is important because perceivers are likely to act upon it. Hence, biased perceptions about women have been implicated as a cause of the under-representation of women in leading political and occupational positions (Kruse and Wintermantel, 1987; Apfelbaum, 1987). Furthermore, a perceiver's beliefs about a target woman can have such a powerful channelling influence on subsequent social interaction that her responses are constrained to confirm them to the extent that she becomes their living embodiment (Snyder, 1981, 1984).

The cognitive mechanisms underlying Handicap 2 are well known. What *is* new about Handicap 2 is the theoretical insights that derive from linking it to Handicap 1. Quite simply, the repertoire of potential social identifications that exists within a given society supplies sets of normative information that are assigned to a given woman when she is socially categorized. However, the content, and indeed the salience, of a relevant social categorization depends not only on the situation and the perceived woman but also on the working self-categorization of the perceiver. Hence, variation in the beliefs that might handicap a given woman is predicted both between and, more importantly, within perceivers. This opens a number of avenues yet to be explored by feminist researchers. In the first instance, variation in the content of a role like 'prostitute' might systematically be related to group memberships (class, ethnic, occupational, political and so on). Perceivers from different groups (doctor, housewife, feminist) are therefore likely to assign different sets of beliefs to a given woman whom they socially categorize as a prostitute. Assuming such beliefs will negatively affect the way they evaluate her, it follows that the nature of Handicap 2 will vary according to the group membership of the perceivers. In the second instance, during the course of an interaction different self-categorizations might become salient for the same perceiver, with the result that the different beliefs about 'prostitute' that appertain to each salient social identification will be applied to the same target woman. This already complex picture is further complicated by the likelihood that a succession of social categorizations will fit the perceived woman with a single situation (prostitute, struggling single-parent and so on).

This conception is entirely compatible with the approach of Oakes (1987) who in addition to considering group memberships *per se*, also takes level of abstraction into account to examine not only the psychological salience of intergroup level categories used in social perception, but also intra-group and 'supra-group' categories, like 'human'. She argues that the social category that a perceiver will employ in a situation depends on its accessibility in his or her repertoire, together with the fit between the observed behaviours and the perceiver's representation of it. However, Oakes also emphasizes that the forms of social perception are determined by the varying content of the perceiver's self-perceptions in such a way as to provide an interpretation of the situation that is functional relative to the perceiver's interests and purposes. She argues that fit not only depends on structural properties of the situation (that is, perceived differences between and within categories) but it also depends on the relevance of perceived dimensions of behaviour to the perceiver's representation of potentially salient social categories.

Clearly, this social identity approach provides a means of conceptualizing changes and perhaps inconsistencies in the beliefs about a sex-typed role expressed by a single perceiver during a single discourse (see Condor, 1987; Wetherell, 1986). The perceiver is conceptualized as actively fitting the developing situation to various stored knowledge representations. To illustrate, a perceiver might categorize a woman as a prostitute and discourse analysis might reveal variations in the meaning of the term. However, these variations are attributed to changes in the perceiver's salient self-categorization (for example, ordinary housewife or oppressed female), which are hypothesized to access different normative representations of 'prostitute'. Thus, as an alternative to Condor's (1987) suggestion, perhaps variation need not imply that perceivers reconstruct social categories during the course of interactions. Perhaps they *do* carry prepackaged sex-typed images, but there might be a vast number of such images, and the speed with which salience shifts between them might be rapid.

The second insight that arises from Handicap 2 concerns the explanation – or lack of one – of how a woman's behaviour that is constrained to fit the beliefs of a perceiver is internalized. Snyder (1984) delineates situational factors that affect the likelihood of internalization, such as consistency and regularity of interactions with the perceiver (whose beliefs are being imposed) and the degree to which the target regards the new behaviour as representative of their underlying disposition; but he does not go on to discuss their psychological underpinnings. Three points seem relevant: first, as the previous discussion suggests, consistency is unlikely to be the rule, since shifts in self- and other categorizations may differently influence interactions within the course of a single encounter. Second, this notion of behavioural confirmation is pitched at an interpersonal level, in the sense that it concerns the way in which individual recipients internalize individual perceivers' beliefs. Since this explanation is *asocial* it seems inadequate to explain how groups of women internalize essentially the same handicapping sets of beliefs as they come to conform to various roles. Third, this view of internalization is passive, assumed to flow from external pressures, and this ignores the active role of the individual in creating his or her own development (Lerner and Busch-Rossnagel, 1981). These points will be addressed during the discussion of Handicap 3 but before dealing with this more fully, it remains to summarize this section.

In Handicap 2, the handicapped woman is viewed as the passive victim of others' beliefs. Through social categorization, evaluation of her behaviour is biased and such biases become an 'undue burden' as they are acted upon by perceivers, or imposed upon and acted out by perceived women, whose performances are determined not so much by their capabilities as by others' beliefs about gender. In this way, Handicap 2 is the first social psychological pathway whereby the beliefs and representations identified as Handicap 1 become reality.

Referent Informational Influence: Handicap 3

So far, the proposed social identity approach to handicap has been like an overheard telephone conversation, since the voice of society in creating handicapping roles as well as the voice of perceivers in imposing them have been heard, but the voice of women, handicapped by their gender, has not. The task of this section is to complete the model and rectify this omission. At the third level, Handicap 3 refers to self-generated handicap – that is, limited opportunities, lowered performances and negative self-appraisals that arise not because of objective limitations but because of conformity to normative beliefs. Hence a woman is handicapped by her gender in this third sense, when a given outcome is poor, not because as a woman she is incompetent, but because as a woman, she *believes* herself to be incompetent.

This social identification approach to self-handicap is rather different from that of Berglas and Jones (1978) and Rhodewalt et al., (1982) who see self-handicap as a manufactured excuse for anticipated failure, created in order to protect self-esteem. In their formulation, a woman would be self-handicapped by her sex if she used it as an explanation for a coming performance that she feared would be inadequate.

Within the present formulation referent informational influence (Turner, 1982; Turner et al., 1987) is understood to be the social psychological mechanism whereby a woman conforms to her representation of a relevant role. Essentially, Turner argues that the function of a salient social identity is to guide behaviour in a situationally appropriate manner and that when a woman defines herself as say 'mother', she will conform to her beliefs about mothers. Since the automatic perceptual effects of social categorization apply to self and ingroup as well as outgroup, cognitive biases serve to enhance this conformity. Furthermore, women who share a particular social identification will assign themselves the same criterial attributes in a situation that enhances its salience, and *social psychologically mediated* (Turner and Giles, 1981) behavioural conformity results. Examples of social representations of women and sex-typed social identifications have already been mentioned, and according to referent informational influence it follows that a salient social identification, 'woman', should lead to the self-assignment of criterial characteristics like less intelligent, more submissive and dependent (whereas self-categorization as a man should lead to self-assignment of characteristics such as competence and assertiveness). Clearly, such self-assignments are expected to have a detrimental effect on women's self-evaluations and performance across a wide range of roles and such effects are defined as Handicap 3.

In this way, referent informational influence provides an explanation of how beliefs about women can become reality that is truly social psychological in nature. It delineates how shared normative expectations may become incorporated into individuals' self-concepts, and *actively* solves the problem of internalization.

Relevant studies comparing women's self-evaluations and performances under conditions of salient personal and salient social identifications seem lacking. Although it is known, for example, that males and females perform better on gender-appropriate tasks (Davies, 1986) or that compared with men, women attribute their own success to external factors (Apfelbaum, 1987; Morant, 1988), the crucial question for present purposes is whether such effects are mediated by a salient 'woman' social identification. This receives little, if any, attention. If the answer is 'yes', increased well-being and better performances may follow emphasis on personal identities or social identifications that are not sex-typed. For example, Hartley (1986) demonstrated with disadvantaged school children that changes in cognitive strategies leading to dramatically improved performances followed role-playing. Similar effects might be mediated by a change in salient social identification. So the exciting conclusion of the proposed approach is that handicap might be alleviated through an active change in self-definition.

Finally, it is worth adding two important qualifications. It has been argued that, generally speaking, beliefs about women entail lower expectations about competence, success, intelligence and so on, and that these will prove disadvantageous to women. However, first, this is not to imply that a woman necessarily suffers a decrease in self-esteem should she assign herself such traits. On the contrary, as social creativity predicts (Brown and Turner, 1981), Condor (1986) demonstrated that 'traditional' women value traits like submissiveness more highly than independence. Second, this also reintroduces the notion of 'positive handicap', in that such self-assignments might *enhance* self-evaluations and performance of traditional women's roles that are consistent with them.

To summarize, through referent informational influence, Handicap 3 provides a social psychological explanation of how beliefs about women, mediated through women's social identities, become real. It stresses the transactional nature of handicap by highlighting the individual as a producer of her own development.

Conclusion

My aim in this chapter was to offer a new approach in which handicap is defined as a socially constructed disadvantage that limits, prevents or devalues outcomes in handicapped people's lives. This contrasts with limitations caused by objective physical or behavioural factors. The approach provided a soundly underpinned working vocabulary to evaluate the way in which physical or performance differences between men and women, or women's failure to fulfil roles are frequently misattributed to female impairments.

Three levels of handicap were identified. The broadest level concerns the repertoire of roles and hence the potential social identities that exist within a society. It was suggested that women are handicapped at this level because social psychological processes restrict their access to roles, thereby limiting their identities, and also because the content of roles to which women have unrestricted access is typically disadvantageous, thereby diminishing their identities. At the second level, social categorization was pinpointed as a mechanism through which a perceiver's representations of social categories bias their perceptions. It was suggested that women are handicapped at this level because expectations associated with sex-typed social categories are likely negatively to bias evaluation of their performances, leading to limited opportunities and constrained interactions and hence self-fulfilment of the expectations. Finally, at the third level, referent informational influence was pinpointed as a mechanism through which an individual's representations of social categories may be internalized as part of their self-concept, in order functionally to guide behaviour. It was suggested that women are handicapped at this level since expectations associated with women and sex-typed roles are likely negatively to bias self-expectations and performances and hence lead to self-generated fulfilment of role expectations.

In identifying three conceptually distinct social psychological pathways in which women are handicapped by their gender, the proposed model also suggests three levels at which attempts to alleviate such disadvantages may be pitched. It suggests that most effort should be directed towards promoting more realistic images of women in the media, since social representations of women are hypothesized to provide the source of handicapping beliefs. Such secular change is likely to be slow, but fortunately the proposed model does not imply that it must be completed before ameliorization at other levels may proceed. On the contrary, it suggests that direct demonstrations of stereotyping, for example, might provide perceivers with the insight to circumvent biased perceptions of women, and such demonstrations could be incorporated into myriad educational programmes. Finally, a woman perceiving herself handicapped by her gender might attempt strategies of individual mobility, social creativity or, perhaps, join a women's movement in an attempt to bring about social change (see Willims and Giles, 1978).

The important point is that the model is transactional. Thus, changes in perceivers' awareness and women's self-definitions contribute to changes in what is expected of women at the level of social representation, which should in turn reinforce changes in self- and perceiver's beliefs. This means that through their own acts of self-definition, women can begin to create a new social reality to shape themselves.

Dedication

This chapter is dedicated to Reubin Randolf St Claire (30 April 1916 to 2 February 1988) and to R.E. St Claire, in loving memory.

References

Apfelbaum, Erika (1987) 'Henri Tajfel Memorial Lecture, 1986: Women in Leadership Positions', *British Psychological Society Newsletter*, 17.

Archer, J. and Lloyd, B. (1982) *Sex and Gender*. London: Penguin.

Badinter, Elizabeth (1981) *The Myth of Motherhood*. London: Sovereign Press.

Berglas, S. and Jones, E. E. (1978) 'Drug Choice as an Externalization Strategy in Response to Noncontingent Success', *Journal of Personality and Social Psychology*, 36: 405-17.

Brown, Rupert, J. and Turner, John C. (1981) 'Interpersonal and Intergroup Behaviour', in J. C. Turner and H. Giles (eds), *Intergroup Behaviour*. Oxford: Basil Blackwell.

Chess, S. and Thomas, A. (1982) 'Infant Bonding: Mystique and Reality', *American Journal of Orthopsychiatry*, 52(2): 213-22.

Collins, A. and Quillian, M. R. (1969) 'Retrieval Time from Semantic Memory', *Journal of Verbal Learning and Verbal Behaviour*, 8: 240-7.

Condor, Susan (1986) 'Sex Role Beliefs and "Traditional" Women: Feminist and Intergroup Perspectives', in S. Wilkinson (ed.), *Feminist Social Psychology: Developing Theory and Practice*. Milton Keynes: Open University Press.

Condor, Susan (1987) 'From Sex Categories to Gender Boundaries: Reconsidering Sex as a "Stimulus Variable" in Social Psychological Research', *British Psychological Society Newsletter*, 17.

Davies, Dilys R. (1986) 'Children's Performance as a Function of Sex-typed Labels', *British Journal of Social Psychology*, 25: 173-5.

Deaux, Kay and Emswiller, T. (1974) 'Explanations of Successful Performance on Sex-linked Tasks: What is Skill for the Male is Luck for the Female', *Journal of Personality and Social Psychology*, 29: 80-5.

Duveen, Gerard and Lloyd, Barbara (1986) 'The Significance of Social Identities', *British Journal of Social Psychology*, 25: 219-30.

Fiske, Susan T. and Taylor, Shelley E. (1984) *Social Cognition*. New York: Random House.

Furnham, Adrian and Schofield, Sandra (1986) 'Sex Role Stereoptyping in British Radio Advertisments', *British Journal of Social Psychology*, 25: 165-71.

Gibbons, F. X. (1981) 'The Social Psychology of Mental Retardation', in S. S. Brehm, S. M. Kassin and F. X. Gibbons (eds), *Developmental Social Psychology*. Oxford: Oxford University Press.

Griffin, Christine (1986) 'Qualitative Methods and Female Experience: Young Women from School to the Job Market', in S. Wilkinson (ed.), *Feminist Social Psychology: Developing Theory and Practice*. Milton Keynes: Open University Press.

Hartley, Robert (1986) 'Imagine You're Clever', *Journal of Child Psychology and Psychiatry*, 27(3): 383–98.

Itzin, Catherine (1986) 'Media Images of Women: The Social Construction of Ageism and Sexism', in S. Wilkinson (ed.), *Feminist Social Psychology: Developing Theory and Practice*. Milton Keynes: Open University Press.

Kruse, Lenelis and Wintermantel, Margaret (1987) 'The Image of the Man', *British Psychological Society Newsletter*, 17.

Kruse, Lenelis, Weimer, Ernst and Wagner, Franc (1988) 'What Men and Women are Said to Be: Social Representation and Language', *Journal of Language and Social Psychology*.

Lerner, R. M. and Busch-Rossnagel, N. A. (1981) 'Individuals as Producers of their own Development: Conceptual and Empirical Bases', in R. M. Lerner and N. A. Busch-Rossnagel (eds), *Individuals as Producers of their own Development*. London: Academic Press.

Livingstone, Sonia and Green, Gloria (1986) 'Television Advertisements and the Portrayal of Gender', *British Journal of Social Psychology*, 25: 149–54.

Mercer, Jane R. (1973) *Labelling the Mentally Retarded*. Berkeley, CA: University of California Press.

Mercer, Jane R (1977) 'Cultural Diversity, Mental Retardation and Assessment: The Case for Nonlabelling', in P. Mittler (ed.), *Research to Practice in Mental Retardation*, vol. I. Baltimore: University Park Press.

Morant, Nicola (1988) 'Subtle Sexism: Attributions of Male and Female Success.' Unpublished Dissertation. Department of Psychology, Bristol University

Moscovici, Serge (1981) 'On Social Representation', in J. P. Forgas (ed.), *Social Cognition: Perspectives on Everyday Understanding*. New York: Academic Press.

Moscovici, Serge (1984) 'The Phenomenon of Social Representations', in R. Farr and S. Moscovici (eds), *Social Representations*. Cambridge: Cambridge University Press.

Moscovici, Serge and Hewstone, Miles (1983) 'Social Representations and Social Explanations', in M. Hewstone (ed.) *Attribution Theory: Social and Functional Extensions*. Oxford: Basil Blackwell.

Nicolson, Paula (1986) 'Developing a Feminist Approach to Depression following Childbirth', in S. Wilkinson (ed.), *Feminist Social Psychology: Developing Theory and Practice*. Milton Keynes: Open University Press.

Oakes, Penelope J. (1987) 'The Salience of Social Categories', in J. C. Turner et al., *Rediscovering the Social Group*. Oxford: Basil Blackwell.

Reiss, S. and Szyszko, J. (1983) 'Diagnostic Overshadowing and Professional Experience with Mentally Retarded Persons', *American Journal of Mental Deficiency*, 87: 396–402.

Rhodewalt, F., Saltzman, A. T. and Wittmer, J. (1982) 'Self-handicapping among 'Competitive Athletes: The Role of Practice in Self-esteem Protection'. Unpublished MS, University of Utah.

Rosch, E. (1973) 'On the Internal Structure of Perceptual and Semantic Categories', in T. E. Moore (ed.), *Cognitive Development and the Acquisition of Language*. London: Academic Press.

Roth, Ilona and Frisby, John P. (1986) *Perception and Representation: A Cognitive Approach*. Milton Keynes: Open University Press.

St Claire, L. and Osborn, A. F. (1987) 'The Ability and Behaviour of Children who have been In-Care or Separated from their Parents', *Early Child Care and Development*, 28(3): 197–354.

Sewell, Sally (1988) 'Women in Sport'. Unpublished Dissertation. Department of Psychology, University of Bath.

Snyder, Mark (1981) 'On the Self-perpetuating Nature of Social Stereotypes', in D. L. Hamilton (ed.), *Cognitive Process in Stereotyping and Intergroup Behaviour*. Hillsdale, NJ: Erlbaum.

Snyder, Mark (1984) 'When Belief Creates Reality', in L. Berkowitz (ed.), *Advances in Experimental Social Psychology*, vol. 18. London: Academic Press.

Tajfel, Henri (1972) 'La catégorisation sociale', in S. Moscovici (ed.), *Introduction à la Psychologie Sociale*. Paris: Larousse.

Tajfel, Henri (1981) *Human Groups and Social Categories*. Cambridge: Cambridge University Press.

Tajfel, Henri and Turner, John C. (1979) 'An Integrative Theory of Intergroup Conflict', in W. G. Austin and S. Worchel (eds), *The Social Psychology of Intergroup Relations*. Monterey, CA: Brooks-Cole.

Tajfel, Henri and Wilkes, A. L. (1963) 'Classification and Quantitative Judgement', *British Journal of Psychology*, 54: 101–14.

Taylor, Shelley E., Fiske, Susan T., Etcoff, N. L. and Ruderman, A. J. (1978) 'Categorical Basis of Person Memory and Stereotyping', *Journal of Personality and Social Psychology*, 36: 778–93.

Turner, John C. (1982) 'Towards a Cognitive Redefinition of the Social Group', in H. Tajfel (ed.), *Social Identity and Intergroup Relations*. Cambridge: Cambridge University Press.

Turner, John C. and Giles, Howard (1981) 'Introduction: The Social Psychology of Intergroup Behaviour', in J. C. Turner and H. Giles (eds), *Intergroup Behaviour*. Oxford: Basil Blackwell.

Turner, John C., Hogg, M. A., Oakes, P. J., Reicher, S. and Wetherell, M. (1987) *Rediscovering the Social Group: A Self-Categorization Theory*. Oxford: Basil Blackwell.

Walkerdine, Valerie (1986) 'Post-structuralist Theory and Everyday Social Practices: The Family and the School', in S. Wilkinson (ed.), *Feminist Social Psychology: Developing Theory and Practice*. Milton Keynes: Open University Press.

Wetherell, Margaret (1986) 'Linguistic Repertoires and Literary Criticism: New Directions for a Social Psychology of Gender,' in S. Wilkinson, (ed.), *Feminist Social Psychology: Developing Theory and Practice*. Milton Keynes: Open University Press.

Williams, J. and Giles, H. (1978) 'The Changing Status of Women in Society: An Intergroup Perspective', in H. Tajfel (ed.), *Differentiation between Social Groups*. London: Academic Press.

Williams, John E. and Best, Deborah L. (1986) 'Sex Stereotypes and Intergroup Relations', in S. Worchel and W. G. Austin (eds), *Psychology of Intergroup Relations*. Chicago: Nelson-Hall.

Wood, Philip H. N. and Badley, Elizabeth E. M. (1978a) 'Size of the Problem and Causes of Chronic Sickness in the Young', *Journal of the Royal Society of Medicine* 71: 437–41.

Wood, Philip H. N. and Badley, Elizabeth E. M. (1978b) 'Setting Disablement in Perspective', *International Rehabilitation Medicine* 1(1): 32–7.

Wood, Philip H. N. and Badley, Elizabeth E. M. (1978c) 'An Epidemiological Appraisal of Disablement', in A. E. Bennett (ed.), *Recent Advances in Community Medicine*. Edinburgh: Churchill Livingstone.

Wood, Philip H. N. and Badley, Elizabeth E. M. (1980) *People with Disabilities*. World Rehabilitation Fund, Inc.

8

Cognitive Consequences of Gender Identity

Patricia Gurin and Hazel Markus

In essays that profoundly influenced the social sciences at the end of World War II, Erikson (1946, 1956) introduced the concept of ego-identity. Deliberately vague in defining its meaning, Erikson alluded to two of its aspects: a persistent sameness within oneself, and a persistent sharing of some kind of essential character with others. On the one hand, ego-identity represents a psychological achievement of the individual – a sense of being unique and the same person now as in the past and continuous into the future. On the other hand, ego-identity is inextricably embedded in social life, limited by as well as fitted to the socio-historical moment in which the individual lives. This duality and bridging of the personal and social is what proved attractive to social scientists in the 1950s and explains the enduring, if often elusive, appeal of the concept.

Sociologists and psychologists have continued to employ the concept, sometimes referring to identity and sometimes to self or self-concept, and usually emphasizing one or the other of its dual meanings. For sociologists, the idea of a niche – the sense of self as fitting in a place, social position, and history – has predominated. So, for example, in the identity theory of structural symbolic inter-actionists, identity is defined as an internalized role designation that corresponds to a social location of the person in a network of interactions (Stryker, 1968; Burke, 1980). For psychologists, it is the idea of distinctiveness – the sense of self as unique and continuous across time – that has been most compelling. The two traditions have also investigated different consequences, sociologists concerned more with role performance, psychologists more with affective and cognitive functions of the self-concept.

Both disciplines treat the self as something one has as well as something that constitutes a social process. Having a self means one can act toward oneself with the same mechanisms, such as symbolic communication and role-taking, that one uses to act toward other individuals. We can perceive, define, and evaluate ourselves just as we perceive, define, and evaluate others (Lester, 1984). However, within this shared meaning of the term 'self' there has been little agreement about a precise distinction between self and identity. The term 'identity' generally suggests the meaning the self acquires when situated in social roles or groups (Stone, 1962; Tajfel, 1974). For structural symbolic interactionists, the self is a set of responses of the organism and is comprised of many parts that are called identities, each representing one's participation in structural social relations (McCall and Simmons, 1966; Stryker, 1968; Burke and Tully, 1977). Although this conceptualization implies that the self is limited to role-identities, Stryker (1984) argues that the processes by which the self develops sometimes results in self-concepts organized around master statuses (such as gender, age, race, social class), personal traits, or some combination of the two. This formulation brings the work of the structural symbolic interactionists close to the current work in psychology on self-schemata.

In this article, we draw from sociological and psychological perspectives and explore the possibility of integrating the bodies of work on self-concept and identity to make them mutually illuminating. We focus on the *social* content of identity and look into its *cognitive* functions. The study investigates women's gender identity. Gender is examined not just as a trait characterizing the individual (Bem, 1981; Markus et al., 1982) but as an internal representation of belonging to the social category, women. Tajfel's social identity theory (1974, 1978) provides the framework for examining gender as one of women's possible social identities – that is, as part of their self-concepts that derives from membership in a gender category.

The study probes the question of whether women's gender identity increases efficiency of information-processing and thus serves the type of cognitive function attributed to self-schemata. Self-schemata, which are cognitive generalizations about the self in particular domains, lend organization to experience. They shape expectations; they determine which stimuli are selected for attention; they guide the processing of new information, the retrieval of stored information, and constitute a basis for inference or going beyond the information given (Markus and Zajonc, 1985; Stryker, 1968, 1980; Taylor and Crocker, 1981).

We also extend the study of cognitive functions to include the implications of gender identity for *political* cognitions. These cognitions include discontent with women's collective status in society and a causal theory of economic and power disparities between men and women.

Our hypothesis is that gender identity depends on (1) how *central* being a woman is to the self-structure, and (2) the extent to which a woman has a *sense of common fate* with other women. We assume that the cognitive consequences of gender identity are dependent on where women locate themselves in socially structured gender roles – whether they have traditional or non-traditional work and family roles. In other studies we have treated role-orientation as both a cause and a consequence of gender identity (see Gurin, 1985). Because this study focuses on information-processing, we believed that the function of role-orientation as a possible conditioner of the meaning of being a woman was the most critical of the various functions it might have in the identities of women.

Laboratory and questionnaire measures taken on undergraduate women students are used to address three sets of questions: (1) Does gender identity function as a self-schema by influencing how group-relevant information is processed? Which of the hypothesized properties of gender identity – cognitive centrality or a sense of common fate – is more important in schematic functioning? (2) What properties give gender identity political significance and are associated with political consciousness? (3) What is the impact of the traditionality or non-traditionality of the woman's career and family plans on the functioning of gender identity?

Subjective Membership – A Self-Schema?

With respect to the first question, Tajfel and colleagues have shown that various bases of categorizing individuals into groups (even assigning them to groups randomly) promote feelings of being an ingroup, and that these ingroup identifications have numerous effects on intergroup relations. Other research shows that people spontaneously describe themselves in categorical terms and that these categorical references typically precede particularistic descriptors (Kuhn and McPartland, 1954; Gordon, 1968). When asked to list words or phrases that describe how they think of themselves (the Twenty Statements Test), individuals usually mention being a woman or a man, a person born into a particular ethnic group, race, or nationality, a member of a particular language community. But do these categorically based identities function as self-schemata?

Self-schemata in particular domains sensitize the individual to information that is relevant to these domains. This heightened interest in and attention to a particular domain produces a dense and well-organized store of knowledge. Those with self-schemata in particular domains (such as independence, creativity, competitiveness) develop a type of expertise for the domain, and such expertise has a number of consequences for subsequent information-processing. Specifically, they can make judgements about the self quickly and confidently in the domain, are consistent in their responses, evaluate new information for its relevance to the given domain, have relatively better memory for information relevant to the domain, and can resist information that contradicts a prevailing schema.

Is there evidence that role- and categorically based identities function in these ways? That is, does thinking of oneself as a woman, or a black, or a worker, parallel the cognitive consequences that have been observed for trait-based characteristics of the self? Solidarity theories of social movements (Tilly, 1978; Fireman and Gamson, 1979), identity theory of role performance (Stryker, 1968; Burke, 1980), and social identity theory of intergroup relations (Tajfel, 1978; Tajfel and Turner, 1986) all assume that they do. Several psychological effects are attributed to a person's representation of his/her group memberships or social roles. These representations become anchors for social judgements, sharpen perception of the boundaries between groups and social positions, provide yeast for action, and shape the course of intergroup and role relations.

The critical question is what properties of group and role identities give these identities psychological significance. Virtually all group members have some awareness of their group membership and thus have a group identity. Some group members seem to possess antennae that are tuned to receive group-relevant information that others miss. It is most often assumed that for these people group membership has become central to the self and thus the identity can be activated by minimal cues (see Sherif, 1980). Yet, experimental studies usually do not evaluate if the impact of group membership is greater when it is more central to the sense of self.[1] Tajfel (1978) suggests that identity centrality (salience in Tajfel's terminology) depends on the clarity of the member's awareness of membership, extent of positive feeling associated with membership, and level of emotional investment in being a member. However, research conducted within the Tajfel framework until recently did not measure either centrality or the psychological characteristics on which it rests. Nor has the emphasis in sociological work on salience, dominance, centrality, and prominence of identity produced a test of their precise effects on social perception and cognition.[2]

The goal of our research is to determine whether group identity has systematic effects on perception and cognition. We hypothesized that when gender is cognitively central to the self-structure, it would function as a self-schema. Guided by the work of Converse (1970), we defined cognitive centrality as the amount of thought the individual reports devoting to gender. Converse argues that mental preoccupation with a social object, issue, or relationship reflects its centrality to self, which in turn makes the internal representation of the object more durably salient, internally consistent with other representations, and more stable across time.

Properties of Identity and Feminist Political Consciousness

Does a self-definition that prominently features a woman's gender ensure that she will develop ideas about the politics of gender relations? A second goal is to determine what properties of gender identity are related to political cognitions.[3] It is usually assumed that centrality of the group identity should play some role in political consciousness. The group's centrality in thought should increase a member's awareness of the group's societal status by heightening the member's interest in the group, by focusing attention on issues that group leaders and the media project as being in the group's interest (Conover, 1984; Conover and Feldman, 1984), and by activating political analyses, causal theories, and expectancies about intergroup life (Gurwitz and Dodge, 1977; Stephan, 1985). But surely it takes more than defining oneself as a woman and thinking about being a woman to develop political consciousness of intergroup relations.

Based on earlier studies of several social categories prominent in American life (blacks and whites, working- and middle-class people, the poor and businessmen, older and younger people), political consciousness for subordinate groups is defined as including: a sense of collective discontent, rejection of the legitimacy of group disparities, and approval of collective strategies to reduce these disparities (Gurin et al., 1980; Gurin, 1985).

These dimensions of political consciousness are similar to what Tajfel and Turner (1986) mean by cognitive alternatives to accepting a group membership that does not provide positive psychological distinctiveness. Research conducted in the Tajfel tradition, however, has not clarified which properties of social identity help members develop these political cognitions that make group membership positive and transform the member's understanding of intergroup relations.

We hypothesize that it is the sense of being connected and interdependent with other group members that galvanizes the politicalization of group membership. A woman can treat her gender almost as a physical trait, like being tall or fat or young. When she does, gender identity, even if central to her self-conception, is not likely to generate beliefs about the social and political significance of gender. It is when her gender identity includes representations of relations to other women, particularly that of shared fate, that it propels her to ponder intergroup relations. The consciousness-raising groups in the 1970s were based on this premise. Through group discussion individuals were helped to see that their experiences were common, not idiosyncratic, and that their fates as women were intertwined by social definitions of gender roles. The strategy was to make 'the personal political' by perceiving commonality and becoming aware that their gender inevitably shapes the fortunes of women and men because gender functions as a social categorization and not merely as an individual characteristic. This was the heart of feminist consciousness-raising.

With respect to collective discontent, the sense of common fate provides an intergroup perspective that is necessary to perceive group disparities. Experimental studies of social categorization repeatedly show, for example, that being labelled a member of an ingroup and drawing attention to commonalities among members also fuels comparisons *between* groups (Wilder, 1978; Allen and Wilder, 1979). And this helps women overcome some of the structural constraints that depress development of political consciousness (Merton, 1968). The structure, frequency and intimacy of their relations with men, and their interdependence with men in families, ethnic groups, and social classes tend to inhibit women from comparing themselves with men or appreciating the extent to which men and women are treated categorically (Williams, 1975; Crosby, 1982; Gurin, 1985).

When women become aware that they are treated categorically rather than individually and that their fates are similar despite variability in their personal qualities, they also begin to raise questions about the legitimacy of group disparities. Wage disparity is likely to be considered fair if it is thought to result from the inadequacies of women or the greater endowments of men. The same discrepancy will be judged illegitimate if it is thought to result from structural or situational factors that limit women or favour men. However, people generally tend to underestimate the importance of social circumstances and exaggerate the causal role of personal qualities of individuals (Nisbett and Ross, 1980; Kelley, 1972). By hypothesis, becoming aware of common fate should lead group members to overcome these attributional biases that limit perception of structural, illegitimate causes of gender-based disparities.

Finally, a positive attitude toward collective action is more likely to develop when gender identity is based on perceived interdependence within the group. When members of a group understand that success and failure depend not only on individual performance but also on group membership, they are motivated to endorse collective strategies to remove the external category-based barriers. Women who treat their gender more as a defining trait than as a relationship to other women are not as likely to see the value of group action.

Structural Divisions among Women:
The Import of Gender Roles

Because large social categories are internally differentiated, group identity is rarely a simple matter of identifying with a whole category. Individuals may identify with members who share similar social origins, experiences, roles, or life-styles, but will not identify with others whose lives are different in these ways. Zavalloni (1973) reminds us that WE and THEY may coexist within a single group membership. WE women are an internal ingroup and THOSE women an internal outgroup within the broader category usually considered the ingroup for women. A cognitive analysis of identity should be sensitive to these internal structural divisions.

Of all the ways that women are differentiated, gender role is one of the most important. Women are distinguished by others and distinguish themselves as traditional or non-traditional depending primarily on their roles as homemakers or as combining family and work. Despite dramatic changes in societal views of appropriate roles for women and men (Mason et al., 1976; Thornton and Freedman, 1979), and the equally dramatic rise in employment of mothers of young children, a significant minority of men and women in both the United States and Europe still adhere to traditional self-role standards (Thornton et al., 1983; Commission of the European Communities, 1984). And while higher education substantially increases approval of non-traditional roles, even young women currently attending college vary widely in their attitudes towards gender roles. Of the college women we surveyed in 1981 for possible inclusion in this study, a fifth described themselves as not career-minded; a fifth thought a working mother cannot establish as warm and secure a relationship with her children; a third that a pre-school child is likely to suffer if his/her mother works; and slightly over a third did not plan to work when their own children were pre-school age. Controversy over gender-role differentiation makes this structural feature of women's lives, even at a large liberal university, a potentially criticial conditioner of the meaning of gender identity. For this reason, we included gender role-orientation in the design to examine whether gender identity did function similarly for traditional and non-traditional women.

Method

On the basis of questionnaire responses, 126 college women (63 with traditional and 63 with non-traditional role orientations) were selected to participate individually in a laboratory study. The questionnaires were administered in classrooms approximately three weeks before the laboratory session, which consisted of two sets of cognitive tasks: one assessed the influence of gender identity on processing information about the self, the other assessed its impact on feminist political consciousness.

Measures
The two properties of gender identity were measured in self-report questionnaires. Following Converse, we measured *cognitive centrality* of gender identity by asking 'How often in your everyday lives do you have to think about being a woman and what you have in common with women and men?' Response categories ranged from 'a lot' 'some', to 'a little', or 'hardly at all'. *Sense of common fate* was measured by a four-point index averaging responses to two questions, one that asked 'How much do you have in common with most women?' and another that asked 'To what extent will what happens to women generally in this country affect what happens in your life?'

Gender role-orientation was measured from four questions about work and family. Two questions, which have been used in several national studies in the United States (Mason and Bumpass, 1975; Thornton and Freedman, 1979), tap role attitudes; two others, future personal plans. Responses were classified as either traditional or non-traditional as follows: *Traditional role-orientation* – Agreed that 'A pre-school child is likely to suffer if his/her mother works'; disagreed that 'A working mother can establish as warm and secure a relationship with her children as a mother who does not work'; did *not* plan to work when her children were pre-school age or when she was 30 years old, presumably a time when children would still be at home. (Respondents who answered inconsistently were dropped.) *Non-traditional role orientation* – Did not feel that a pre-school child suffers if the mother works or that working interferes with a woman's ability to establish a warm and secure relationship with her children; did plan to work even when her children were young.

Convergent validity for this classification was demonstrated by responses to a questionnaire administered during the laboratory session in which subjects were asked if 'they thought of themselves as having a career, working but not really career-minded, or primarily as homemakers'. All of the non-traditional, but only a third of the traditional, subjects selected 'having a career'.

Subjects were selected to give an equal number with traditional and non-traditional role-orientations, but we did not pre-select subjects on the basis of the identity measures. Not surprisingly, traditional and non-traditional women differed significantly on the cognitive centrality and common fate measures of gender identity. Thirty per cent of the non-traditional, but only 10 per cent of the traditional, women said they thought 'a lot' about being a woman (difference significant at p = 0.0001); and 45 per cent of the non-traditional, compared to 26 per cent of the traditional, women felt their fates highly connected to other women (difference significant at p = 0.0001).

Procedures

When students arrived at the laboratory, they were told they were taking part in a social impression study. As many as six subjects participated in a session. Each was placed in a cubicle which contained a computer terminal.

Task 1: processing gender-relevant information about the self Once in the cubicles, subjects were told that phrases would appear on the computer screen and they were to push a 'me' button if a phrase was self-descriptive, or a 'not me' button if it was not. Each phrase appeared on the screen for two seconds or until the subject responded, whichever came first. Both the latency and the response were recorded (although the subjects were not aware that latencies were being measured). For each subject, the 'me' button was placed on the side of the dominant hand. After the subject responded 'me' or 'not me' to each phrase, the question 'How confident are you?' appeared on the screen. Subjects responded by pushing buttons on a six-point scale ranging from 'not at all confident' to 'very confident'. To ensure that individuals associated similar types of behaviour with the phrases, a particular context was specified for the self-judgements. Subjects were told that 'When you are making these decisions about yourself, try to imagine yourself in a typical situation here at college – in a classroom, in a dorm'.

Ten descriptors appeared on the screen in one of four randomly determined orders of presentation. Five phrase-length descriptors had previously been judged to be related to identification with women. These were, 'more in common with women than men'; 'identified with other women'; 'feel obligated to other women'; 'feel close to women'; 'rarely think about women as a group'. Five adjectives drawn from other self-schema studies and judged to be neutral with respect to gender were included to show the discriminant effect of gender identity, that it influences the processing of relevant but not irrelevant information. These were: 'easy going'; 'calm'; 'serious'; 'thrifty'; and 'happy'.

Task 2: political cognitions After completing this task, subjects carried out a social judgement task (see Gurin and Markus, 1988), and then answered a questionnaire about topics of political significance in the United States. Included were questions that have previously been asked of national samples to measure three dimensions of group consciousness (Gurin et al., 1980; Miller et al., 1981; Gurin, 1985).

Collective discontent was measured from evaluations of the influence of various groups in American society. The stimulus stated that 'Some people think that certain groups have too much influence in American life and politics, while other people feel that certain groups don't have as much influence as they deserve. How about you? Do (group labels) have "too much influence", "just about the right amount", or "too little influence"?' Collective discontent is the discrepancy between judgements of how much influence women and men ought to have.

Evaluation of legitimacy was derived from responses to three forced-choice causal attribution questions in which subjects were asked to identify the sources of gender differences in income, occupational status, and general position in American life. For each question, one alternative attributed these differentials to women's personal deficiencies (dispositional attribution) or to structural obstacles (situational attribution). Choosing the dispositional attribution indicates a belief that gender disparities are legitimate in that the rules by which rewards are distributed are fair – women just need to be more ambitious, work harder, or be more like men. Choosing the situational attribution indicates a belief that discrimination and role constraints make gender disparities illegitimate. People can subscribe to both beliefs, of course, and forcing them to choose may not represent the subtlety of their beliefs. However, forced-choice questions are useful to press people to decide which of two accepted beliefs is more dominant.

Approval of collective action was measured by a question that asked subjects to show their feelings towards the 'Women's Liberation Movement', using a 'feeling thermometer' on which less than 50 degrees represented a cold feeling, 50 a neutral feeling, and 51 to 100 a warm feeling. Women who felt warmly toward the Movement were considered the most positive toward collective action.

Results

Endorsement of Self-Descriptors
If gender identity functions as a self-schema, subjects for whom being a woman is cognitively central and who have a sense of common fate with other women ought to endorse as self-descriptive more of the phrases that denote acceptance of their membership in the category 'women'. The five gender-identification descriptors that were presented in the laboratory task may be construed as providing a test of convergent validity for the two measures of gender identity. Equally important, the gender identity measures should *not* correlate with endorsing neutral traits, thus demonstrating discriminant validity.

Both predictions were supported. With respect to discriminant validity, the results show that neither of the identity measures were significantly related to endorsing the neutral traits. With respect to convergent validity, cognitive centrality and common fate were both significantly related to endorsing more of the gender-identification phrases.

Figure 8.1 shows the size of the cognitive centrality and common fate effects. Subjects who thought a lot about being a woman endorsed significantly more of these phrases (eta = 0.323, F[2,123] = 6.44, p = 0.002), as did subjects for whom a sense of common fate was strong (eta = 0.426, F[3,122] = 8.66, p = 0.0001). Of course, since cognitive centrality and common fate were themselves correlated, their independent effects were smaller, although still statistically reliable. (See betas in Figure 8.1.)

We also tested whether the results were similar for traditional and non-traditional women. None of the interaction terms was statisically significant, showing that, for both groups of women, thinking about one's gender identity and having a sense of common fate with other women were related to endorsing more of the group-identity phrases.

Processing of the Self-descriptors
If gender identity functions as a schematic aspect of the self, women for whom gender was central should have responded to the gender-relevant descriptors more quickly and with greater confidence than women for whom it was not central. And the two groups should *not* have differed in reacting to neutral descriptors.

We found strong support for the hypothesis that gender identity would influence the efficiency of information processing, especially when gender identity was cognitively central. Evidence was also strong that gender identity did not influence the speed and confidence of processing the neutral traits – again showing discriminant validity for our measures of gender identity.

The effects of cognitive centrality were quite strong. Subjects who thought a lot about being women decided more quickly than others that the identification phrases applied to them (F[2,123] = 3.85, p = 0.05). They were also more confident that these phrases applied (F[2,123] = 11.51, p = 0.001); and made confidence judgements faster (F[2,123] = 3.68, p = 0.05).

The effects of common fate were less strong. Women who had a sense of common fate were more confident that the gender-descriptors applied to them (F[3,122] = 6.01, p = 0.001), but they were not faster than other women in making this judgement. Nor were they faster in making the confidence judgement. This aspect of identity helped women see the self-relevance of the identification phrases but did not produce more efficient processing. It was especially *cognitive* involvement – thinking about gender identity – that fostered quick processing.

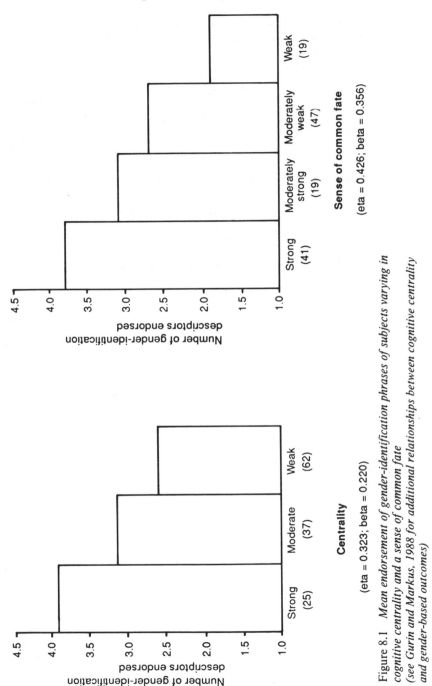

Figure 8.1   *Mean endorsement of gender-identification phrases of subjects varying in cognitive centrality and a sense of common fate*
(see Gurin and Markus, 1988 for additional relationships between cognitive centrality and gender-based outcomes)

We again tested for possible interactions with role-orientation but found that the relationships between gender identity and the processing measures were similar for traditional and non-traditional women.

Feminist Political Consciousness

Feminist political consciousness was much stronger among women who expected to combine work and family and did not believe that working jeopardizes the relationship between a mother and child. The main effect of role-orientation was significant on all three measures of political consciousness at a probability level of less than 0.0001. The size of the associations was impressive: eta = 0.44 with collective discontent; 0.32 with illegitimacy of gender disparities; and 0.43 with approval of collective action.

As we suspected, role-orientation was also a critical conditioner of the relationship between gender identity and political consciousness. In particular, the political meaning of cognitive centrality depended on the woman's role-orientation. (The political meaning of sense of common fate was similar for both groups of women.)

We consider the implications of cognitive centrality for *traditional* women first. These were women who had traditional work intentions and traditional attitudes toward family and work roles. In general, they voiced much less criticism than non-traditional women of gender-based stratification and of power differences between men and women, and they less often approved of collective action. Traditional women for whom gender identity was cognitively central were even less feminist in their views of gender relations. The cognitive centrality measure was *negatively* related to all three dimensions of feminist political consciousness. The correlation between a summary index of these political measures and cognitive centrality was –0.219 (significant at 0.0001). Thus, when traditional women think a lot about being women, their proclivities to accept traditional gender relations and oppose collective change are considerably increased. Consciousness of themselves as women produces stronger anti-feminism among these women.

The opposite pattern characterized the relationship between consciousness of thought and feminist political consciousness for *non-traditional* women. The generally higher levels of feminism among non-traditional women were considerably higher for those who thought a lot about being women. The correlation between the summary feminist political index and cognitive centrality was +0.377 (significant at less than 0.0001).

In marked contrast to the results on cognitive centrality, *none* of the interaction tests involving the sense of common fate proved statistically reliable. For both groups, a sense of common fate was positively related to all three dimensions of feminist political consciousness. Of course, as already noted, sense of common fate was less frequent among traditional women. However, those who did feel that they had a lot in common with other women and that their fates depended on what happens generally to women were more critical of gender-based stratification, discontented with women's limited political influence, and supportive of the Women's Movement.

Overall, the results for non-traditional women were consistent and straightforward. The two properties of gender identity were positively related to each other and each was positively related to all dimensions of feminist political consciousness. A regression equation predicting political consciousness scores shows that the effects of cognitive centrality and common fate were smaller when their joint variance was controlled, but that each effect was still statistically significant and that they together explained 45 per cent of the variance in political consciousness (see Table 8.1). The results for traditional women were inconsistent and complex. Although the cognitive centrality and common fate measures were positively correlated for them as well, these two properties of identity had very different political implications. The generally weaker feminism of these women was even weaker when they thought a lot about being women, while a sense of common fate had the opposite effect – strengthening their feminism. The regression results therefore show that the controlled effects of

Table 8.1 *Regression coefficients for measures of identity in predicting feminist political consciousness*

	Traditional women			Non-traditional women		
	r	metric	beta	r	metric	beta
Cognitive centrality	−0.219	−0.435	−0.235* (0.123)	0.377	0.383	0.313*** (0.121)
Sense of common fate	0.319	0.470	0.380**** (0.123)	0.332	0.257	0.256** (0.119)
		$R^2 = 0.473$			$R^2 = 0.450$	

Standard errors are in parentheses. The unstandardized (metric) and standardized (beta) regression coefficients come from equations in which the measures of cognitive centrality and a sense of common fate were the predictors of the summary index of feminist political consciousness.

* significant at 0.05
** significant at 0.01
*** significant at 0.001
**** significant at 0.0001

cognitive centrality and common fate were larger than their uncontrolled effects. Together, these two properties of identity explained as much variance as they did for non-traditional women. Thus, gender identity was not less politically implicated but its meaning was much more complicated for traditional than for non-traditional women.

Summary and Discussion

The central question of whether gender identity functions as a self-schema is answered affirmatively. The information-processing results show that gender identity influenced the speed and confidence with which women processed gender-relevant material and that cognitive centrality was the critical property of identity in these effects.

Why should cognitive centrality be so important? Mental time – thinking a great deal about a particular domain – is usually associated with acquiring a large store of knowledge about that domain. Although nearly everyone can be expected to have some knowledge about the domain of gender, those women who have thought a great deal about being women will have a particularly dense and well-organized store of knowledge (Chi, 1979; Markus et al., 1985). This knowledge includes generalizations and hypotheses deriving from past social experiences about what it means to be a woman, as well as gender-relevant goals, plans, and strategies. As a consequence of this richly textured accumulation of knowledge, attention to the gender domain and interest in it will be heightened. Those for whom the gender domain is central will be 'tuned in' and sensitive to gender, and events will tend to be framed and interpreted according to their relevance to gender. Social experiences will have order, meaning, and structure by virtue of what they reveal about gender. In short, these individuals can be characterized as experts with respect to gender (Chase and Simon, 1973; Fiske and Kinder, 1981).

Relative to other domains that have not been the focus of so much cognitive activity, the structures related to the gender domain will be easily accessible, perhaps chronically accessible (Higgins et al., 1982), for organizing one's experiences. The accessibility of these structures was reflected in this study in the fast processing times and confident decisions of the women for whom gender was cognitively central.

The significance of these results is twofold. First, with reference to the psychological literature, they extend findings on cognitive consequences of self-concept by demonstrating that identities which derive from social categories function as self-schemata. With respect to the sociological literature, these findings suggest that group identities affect role performance by functioning as self-schemata. As such, group identity sensitizes the individual to group cues and events in the social environment, and contributes group-relevant meaning and structure to ambiguous or confusing social situations. The self-schema is associated with this selective and differential processing of information because it includes well-organized and integrated information about the group which in turn allows for rapid and confident encodings, interpretations, and decisions in new situations. It also includes representations of possible courses of action that are crucial to selecting and directing the behaviour to be carried out (see Burke and Reitzes, 1981).

Stryker (1984: 8) has called for attention to the processes that 'underwrite the linkage between identity salience and role performance'. The cognitive consequences of group identity examined here are thus some of the mechanisms that provide this connection. That individuals *want* to live out particular roles, or believe them to be important, does not adequately explain role performance. It is the cognitive structure and processes that accompany and articulate one's group identity that create the link between identity and role performance.

A second question in this study probed cognitive effects of identity that have not been studied in previous research on self-schemata. Gender identity not only increased efficiency of processing but also provided a framework for interpreting the political situation of women. As predicted, we found that the sense of common fate would be influential in political consciousness because it involves an awareness of categories and of categorical treatment that is necessary to perceive group disparities; it helps members overcome attributional biases that limit perception of structural and therefore illegitimate causes of these disparities; and it stimulates collective approaches to the removal of barriers now perceived as categorically based. The results supported all these predictions. Regardless of role-orientation, when gender identity included representations of common fate, women were more discontented with the limited power of women, more critical of gender-based stratification, and more supportive of collective action. As predicted, we also found that cognitive concern with one's gender influenced these political cognitions, making non-traditional women more feminist, traditional women less feminist.

A third question we raised is whether the traditionality/non-traditionality of a woman's career and family commitments altered the impact of her gender identity. We found that role-orientation did condition the impact of gender identity on political cognitions.

The results for the non-traditional women showed that the two dimensions of identity functioned in similar ways. Centrality and sense of common fate were both influential. Non-traditional women who said they thought a lot about being women and felt themselves interdependent with other women displayed these features of their identities by endorsing more of the phrases indicating closeness and obligation to women and identification and commonality with them. Of the two properties, consciousness of thought was the more influential, however, in helping these women process gender-related material efficiently. Both properties of identity promoted feminist attitudes, and when the shared variance between common fate and centrality was controlled each still had significant effects on the feminist political consciousness of non-traditional women.

In general, the results for traditional women were more complicated. Cognitive centrality in particular had a complex pattern of effects for these women. On the one hand, traditional women who thought a lot about being women endorsed more self-descriptors showing that they felt identified with other women. They also processed these identification phrases more effectively than other traditional women. On the other hand, consciousness of thought about their identities made their already weak feminism even weaker. In this way, a central gender identity seems to help traditional women maintain their gender role commitments. Preserving their own role stance almost requires that they explicitly or implicitly reject ideas that women are deprived of power or that they are treated illegitimately in the marketplace or that women owe something to each other to improve women's collective condition. To do otherwise would begin the process of eroding their role-orientations.

Only those women who have not been required to confront these feminist ideas, or can effectively refute them, can maintain a traditional role-orientation. Moreover, it is not simply that cognitive centrality had complex effects for traditional women. In addition, the sense of common fate conflicted with cognitive centrality. Centrality had negative effects and common fate had positive effects on feminist political consciousness. Of course, common fate representations were less prevalent in the identities of traditional women. But when they were present, they promoted feminist, not anti-feminist, political cognitions. Thus, for traditional women, some elements of gender identity pressed toward feminism, others toward maintenance of traditional gender relations in line with their own traditional role-orientations. In this way, the identities of traditional women seem less coherent, or perhaps their role-orientations are so much in flux that they do not provide them a consistent framework for interpreting intergroup affairs.

Evidence supporting the idea that traditional women are less clear-cut about their role orientations is provided in a study of information-processing carried out by Trautmann (1984). In that study, traditional and non-traditional role-orientation was defined and measured as in the study reported here, and the two groups of women were asked to process information related directly to gender roles. Some of the information was congruent, some incongruent with the woman's own role-orientation. Non-traditional women showed the pattern expected of schematic processing. They endorsed schema-congruent descriptors efficiently and confidently and, on the few occasions that they endorsed schema-incongruent descriptors, they did so with difficulty and lack of confidence. They appeared to have a clear vision of themselves along the dimension of non-traditionality. In contrast, the traditional women did not show the differential pattern of responding to congruent and incongruent material that would be expected if their role-orientations were self-schematic and thus likely to guide their social perceptions.

The internal contradictions in the gender identities of some traditional women also suggest that some of these women will be psychologically open to social experiences that offer new interpretations of gender role. As the culture shifts towards greater gender egalitarianism in public and domestic spheres, some traditional women are likely to notice and grapple with the personal challenge that these shifts involve. The very incoherence in the identities of those who combine a strong sense of common fate with traditional role-orientations should help them perceive rather than ignore discordance and make them more responsive to expanded opportunities for women.

Notes

1 Sometimes reference is made to properties of group schemata that enhance their activation or tuning: for example, their level of development and richness, self-relevance, importance of categorical distinctions in the person's value system, complexity of the group schemata (Markus and Zajonc, 1985; Stephan, 1985). But these properties are rarely if ever directly assessed. Even the vast experimental literature on the effects of social categorization does not answer our question definitively. In the first place, most laboratory studies (reviewed by Stephan, 1985, for the latest edition of the *Handbook of Social Psychology*) simply manipulate conditions that should make subjects aware of group membership or give them self-schemata as group members, but typically do not assess if subjects actually accept the categorizations or group labels applied to them. Second, the very ambiguity of the laboratory situation may exaggerate the schematic effects of group membership. Usually, group membership is the only cue available to subjects for interpreting and organizing their experiences in the laboratory. Outside the laboratory, the schema of self as a member of a social category may vary greatly in salience or centrality and only occasionally influence social cognition and perhaps only for some group members.

2 These terms are used by structural theorists to differentiate statuses in the social environment. For example, Merton designates a particular status in a status-set

salient when it is the one to which others primarily respond; central when it constrains the probability of acquiring others; and dominant when other statuses are subordinated to it in case of conflict. The terms are used by symbolic interactionists to delineate multiple identities, defined as internalized statuses or roles (McCall and Simmons, 1966). Linking the social and individual levels of analysis, these concepts have been critical in structural symbolic interactionalism. Research from that perspective has demonstrated the salient identities have greater impact on role performance, but the mechanisms by which this happens are yet little studied (Stryker, 1984).

3   See especially Jackman and Jackman, 1983; Conover, 1984; and Gurin et al., 1980, for development of the distinction between identification and consciousness.

References

Allen, V. L. and Wilder, D. A. (1979) 'Group Categorization and Attribution of Belief Similarity', *Small Group Behaviour*, 10: 73–80.

Bem, S. L. (1981) 'Gender Schema Theory: A Cognitive Account of Sex Typing', *Psychological Review*, 88: 354–64.

Burke, P. J. (1980) 'The Self: Measurement Requirements from an Interactionist Perspective', *Social Psychology Quarterly*, 43: 18–22.

Burke, P. J. and Reitzes, D. C. (1981) 'The Link between Identity and Role Performance', *Social Psychology Quarterly*, 44: 83–92.

Burke, P. J. and Tully, J. C. (1977) 'The Measurement of Role Identity', *Social Forces*, 55: 881–97.

Chase, W. G. and Simon, H. A. (1973) 'Perception and Chess', *Cognitive Psychology*, 4: 55–81.

Chi, M. T. H. (1979) 'Exploring a Child's Knowledge of Dinosaurs: A Case Study'. Paper presented at the Annual Meeting of the Society for Research in Child Development, March.

Commission of the European Communities (1984) *European Men and Women in 1983*. Brussels: Commission of the European Communities.

Conover, P. J. (1984) 'The Influence of Group Identification on Political Perception and Evaluation', *Journal of Politics*, 46: 760–85.

Conover, P. J. and Feldman, S. (1984) 'Group Identification, Values and the Nature of Political Beliefs', *American Politics Quarterly*, 12: 151–75.

Converse, P. E. (1970) 'Attitudes and Non-attitudes', in E. R. Tufte (ed.), *The Quantitative Analysis of Social Problems*. Reading, MA: Addison-Wesley.

Crosby, F. J. (1982) *Relative Deprivation and Working Women*. New York: Oxford University Press.

Erikson, E. (1946) 'Ego Development and Historical Change', *Psychoanalytic Study of the Child*, 2: 359–96.

Erikson, E. (1956) 'The Problem of Ego Identity', *Journal of the American Psychoanalytic Association*, 4: 56–121.

Fireman, B. and Gamson, W. A. (1979) 'Utilitarian Logic in the Resource Mobilization Perspective', in M. Zald and J. McCarthy (eds), *The Dynamics of Social Movements*. Cambridge, MA: Winthrop.

Fiske, S. T. and Kinder, D. R. (1981) 'Involvement, Expertise and Schema Use: Evidence from Political Cognition', in N. Cantor and J. Kihlstrom (eds), *Personality Cognition and Social Interaction*. Hillsdale, NJ: Erlbaum.

Gordon, C. (1968) 'Self-Conceptions: Configurations of Content', in C. Gordon and

K. Gergen (eds), *The Self in Social Interaction,*, vol. I: *Classic and Contemporary Perspectives.* New York: Wiley.

Gurin, P. (1985) 'Women's Gender Consciousness', *Public Opinion Quarterly*, 49: 143–63.

Gurin, P. and Markus, H. (1988) 'Group Identity: The Psychological Mechanisms of Durable Salience', *Revue Internationale de Psychologie Sociale*, 1: 257–74.

Gurin, P., Miller, H. and Gurin, G. (1980) 'Stratum Identification and Consciousness', *Social Psychology Quarterly*, 43: 30–47.

Gurwitz, S. B. and Dodge, K. A. (1977) 'Effects of Confirmations and Disconfirmations on Stereotype-based Attributions', *Journal of Personality and Social Psychology*, 35: 495–500.

Higgins, E. T., King, G. A. and Mavin, G. H. (1982) 'Individual Construct Accessibility and Subjective Impressions and Recall', *Journal of Personality and Social Psychology*, 43: 35–47.

Jackman, M. R. and Jackman, R. W. (1983) *Class Awareness in the United States.* Berkeley, CA: University of California Press.

Kelley, H. H. (1972) *Causal Schemata and the Attribution Process.* Morristown, NJ: General Learning Press.

Kuhn, M. H. and McPartland, T. S. (1954) 'An Empirical Investigation of Self-Attitudes', *American Sociological Review*, 19: 68–76.

Lester, M. (1984) 'Self: Sociological Portraits', in J. A. Kotarba and A. Fontana (eds), *The Existential Self in Society.* Chicago: University of Chicago Press.

McCall, G. J. and Simmons, J. L. (1966) *Identities and Interactions.* New York: Free Press.

Markus, H. (1977) 'Self-Schemata and Processing Information about the Self', *Journal of Personality and Social Psychology*, 35: 63–78.

Markus, H. (1980) 'The Self in Thought and Memory', in D. M. Wegner and R. R. Vallacher (eds), *The Self in Social Psychology.* New York: Oxford University Press.

Markus, H. and Zajonc, R. B. (1985) 'The Cognitive Perspective in Social Psychology', in G. Lindzey and E. Aronson (eds), *The Handbook of Social Psychology.* New York: Random House.

Markus, H., Crane, M., Bernstein, S. and Siladi, M. (1982) 'Self-schemas and Gender', *Journal of Personality and Social Psychology*, 42: 38–50.

Markus, H., Smith, J. and Moreland, R. J. (1985) 'The Role of the Self-concept in the Perception of Others', *Journal of Personality and Social Psychology*, 49: 1499–512.

Mason, K. O. and Bumpass, L. L. (1975) 'US Women's Sex-role Ideology, 1970', *American Journal of Sociology*, 80: 1212–19.

Mason, K. O., Czajka, J. L. and Arber, S. (1976) 'Change in US Women's Sex-role Attitudes, 1964–1974', *American Sociological Review*, 81: 573–96.

Merton, R. K. (1968) *Social Theory and Social Structure.* New York: Free Press.

Miller, A. H., Gurin, P., Gurin, G. and Malanchuk, O. (1981) 'Group Consciousness and Political Participation', *American Journal of Political Science*, 25: 494–511.

Nisbett, R. E. and Ross, L. (1980) *Human Inference: Strategies and Shortcomings.* Englewood Cliffs, NJ: Prentice-Hall.

Sherif, C. W. (1980) 'Social Values, Attitudes and Involvement of the Self', in M. M. Page (ed.), *Nebraska Symposium on Motivation.* Lincoln, NE: University of Nebraska Press.

Stephan, W. G. (1985) 'Intergroup Relations', in G. Lindzey and E. Aronson (eds), *The Handbook of Social Psychology.* New York: Random House.

Stone, G. P. (1962) 'Appearance and the Self', in A. M. Rose (ed.), *Human Behaviour and Social Processes.* Boston, MA: Houghton Mifflin.

Stryker, S. (1968) 'Identity, Salience and Role Performance: The Relevance of Symbolic Interaction Theory for Family Research', *Journal of Marriage and the Family*, 30: 558–64.

Stryker, S. (1980) *Symbolic Interactionism: A Social Structural Version*. Menlo Park, CA: Benjamin-Cummings.

Stryker, S. (1984) 'Identity Theory: Developments and Extensions'. Paper prepared for Symposium on Self and Social Structure, British Psychological Society, University College, Cardiff, Wales.

Tajfel, H. (1974) 'Social Identity and Intergroup Behaviour', *Social Science Information*, 13: 69–89.

Tajfel, H. (1978) 'Social Categorization, Social Identity, and Social Comparison', in H. Tajfel (ed.), *Differentiation between Social Groups*. New York: Academic Press.

Tajfel, H. and Turner, J. C. (1986) 'The Social Identity Theory of Intergroup Behaviour', in S. Worchel and W. G. Austin (eds), *Psychology of Intergroup Relations*. Chicago: Nelson-Hall.

Taylor, S. E. and Crocker, J. (1981) 'Schematic Bases of Social Information Processing' in E. T. Higgins, C. P. Herman, and M. P. Zanna (eds), *Social Cognition: The Ontario Symposium*, vol 1. Hillsdale, NJ: Erlbaum.

Thornton, A. and Freedman, D. (1979) 'Changes in the Sex-role Attitudes of Women, 1962–1977: Evidence from a Panel Study', *American Sociological Review*, 44: 831–42.

Thornton, A., Alwin, D. F. and Camburn, D. (1983) 'Causes and Consequences of Sex-role Attitudes and Attitude Change', *American Sociological Review*, 48: 211–27.

Tilly, C. (1978) *From Mobilization to Revolution*. Reading, MA: Addison-Wesley.

Trautmann, M. H. (1984) 'Role Orientations in Women: Some Evidence for Schematic Effects in Information Processing'. Unpublished paper.

Wilder, D. (1978) 'Perceiving Persons as a Group: Effects on Attributions of Causality and Beliefs', *Social Psychology Quarterly*, 41: 13–23.

Williams, R. M., Jr (1975) 'Relative Deprivation', in L. A. Coser (ed.), *The Idea of Social Structure: Papers in Honor of Robert K. Merton*. New York: Harcourt Brace.

Zavalloni, M. (1973) 'Social Identity: Perspectives and Prospects', *Social Science Information*, 12: 65–91.

9

'I'm not a Women's Libber, but . . .': Feminism, Consciousness and Identity

Christine Griffin

The original impetus for this chapter came from a conversation I overheard on a train during the summer of 1986. Three women were discussing their work as librarians in Birmingham Reference Library, when the male friend of one interjected with a 'joke':

> What's the difference between a feminist and a bin-liner?
> A bin-liner gets taken out at least once a week.

This was greeted by a stunned silence, but no laughter. The young man had managed to interrupt the flow of female conversation, and he then directed the discussion towards another unrelated topic, in which he was able to take a more active part.

There were a number of surprising aspects to this brief exchange. Firstly, the conversation prior to this interjection had not been concerned with feminism, gender relations, or anything which might be termed a woman's subject. The three young women were talking about people and events from their shared workplace. The young man, who did not work at the library, appeared to be the partner of one of the young women, since they were holding hands and he had his arm around her shoulders. As to his reason for making that particular joke, I can only assume that he wanted to break into the young women's conversation.

The second issue concerns why he chose a joke against feminists which was based on assumptions about their supposed unattractiveness to men. This was totally irrelevant to their earlier conversation, and to any of the group's previous interactions. At this point, I remembered a phrase which I had heard from many of the female participants in a research project on young women and the transition from school to the job market: 'I'm not a women's libber but . . .' This sentence usually ended with statements such as 'women work much harder than men' or 'there's a lot of prejudice against women still', which could, in certain contexts, be viewed as reflecting feminist ideas. This set me thinking about the ways in which feminisim is constructed, understood and experienced in such everyday interactions.

My study, henceforth referred to as the Young Women and Work project, was concerned with the transition from school to the job market for young working-class women, with particular reference to the role of family life and gender socialization. A comprehensive analysis of the research is available elsewhere (Griffin, 1985). Although this study was not intended to be an investigation of feminist identity or consciousness, the issue was unavoidable. When I came to look at the meanings and implications of feminism for the research participants, I realized that many aspects of their experiences could not be readily explained via social psychological theories of identity.

My main argument is that feminism is not a unitary category which encapsulates a consistent set of ideas within a readily identifiable boundary. Most studies concerned with feminist identification have used structured attitude questionnaires within a positivist framework, reinforcing the notion that feminism represents a neat and coherent phenomenon which can be measured in quantitative terms. When more open and qualitative methods are used, the picture which emerges is far less clearcut. There is not one feminism but many, the concept is under a continual process of negotiation, and for most women, the identification of oneself as a feminist is not a straightforward process.

In addition, gender and feminism are often interrelated: the experience of being female varies with class, age, race, sexuality and region; and it must be understood in social and historical context. Many studies employ generalized definitions of womanhood, losing that social context, and minimizing the role of ideology in constructions of femaleness, feminism and feminity (Wetherell, 1986). So this chapter will not end with a final definition of feminist consciousness or identity, but will aim to open up for discussion some of the issues that more traditional social psychological research in this area has tended to close off.

The Young Women and Work Study

This project was set up as a female equivalent to Paul Willis' (1977) study of pro- and anti-school cultures amongst young white working-class men. Willis conducted informal interviews and observation in a West Midlands boys' secondary school over a one-year period during the mid-1970s. He argued that there was a powerful cultural connection between school and the job market for these young men. Focusing on the anti-school group, he traced the links between their creative resistance to the authority of the school, pride in their own working-class competence and abilities, and a macho bravado which often took racist and sexist forms (see Griffin, 1987 for an analysis of the problems involved in applying Willis' thesis to young women's experiences).

The Young Women and Work study covered the periods immediately before and after leaving school, involving interviews with a wider range of young women. As the sole research worker, I visited six schools in early 1979; including single-sex (girls') schools and co-educational; Catholic, Church of England and non-denominational; ranging in size from 500 to over 1900 students. Each school was visited at least three times for interviews with headteachers, careers and form teachers and careers officers. I talked to 180 fifth and sixth form girls – and some boys – either individually or in groups. This first stage included interviews with young working- and middle-class women and Asian, white and Afro-Caribbean students, from a range of academic levels.

The second stage of the research involved following 25 female fifth formers from five of these schools into their first two years in the full-time labour market. This group were all young white working-class women with few or no academic qualifications, and I visited them every two or three months at home, in local coffee bars and pubs, and in their workplaces wherever possible. I talked to most of the young women's mothers, sisters and girlfriends; male relatives and friends proved far more elusive and wary of my presence. I also visited ten of the young women's workplaces to provide case studies of a range of jobs: traditional female jobs in offices and factories and men's work in engineering, as well as young women's experiences of unemployment.

Before looking at the ways in which feminism was constructed and experienced in the Young Women and Work study in more detail, I want to review one of the main frameworks in which social identity and intergroup relations has been conceptualized in European social psychology: Tajfel's social identity theory (SIT; Tajfel, 1974). The various theoretical and methodological limitations of this approach have restricted its potential value for the understanding of feminist consciousness and gender identifications. I then turn to Billig's study of fascism and the National Front, and Gramsci's notion of hegemony, to provide broader and more flexibile analyses of political affiliation and the role of ideology (Billig, 1978a; Gramsci, 1971). Finally, I shall consider work on the nature of feminist consciousness and identi-fication from the feminist research literature (Stanley and Wise, 1983; Condor, 1986).

The Social Identity Perspective

Tajfel's work on social identity has already been rehearsed elsewhere in this book. The analysis of gender relations has scarcely figured in the academic literature on SIT.[1] One of the earliest and most influential attempts to consider this area was the work of Jenny Williams. Briefly, she argued that SIT rests on gender-specific assumptions about the process of social identity construction (Williams, 1984). It emphasizes agentic rather than communal modes of social identification, and the former is a prototypically masculine form. For Jenny Williams, SIT in its current state is not equally applicable to women and men, and this limited the value of her own earlier work, which aimed to understand various feminist strategies according to the social identity perspective (Williams and Giles, 1978). The latter's focus on strategies of assimilation reflected the agentic framework of SIT, and the emphasis on liberal definitions of feminism in most social psychological research (Condor, 1986).

SIT has also tended to treat the key social group 'women' as a relatively static and unitary category. Glynis Breakwell was relatively unusual in considering this issue in some detail (Breakwell, 1979). Although some aspects of womanhood are common to all women, the group 'women' includes a multitude of sub-groups, some in direct contradiction to one another. The opposition between idealized notions of the busy housewife and mother and the successful career woman is one example here (Wetherell, 1986).

The methodological limitations of SIT research are exemplified by recent American work on gender identity and consciousness (for example, Gurin and Townsend, 1986). Gurin and Townsend began with the common definitions of group identity as 'the [group] member's awareness of membership and feelings attached to being a member'; and of group consciousness as 'the member's ideology about the group's position in society', drawing on Tajfel's approach as one of several in the literature on 'the political mobilization of collectivities' (1986: 139). Their study is one of the more sophisticated attempts to examine the relationship between gender identity and consciousness using quantitative survey methods, although I am still confused by their use of the term 'ideology' in this context.

Gurin and Townsend used multidimensional definitions of both gender identity and consciousness, rather than the more usual unidimensional definition of identity. They employed three properties of group identity: the perceived similarities in the personal characteristics of members; an awareness of common fate; and how central group membership is to the way the member thinks of the self. Their three dimensions of group consciousness were collective discontent, appraisal of legitimacy, and belief in collective action. I am less concerned here with the precise results and conclusions of Gurin and Townsend's study, and more interested in the extent to which the use of quantitative techniques placed limitations on their understanding of gender identity and consciousness.

Gurin and Townsend conducted a telephone survey of women who had taken part in a nationally representative panel survey during the American elections of 1972 and 1976. They experienced considerable problems in measuring these dimensions of identity and consciousness, related to the use of such structured research techniques, and especially in operationalizing the centrality of gender to women's social identities. This was measured by asking respondents 'How often in their everyday lives they thought about being a woman and what they have in common with women and men' (Gurin and Townsend, 1986: 142). This dimension of gender identity was measured in terms of the amount of time spent thinking about being a woman. This approach was adopted after an earlier attempt to operationalize the concept of centrality had failed (Townsend, 1982, cited in Gurin and Townsend, 1986).

The Young Women and Work study indicated the centrality of gender to young women's experiences is an extremely complex and contradictory phenomenon, which was highly situation-specific. This study was not set up to ask the same questions as Gurin and Townsend's work, but it did cover aspects of 'what it means to be female' in the course of investigating the move from school to the job market for young working-class women. During interviews in Birmingham schools and immediately after the young women had left, I asked about their experiences of 'being a girl'; reactions to being in mixed or single-sex (girls') schools; and perceptions of female and male peers in and out of the school (Griffin, 1985). For these young women, the meanings associated with 'being a girl' emerged most clearly in discussions about mixed and single-sex schooling and traditionally female and male jobs (Griffin, 1985:191).[2]

> *CG*: Do you think there is any difference between women's and men's jobs?
> *Tracey*: Well, I think girls are more closer, they stick together and talk more easily to each other. But blokes all like to show off in front of their mates, they don't like to look sissy. I wouldn't like being a fella [laugh], I like being a girl, I'm glad I'm a girl.

This was in sharp contrast to the young women's views of their immediate male peers (1985: 76).

> *CG*: What about being at school with boys?
> *Sharon*: They just run around and get in your way, and they always hit yer.
> *Marion*: Boys are violent. When we want some peace we go and sit in the toilets.
> *Ann*: It doesn't bother us. We [laugh] just stay away from them most of the time. Don't really mix, but we do talk to them. Girls seem to stick to their own group, but boys aren't really fussy.

Of course, it is not possible to make direct comparisons between Gurin and Townsend's study and the Young Women and Work project. The latter was not concerned with issues of gender identity *per se*, the examples quoted above are responses to different questions, and each study used different research methods. I am not sure how these young women would have reacted to the type of questions asked by Gurin and Townsend. Even in the few examples quoted above, it is notable that one question about women's and men's jobs produced a reply which concerned the experience of being female, and the nature of female and male cultures and friendship groups. Gurin and Townsend themselves expressed concern about the difficulty of investigating social identity using structured questionnaires in a telephone survey, and I remain unconvinced that traditional survey techniques can adequately reflect the full complexity of women's – or indeed men's – experiences. I am not arguing that Gurin and Townsend's work is mistaken or worthless, simply that it is unavoidably limited by the nature of the research techniques they employed and the questions they were able to ask.

The Young Women and Work study indicated that young women's responses must be situated in the context of institutions and cultures which are sharply divided according to sex and gender, before we even consider the question of gender identity. Even in mixed schools, young women's main friendship groups were predominantly or entirely female; academic and vocational subjects were differentiated along gender lines, as were their prospective occupations. Gender was experienced at a general level in terms of *differences* between girls and boys, women and men, femininities and masculinities.

Gender was also overlaid by race, class and age, such that being female and identifying as female had different implications for different groups of young women (Griffin, 1987; Frazer, 1988). The move from school to the job market was experienced quite differently by young Asian fifth formers in inner city schools, compared to their more affluent white and middle-class peers in the sixth form of an independent girls' school (Griffin, 1985). This is not to imply that gender was experienced simply in terms of different social situations which varied in a random manner. What is missing from most social psychological approaches is a recognition of the far from random sets of power differentials on which these social situations rest.

Political Affiliation

Apart from research on social identity and intergroup relations, the analysis of feminist consciousness and gender identity is also relevant to theories of political socialization and affiliation. Unsurprisingly, few studies on political attitudes have recognized feminism as a political issue, or examined the gender aspect of traditional political affiliations. Most studies in this area have used structured interviews and attitude scales, which cannot always reflect the complex and contradictory nature of political affiliations (Cochrane and Billig, 1983).

Mick Billig, for example, in his study of British fascism and the National Front, did not start with a relatively static definition of fascism. He did not aim to identify which individual National Front members were fascist or whether the National Front as a whole could be described as a fascist group (Billig, 1978a). He adopted a more flexible approach, noting the considerable variation in the ideologies and programmes of self-styled fascist groups, as well as the use of 'fascism' as both a complimentary and a pejorative term – an approach that Billig admits could equally be applied to 'democratic', 'socialist' and 'communist'. It is not enough to develop a consensual definition: this will vary in different historical contexts. In order to understand the meanings and implications of any political movement or category, we need to know how such a category is actually used in practice.

Billig's study relied on informal interviews with 11 male National Front members and value analysis of National Front literature. Although gender is an important theme in fascist ideology, this was seldom addressed in Billig's text. Obviously, gender is less central than race in fascist ideologies and programmes, but the themes of violence and authoritarian control have specifically masculine connotations (CCCS, 1980). Billig's analysis of support for the National Front might not be equally applicable to female sympathizers (cf. a study of support for the Ku Klux Klan by Seltzer and Lopes, 1986). I have found this flexible and qualitative approach more useful for understanding the nature of gender, feminism and feminist consciousness, compared to the perspective developed by the Tajfel school or that adopted by Gurin and Townsend.

I also found Gramsci's concept of hegemony more useful in this respect than traditional social psychology approaches to political socialization and identity. In brief, Gramsci argued that in capitalist societies, the ruling class maintain control partly by coercion through state institutions such as the police and the judico-legal system. They can also achieve hegemony (or dominance) through ruling by 'consent', but this consent is based on the mystification of existing power relations as natural and inevitable, and the concealment of opposition and oppression (Gramsci, 1971). The notion of hegemonic ideologies allows us to make connections between women's identification as feminists and dominant negative representations of 'women's lib' in the popular media, for example. Feminist identification can be treated as more than a matter of individual preference or attitudes towards sex-roles.

Hegemony operates at the ideological level as well as the political and the economic, and struggles over the gaining of 'consent' through Thatcherite ideologies have been the focus of much recent debate (Hall, 1988). Hegemony is concerned with the production and reproduction of forms of consciousness, as a form of domination which is imposed through a mixture of persuasion and coercion. The notion of hegemony can be applied to patriarchal and imperialist social relations as well as to capitalism (Arnot, 1982; Race and Politics Group, 1982). It is the ways in which hegemonic ideologies can conceal and deny women's experiences and resistances, constructing traditional gender divisions as 'natural', for example, which is most relevant to gender relations and feminist consciousness.

The Definitions of Feminism(s): Construction and Consciousness

Feminists have also adopted a flexible approach to the understanding of feminist consciousness, arguing that there are not one but many feminisms, which can best be understood in political and historical context (Stanley and Wise, 1983; Davis, 1982). An analysis of explicitly feminist publications provides a diverse picture of contemporary Western feminism, but this is only part of the story, as many feminists would themselves argue (Bowles and Klein, 1983). Women with time, money, jobs and access to higher education are the most likely to get into print, and these women are predominantly white and middle class (Attar, 1987). Whilst the available publications on feminism do not necessarily represent the full diversity of the Women's Liberation Movement (WLM), consideration of dominant popular representations of 'women's lib' would present an even more misleading and inaccurate picture (Mitchell and Oakley, 1986).

The definition of feminism is no easy matter. In the British context, Sue Wilkinson took as a starting point Renata Duelli Klein's definition that: 'feminism for me implies assuming a perspective in which women's experiences, ideas and needs . . . are valid in their own right' (in Bowles and Klein, 1983: 89); and developed this to refer to 'taking conscious political action to change women's position in society' (Wilkinson, 1986: 8). American feminist Barbara Smith put it even more concisely when she stated that 'feminism is the political theory and practice that struggles to free *all* women' (Smith, 1982: 27, original emphasis). The WLM, the second wave of twentieth-century Western feminism, has not operated as a traditional political party. Indeed it originated in a determination to avoid the formalized structures and practices of most male-dominated political groups. The commitment to collective action, valuing personal experience, and consciousness-raising, have all made feminism difficult to classify and investigate using the traditional research techniques of political science (Mitchell and Oakley, 1986).

It is inappropriate to treat feminism as a unitary category reflecting a consistent set of beliefs, or even as a coherent social identity. Feminism is a contested space, a category under continual dispute and negotiation. I have adopted the flexible approach of Stanley and Wise, who used the term 'consciousness' rather than 'identity'. They were critical of the linear sequential model of consciousness borrowed from marxist analysis through which women are supposed to progress from false consciousness, partial consciousness or consciousness-raising, to revolutionary or feminist consciousness. In this model, ordinary or traditional women are placed in the former category, with feminists treated as a uniform group whose consciousness has been raised and will presumably stay raised. Stanley and Wise (1983: 117) preferred to define feminist consciousness as:

> an entirely different 'ontology' or way of going about making sense of the world . . . [which] makes available to us a previously untapped store of knowledge about what it is to be a woman, what the social world looks like to women, how it is constructed and negotiated by women . . . This knowledge is made available to us through feminism's insistence on the importance of 'the personal'.

They saw feminist consciousness not as a linear progression but a circle or spiral: 'there's no such creature as a "sorted-out feminist" ' (1983: 120). Similarly, women who would not identify themselves as feminist (or even anti-feminist), cannot be dismissed as falsely conscious, since this overlooks the reasons for their denial of an explicit feminist allegiance The close links between gender relations and feminist consciousness are recognized, as is the emphasis on experience and meanings rather than a set of pre-determined categories imposed by the researcher.

Research on feminist consciousness and identification has tended to distinguish between non-feminist, anti-feminist and feminist women – and sometimes men (McClain, 1978; De Man and Benoit, 1982). The former two groups are usually assumed to hold traditional attitudes to sex-roles and gender stereotypes, whilst self-defined feminists are expected to hold liberal or radical views (Renzetti, 1987). Attitudes towards feminism and gender roles are measured using the type of generalized statements employed by Gurin and Townsend. In most cases, feminism is defined in terms of one relatively specific area: liberal feminism. In Renzetti's study, one of the five statements designed to indicate a feminist attitude towards gender roles was 'If there is a military draft, both men and women should be included in it' (Renzetti, 1987: 267). As a feminist, I certainly would not agree with that statement, nor, I imagine, would those involved in the women's peace movement or anti-imperialist campaigns.

Sue Condor's work has provided a more detailed and interesting understanding of differences and similarities between traditional and feminist women. Condor (1986) was concerned with those women who appeared to be traditional according to quantitative measures of gender identity and beliefs about women, men and sex-roles. In less-structured interviews, these women did not necessarily view women and femininity as negative with respect to men and masculinity. They were predominantly anti-feminist but pro-women, upholding traditionally feminine values. These women also held men and most masculine qualities in low esteem. Condor's work is a powerful critique of mainstream quantitative psychological research techniques, but it also tells us something about the world views of traditional women – especially white middle-class ones.

Sue Condor's work questioned the validity of making a neat distinction between feminists and traditional women. The uncritical nature of this division carries some unfortunate consequences. It misses the various meanings which feminism might have for women who would not necessarily identify themselves as feminists. It also loses a sense of those pressures which might prevent or discourage women from expressing an explicit allegiance with feminism, or an agreement with feminist ideas.

Feminism in the Young Women and Work Study

The negotiable nature of feminism as a category, and the connections between feminism and gender, became increasingly obvious as the Young Women and Work study progressed. The very objectives of the project (and my own political affiliations) were defined by participants and other researchers as feminist simply because I was a female researcher interested in the experiences of young women. This was not a consequence of my appearance, or even my voice, since in many cases these assumptions were made before people had met, or even spoken to me. Despite this, both the project and myself were assumed to have political intentions in a way that Willis' all-male study never was (Griffin, 1986).

I had decided not to ask direct questions about feminism, due to the overwhelmingly negative representations of 'women's lib' in the media, and because the project was not primarily concerned with feminist identification or consciousness. However, feminism was a significant item on the hidden agenda of the study from the outset. One headmaster took me into his office on my first visit to his school, a small mixed comprehensive, to tell me exactly why he thought 'this equal opportunities thing is a waste of time'. I had never mentioned equal opportunities, nor even the proportion of young women entering non-traditional jobs. At that stage, I had not even asked anyone in the school a question, yet I was given a detailed description of his daughter's child-care arrangements as a justification for the status quo.

For the headmistress of the large girls' comprehensive in the same area of Birminghan, the project had far more positive connotations, which were expressed in relation to her own experiences in the teaching profession. Ms Evans felt that 'girls are so unsure of themselves and so unconfident, I do think this study needs to be done'. She went on to complain about the speed with which younger, less-experienced male teachers were promoted over their female peers. On another occasion, a young white working-class woman named Jeanette introduced me to her workmates in a small printing company as follows: 'This is Chris, she's doing a project on me – women's lib!' All this was spoken, or rather shouted, with her clenched fist raised in the air. We had never discussed, or even mentioned 'women's lib' or any explicitly feminist issue (Griffin, 1986).

I should add that I would describe myself, then and now, as conducting research from a feminist perspective. As such, I did not try to adopt a pretence of objectivity or invisibility. The research perspective I employed would challenge the notion that objective research is ever possible (Stanley and Wise, 1983; Bowles and Klein, 1983). The relevant issue is that many respondents had decided that I was part of a feminist project, simply because I was a female researcher engaged in a study of young women's experiences.

There was no clear consensus on the definition of feminism, and it was often used by men to obscure and overcome potential female opposition. The very use of the category feminist was subject to dispute. At Midlands Stationers, where Clare worked as an office junior, the predominantly male sales team visited the office every Friday. Over lunch in a nearby pub, Bob and Jill from Midlands Stationers were talking to Jim, a salesman from an advertising agency which was dealing with a contract for Birmingham's National Exhibition Centre (NEC):

> *Jim*: It's not often we use a bit of cheesecake on our conference manual. We never have before. It's very tasteful, we use Cathy James – Miss European something. We've got her in a singlet and bowler hat and brolly to emphasise the business side of it. It's only down to the waist, so she could have jeans on. We'll do a full frontal shot too, with the singlet pulled

down, for people to buy. There might be a few problems with it, 'cos we usually use conference shots, but I expect the feminists will get onto it.

Jill: And the women in Personnel might not want to handle it.

Jim: No, it's these feminists, but we can ignore them. It'll be OK. It's very tasteful. What you have to do is to think how to get a man going round your conference to keep your manual. It looks like one of those porno mags, and that means he'll be more likely to read it, or at least open it and look through.

This was part of a long and heated discussion about the use of such images in advertising, in which the labelling of specific women as feminists was a recurring theme. Jim was using the term 'feminist' as a derogatory term, forcing Jill to argue that her objections were not associated with such a negative label, and were not feminist according to Jim's definition of the term. Feminism retained a negative label, and women's objections could be construed as individual, biased and unreasonable moral judgements, rather than as collective political opposition. Jim's definition of feminism dominated the whole discussion.

'It's all Different Now'

Feminism, or rather the presumed impact of feminism, was also mentioned in relation to the assumption that 'it's all different now' in the era of 'equal opportunities'. The former theme was not always shared by young women and men, however. During a discussion of domestic responsibilities, one group of white middle-class sixth form boys argued that this supposed improvement was specific to their own cultural group. Three young Afro-Caribbean women in the same group definitely did not agree:

Vanessa: It's always us girls that have to do the cleaning and cooking, boys never do any.

Terry: But it's not like you say really. Middle class men are different. Things have changed now, it's more equal. What you say sounds very old-fashioned. When most married women go out to work, fathers help out in the house more now.

Vanessa, Jacinta and Penny: [shouting] No! Rubbish! When did men ever do anything? It's helping out that's all – not cleaning up sick. Men never clean the toilets.

When young women talked about 'equal opportunities' (again in a series of unsolicited comments), they used the experiences of older women – especially their mothers – as examples of the 'bad old days'. Their optimistic assumption was that 'it's all different now'. During an interview in Cathy's home, this came up in a discussion of a television programme about pregnant schoolgirls:

Cathy: I want to flit about and enjoy myself while I'm young. While I can. You've got to, haven't you? I want my career. There'll be plenty of time for settling down and saving for your household belongings later. I mean it's different now. Ten years ago or so you just left school and worked for a couple of years to earn a bit of money and then you got married and stopped work and had kids and that was it. But now you can stop and have a career. I mean, women can, there's nothing to stop it.

This same young woman was faced with a challenge to this view when she started work as an office junior at Gaskells, a wholesalers for up-market office furniture. As Cathy puts it: 'there's a lot of prejudice still'. She still argued that the position for young women like herself (white and working class) had improved since her mother's day, especially in education and the job market.

In some cases men used a similar theme when recalling 'the bad old days', but with the emphasis reversed. They were harking back with nostalgia to a mythical past when women knew their place, and looking with regret at the young women of the 1980s, who 'have it made'. Jeanette's supervisor in her job as office junior-cum-dogsbody at Townsend Graphics made the following unsolicited comment during a discussion about the history of the company:

Tom Nicholls: Perhaps I'm just old-fashioned but women have it made now. Here they do all the same jobs, except the heavy lifting of course. If they're attractive – well all girls are attractive – they can go out and get some poor fellas to buy them drinks, and take them out and sponge off these mugs, and then go to the Costa del Sol on their holidays on their ill-gotten gains.

So whilst women and men reacted in different ways to the Young Women and Work study, they all tended to deal with similar themes associated with femininity and masculinity – feminism, equal opportunities and discrimination – albeit from quite different perspectives. I would argue that the hegemonic nature of patriarchal ideologies strives to set the agenda and the boundaries for these constructs. Feminism is renamed as 'women's lib' or 'female chauvinism', and given a whole range of negative associations. Women who might identify as feminists are compelled to deal with these concepts on the latter's terms.

'I'm not a Women's Libber, but . . .'

During a visit to a workshop which was part of the Engineering Industry Training Board (EITB) Girls in Engineering scheme, the supervisor of the scheme expressed her reactions to the research at the end of a long story about her struggles to take an Open University degree in the midst of a traumatic divorce. This included the phrase which I have used in the title of this chapter: 'I'm not a women's libber, but . . .'

> *Ms Webb*: 'I'd be really interested to see the results of your study because I identify with it very strongly. I mean I'm not a women's libber, but I'm a woman in a man's job, and I identify with the young people too.

I am interested in the reasons why women felt that such a disclaimer was necessary, why this phrase was so common, and the meanings it held for different groups of women. In most cases, the phrase 'I'm not a woman's libber, but . . .' was followed by statements which could be taken as sympathetic to feminist ideas. Common themes included the ways in which women 'have a hard time' compared to men in education, family life and employment, complaints about male behaviour and male privilege. There was an important sense in which aspects of the women's experiences had resonances with feminist theories and principles.

I am not arguing that all women are automatically feminists, nor am I adopting a form of false consciousness perspective, viewing women like Ms Webb as ordinary women lacking in a suitably raised feminist consciousness. Nor would I wish to deny that women who make their feminism explicit are making an important political statement: many have lost jobs, promotion, or worse, as a result of such actions. Nor was there an automatic sense of sisterhood or identical experience between young white, Asian and Afro-Caribbean women, or between working- and middle-class school-leavers. Sisterhood *is* powerful, but it is not the whole story (Bhavnani and Coulson, 1987).

Turning now to reasons why the disclaimer, 'I'm not a women's libber' should have been so common. There are several possible reasons for this, including the predominantly negative representation of feminism in the mass media, male intimidation and the threat of lesbianism associated with the label 'feminist'. Gramscian analysis would imply that ideological 'consent' is gained through the denial of opposition and oppression. The Young Women and Work study indicated that patriarchal hegemony is also partly achieved through attempts to obscure women's resistance through the appropriation and attribution of the category of feminism itself. Collective female resistance is defined as negative and unfeminine, implying that feminists are unattractive to men – the very heart of the joke quoted at the start of this chapter. Once such a negative category is in place, feminism can be used as an accusation, and a means of silencing insubordinate women. 'You're not a women's libber, are you?' becomes an insult, a threat with overwhelmingly negative connotations.

Identifying as Feminists: The Engineering Trainees

Hegemony is not achieved so easily, however, and the category of feminism is not totally secured for patriarchy as negative and threatening. There is clear evidence of negotiation and struggle over its construction. During the Young Women and Work study I did meet some young white working-class women who identified explicitly as feminists, defining the category in positive terms. They wore feminist badges and constituted a united and vocal group on the Engineering Industry Training Board's craft technician course for Girls in Engineering. Their tutor, Mr Prestwood, viewed these young women with a mixture of pride and horror: he was so determined that I should hear their views that he provoked a discussion on gender relations. This backfired when he found the role of passive observer too difficult and became engrossed in the extremely heated discussion himself (Griffin, 1985: 166–7):

> *Mr Prestwood*: [to me] I wanted you to see some of these girls because they've got very fixed ideas which they'll modify over the next few years.
> *Young women*: [who had overheard him]: On what?
> *Mr Prestwood*: On what? About these superior men.
> *Kate*: We're just as good as you.
> *Mr Prestwood*: [patronising] You're better, my dear, you're better. My wife has always been on a pedestal in my life. Women are much better than men, they just have problems proving it.
> *Lorna*: We're trying to prove that a woman can do the same things as a man, not that we *are* men.
> *Mr Prestwood*: Yes, but you don't have to prove that you can do a man's job. There are lots of jobs in industry that are suitable for women to do.
> *All*: Aah! [indrawn breath].
> *Kate*: No, but I can do exactly the same job as you. You have no right whatsoever to say 'oh that's a woman's job, that's a man's job'. I think he's trying to get us annoyed [laugh] [. . .].
> *Mr Prestwood*: Yeh but what you're trying to do, you're trying to alter the structure of our society, which has been built up over centuries, and you can't do it.
> *Kate*: But if it needs changing you can't keep it.

We can only speculate on the various factors which might have contributed to these young women's feminist identification. Their position as trainees on a course which was developed to encourage young women to enter a non-traditional and strongly male-dominated occupation no doubt provided a significant contributory factor. Despite the rather superficial support of Mr Prestwood, their political allegiance was based on a common institutional and cultural foundation, and a shared view of the restricted opportunities open to women in the job market. Not all of the groups on this course identified themselves as feminist in this way, however. Most trainees had joined the course out of an active interest in engineering, although a minority gave reasons like 'I didn't know what else to do' (Griffin, 1985).

There is no one factor, or set of factors, which leads neatly to feminist allegiance (Rowland, 1984). There is no clear distinction between feminists and non-feminists that can operate out of social context, based solely on the personal characteristics or idiosyncratic attitude constellations of individual women. It would be foolish to try to identify those attributes which might distinguish between feminist, non-feminist and anti-feminist women, given the complex processes involved in feminist identification, some of which have been discussed in this chapter. We need an approach which sets feminist identification in social context, relating it to relevant ideological formations and social structures.

Summary

In this chapter I have rehearsed the limitations of traditional social psychological research, and particularly of Tajfel's social identity perspective, for the understanding of feminist identification and gender consciousness, looking at the ways in which feminism was reflected in the Young Women and Work study. The limitations of SIT are both methodological and conceptual, with a relevance to research on social identity and intergroup relations in general, as well as the specific area of gender relations and feminist identification.

Unlike other theories of identity and discrimination, SIT allows us to question the construction of those social categories on which group identity and discrimination are based. Unfortunately, many studies take specific social categories (often developed via trivial and arbitrary experimental manipulations), and set them in psychological concrete throughout the research process. As a result, social categorization and intergroup discrimination are represented as almost inevitable aspects of intergroup relations. In addition, the formation and maintenance of a 'positive social identity' has been treated as a relatively linear progression towards 'positive psychological distinctiveness' (Taylor and McKirnan, 1984). This limits the value of SIT for understanding the various ways in which different (and sometimes contradictory) constructs of womanhood, feminism and femininity are struggled over throughout the process of feminist identification.

Research employing SIT has been characterized by an almost obsessive reliance on the most traditional research methods, using experimental designs and quantitative techniques within a strictly positivist framework. All of the empirical contributions to the 1984 *British Journal of Social Psychology* special issue on 'Intergroup Processes', for example, were positivist studies involving quantitative experimental techniques (Brown, 1984). This methodological tunnel vision has been extremely detrimental to the development of Tajfel's original analytic framework. The positivist use of experimental and quantitative methods has its own benefits and limitations, but we need to pay equal attention to the potential contributions of more flexible qualitative methods and non-positivist approaches (Billig, 1978b; Griffin, 1986).

There has also been a marked tendency in social identity research to treat the various social groups under investigation as relatively uniform. This makes it difficult to appreciate the interconnected and often contradictory elements of gender identification. It is equally difficult to appreciate the ways in which the meanings and experiences associated with being female – or male – might vary with race, class, and age in particular. Most studies look at *either* gender *or* race *or* national identification: possible interactions are seldom considered. Just as it would be a mistake to assume that all 'traditional' women are anti-feminist, it would be equally inaccurate to assume that feminism or gender have the same meanings for all women, regardless of class, race or age (Bhavnani and Coulson, 1987). It is not enough to ask generalized questions about 'the position of women', or how often one thinks about 'being a woman', since this takes gender relations out of context.

Equally problematic has been the tendency to focus on individual variability remote from social and historical context, treating psychological processes with minimal reference to ideological formations, institutional structures or material conditions. Feminist identification is not simply an isolated individual phenomenon, but a product of specific social, political and historical conditions (Davis, 1982). Social psychology research in this area has tended to confuse gender and feminism, identity and consciousness, often using the terms interchangeably. Whilst feminism and gender *are* connected, awareness of one's position as a woman is not equivalent to identifying oneself as a feminist, as some studies seem to imply. Social identity is not a tangible entity which can be put on or discarded rather like a hat. I prefer to understand identity not as a noun but as a verb: to look at the *process* of identification rather than the formation of a static social identity.

In this chapter I have looked at the nature of gender consciousness and feminist identification as reflected in disputes over the category of feminism in the Young Women and Work study. Feminism was not a unitary category shared by all, to which some women expressed explicit allegiance whilst others did not. The very definition of feminism was under constant negotiation between different groups of women and men. Feminist identification was not simply a matter of individual attitudes: of agreeing or disagreeing with a set of ideas and principles. It could also be implicit, operating as a powerful under-current behind women's experiences and interactions. Media representations of 'bra-burning' boiler-suited 'women's libbers', and the male challenge 'You're not a women's libber, are you?' to the slightest hint of female insubordination, served to keep feminism hidden beneath the surface of discourse. Those occasions when feminism surfaced, such as the episode of the bin-liner joke, provided access to the hidden face of feminism as it was experienced by women (and men). Feminism, like all major political developments, also had implications for women who would never identify themselves as feminist, sympathetic to feminism, nor even as anti-feminist.

Feminism had meanings far beyond a specific relevance to white middle-class women. In their discussions of equal opportunities, prejudice and discrimination, as well as their reactions to me and to the research project, young white and black working-class women indicated that feminism had impinged on their lives to a significant extent. They may not have expressed overt allegiance to women in a collective political sense, but they did argue that prejudice and discrimination against them as women were wrong and should no longer be endured, and that political, economic and social progress for women had been made, especially compared to the conditions which had prevailed in their mother's youth. For many of the young black women, race and racism were impossible to ignore, and were closely connected with their experiences of prejudice and discrimination.

There was an obvious distinction between women who express an overt allegiance to feminism in all situations, and those who did not, but it would be presumptuous to assume that a denial of feminist identification (that is, 'I'm not a women's libber, but . . .') was synonymous with anti-feminist sympathies. In the Young Women and Work study those women who made such comments often expressed implicit or explicit agreement with feminist ideas on issues as diverse as sexual violence, equal pay, and shared child care. Several recent studies of US college women appear to confirm these findings, arguing that the latter group 'embrace feminist ideals, but do not accept the collective efforts of the women's movement as the appropriate means to achieve their own goals' (Renzetti, 1987: 266; Komarovsky, 1985). Some of this work has recognized the impact of the predominantly negative image of feminism (Jacobson and Koch, 1978), but the use of quantitative survey techniques in a positivist framework imposed considerable restrictions on the analysis. The constraining influence of the agentic orientation discussed by Jenny Williams has appeared here too, when Renzetti defined feminism as a means of 'achieving (women's) goals', or referred to 'tomorrow's feminist leaders' (1987: 276). It is scarcely possible to imagine a less appropriate choice of phrase than the latter, given feminists' determination to avoid the hierarchical structures of male-dominated political groups. This combination of quantitative techniques and a Western liberal definition of feminism is all too common in mainstream studies of gender and feminist identification (Condor, 1986).

What most studies of feminist identification omit is any detailed consideration of those pressures which operate to discourage overt feminist allegiance. These include male intimidation, even physical violence (Hanmer and Maynard, 1987); negative media representations; the implicit association between lesbianism and feminism (Rich, 1981); and sanctions on women's collective cultural practices (such as, the 'deffing out' process: Griffin, 1985).[3] The identification of oneself as a feminist has to be understood in this context. The trivializing image of 'women's lib' is used to make a joke out of women's organized opposition to their oppression; to obscure the potential and actual threat posed by feminism; and to scare women away from expressing an explicitly feminist allegiance.

I can offer no neat alternatives to Tajfel's social identity perspective for our understanding of gender consciousness and feminist identification. In this chapter, I have pointed out some of the major limitations imposed by the former, having found the relatively flexible and sophisticated analyses of Billig, Gramsci, and feminist researchers like Stanley and Wise more useful than the agentic orientation of traditional social psychology. We need more research on feminist identification and consciousness which begins from the perspective of Rebecca West, writing in a 1913 issue of *The Clarion*:

> I myself have never been able to find out precisely what feminism is: I only know that people call me a feminist whenever I express sentiments that differentiate me from a doormat.

Notes

1 This is not the only possible approach to the understanding of gender identification or feminist consciousness within social psychology, of course. Sandra Bem's work on androgyny is the most notable alternative, and does at least have the advantage of being developed out of an explicit focus on gender relations and a feminist perspective (Bem, 1976). This work has not been without its critics (Wetherell, 1986), but to start with Bem's work would form the basis of another chapter in another book.

2 In all of the direct quotes from participants in the Young Women and Work study I have used pseudonyms to maintain anonymity. Where these quotes have previously been published, the reference is given in the text: those quotes without such references have not been published elsewhere.

3 'Deffing out' is the tendency to 'drop' or ignore one's friends, which can occur when one of a group of close girlfriends begins to see a 'steady' boyfriend on a regular basis.

References

Arnot, M. (1982) 'Male Hegemony, Social Class and Women's Education', *Boston University Journal of Education*, 164(1): 25–37.

Attar, D. (1987) 'The Controversial Feminist', *Trouble and Strife*, 12: 16–19.

Bem, S. (1976) 'Probing the Promise of Androgyny', in A. G. Kaplan and J. P Bean (eds), *Beyond Sex-Role Stereotyping*. Boston: Little, Brown.

Bhavnani, K. and Coulson, M. (1987) 'Transforming Socialist Feminism: The Challenge of Racism', *Feminist Review*, 23: 81–92.

Billig, M. (1978a) *Fascists: A Social Psychological View of the National Front*. London: Academic Press.

Billig, M. (1978b) 'The New Social Psychology and "Fascism"', *European Journal of Social Psychology*, 7(4): 393–432.

Bowles, G. and Klein, R. D. (eds) (1983) *Theories of Women's Studies*. London: Routledge & Kegan Paul.

Breakwell, G. (1979) 'Woman: Group or Identity?' *Women's Studies International Quarterly*, 2: 9–17.

Brown, R. (1984) 'Editorial: Social Identity and Social Change: Recent Developments in Intergroup Relations Research', *British Journal of Social Psychology*, 23 (4): 289–90.

CCCS Women and Fascism Study Group (1980) *Breeders for Race and Nation: Women and Fascism in Britain Today*. Bath Printshop Pamphlet.

Cochrane, R. and Billig, M. (1983) 'Youth and Politics', *Youth and Policy*, 2: 31–4.

Condor, S. (1986) 'Sex Role Beliefs and "Traditional" Women: Feminist and Intergroup Perspectives', in S. Wilkinson (ed.), *Feminist Social Psychology: Developing Theory and Practice*. Milton Keynes: Open University Press.

Davis, A. (1982) *Women, Race and Class*. London: Women's Press.

De Man, A. and Benoit, R. (1982) 'Self Esteem in Feminist and Non-feminist French-Canadian Women and French-Canadian Men', *Journal of Psychology*, 111, 3–7.

Frazer, E. (1988) 'Talking about Femininity: The Concept of Ideology on Trial'. Unpublished D.Phil. dissertation, University of Oxford.

Gramsci, A. (1971) *Selections from the Prison Notebooks*, edited and translated by Q. Hoare and G. Smith, based on letters written between 1929 and 1935. New York: Lawrence & Wishart.

Griffin, C. (1985) *Typical Girls? Young Women from School to the Job Market*. London: Routledge & Kegan.

Griffin, C. (1986) 'Qualitative Methods and Female Experience: Young Women from School to the Job Market', in S. Wilkinson (ed.), *Feminist Social Psychology: Developing Theory and Practice*. Milton Keynes: Open University Press.

Griffin, C. (1987) 'Youth Research: Young Women and the "Gang of Lads" Model', in J. Hazekamp, W. Meeus and Y. te Poel (eds), *European Contributions to Youth Research*. Amsterdam: Free University Press.

Gurin, P. and Townsend, A. (1986) 'Properties of Gender Identity and their Implications for Gender Consciousness', *British Journal of Social Psychology*, 25: 139–48.

Hall, S. (1988) 'Thatcher's Lessons', *Marxism Today*, March: 20–7.

Hanmer, J. and Maynard, M. (eds), (1987) *Women, Violence and Social Control*. London: Macmillan Press.

Jacobson, M. and Koch, W. (1978) 'Attributed Reasons for Support of the Feminist Movement as a Function of Attractiveness', *Sex Roles*, 4: 169–74.

Komarovsky, A. (1985) *Women in College*. New York: Basic Books.

McClain, E. (1978) 'Feminists and Non-feminists: Contrasting Profiles in Independence and Affiliation', *Psychological Reports*, 43: 435–41.

Mitchell, J. and Oakley, A. (eds) (1986) *What is Feminism?* Oxford: Basil Blackwell.

Race and Politics Group, CCCS (eds) (1982) *The Empire Strikes Back: Race and Racism in '70s Britain*. London: Hutchinson.

Renzetti, C. (1987) 'New Wave or Second Stage? Attitudes of College Women Toward Feminism', *Sex Roles*, 16 (5/6): 265–77.

Rich, A. (1981) 'Compulsory Heterosexuality and Lesbian Existence', London: Onlywomen Press phamplet.

Rowland, R. (ed.) (1984) *Women who Do and Women who Don't Join the Women's Movement*. London: Routledge & Kegan Paul.

Seltzer, R. and Lopes, G. (1986) 'The Ku Klux Klan: Reasons for Support or Opposition among White Respondents', *Journal of Black Studies*, September: 91–109.

Smith, B. (1982) 'Racism and Women's Studies', in G. T. Hull, P. B. Scott and B. Smith (eds), *All the Women are White, All the Blacks are Men, but Some of Us are Brave*. New York: Feminist Press.

Stanley, L. and Wise, S. (1983) *Breaking Out: Feminist Consciousness and Feminist Research*. London: Routledge & Kegan Paul.

Tajfel, H. (1974) 'Social Identity and Intergroup Behaviour', *Social Science Information*. 13: 65–93.

Taylor, D. and McKirnan, D. (1984) 'A Five-Stage Model of Intergroup Relations', *British Journal of Social Psychology*, 23: 291–300.

Townsend, A. (1982) 'The Effects of Gender Centrality on Women's Gender-related Attitudes'. Unpublished Ph.D. dissertation, University of Michigan.

Wetherell, M. (1986) 'Linguistic Repertoires and Literary Criticism: New Directions for a Social Psychology of Gender', in S. Wilkinson (ed.), *Feminist Social Psychology*. Milton Keynes: Open University Press.

Wilkinson, S. (ed.) (1986) *Feminist Social Psychology: Developing Theory and Practice*. Milton Keynes: Open University Press.

Williams, J. (1984) 'Gender and Intergroup Behaviour: Towards an Integration', *British Journal of Social Psychology*, 23: 311–16.

Williams, J. and Giles, H. (1978) 'The Changing Status of Women in Society: An Intergroup Perspective', in H. Tajfel (ed.), *Differentiation between Social Groups*. London: Academic Press.

Willis, P. (1977) *Learning to Labour: How Working Class Kids Get Working Class Jobs*. Farnborough: Saxon House.

10

Conclusion

Suzanne Skevington and Deborah Baker

This book took as its starting point the theory of social identity originated by Tajfel. Social identity has been defined as 'that part of an individual's self-concept which derives from his or her knowledge of his or her membership of a social group (or groups), together with the value and emotional significance attached to that membership (Tajfel, 1978). More particularly, we have been concerned with the applications of social identity theory to the study of gender relations between women and men outlined by Williams and Giles (1978), with reference to the position of women as a result of changes made by the Women's Movement at that time. Ten years on, the study of women and gender relations has been transformed, and in this chapter we aim to draw together the different strands of thought that have been developed throughout this book. First of all we consider whether there is a social identity of women. Then we take a critical look at the value of social identity theory for a study of women and why it is necessary to study women within their social context. Later we contrast positive aspects of women's social identity with the more familiar negative view. Finally, in predicting the way forward for the study of women, we focus on the implications of the findings of this book for feminist consciousness and the need to integrate ideology into a new theoretical framework.

Women are probably the single most important natural grouping to be studied within social identity theory. The complexity of the subject matter has been shown here to demand a variety of multivariate field-work methods or quasi-experimental approaches to tap the richness of the data available. One of the reasons for writing this book was that we think not only are women of intrinsic interest as a group for study but also, as we hope has been demonstrated, there is a lot of good research going on in this still-developing area.

The major criticisms of the theory have revolved around the exclusion of the social context, the over-reliance on positivistic methodologies and the treatment of social groups as relatively uniform, and it is clear from this critique that social identity theory, as it stands, is inadequate to meet the criteria necessary for doing research on womens' lives. So it is perhaps unsurprising that the formalized theory and methods do not meet the criteria set out for feminist research either (Stanley and Wise, 1983), as Henri Tajfel had issues of race and class conflict more in mind at the time of writing. Consequently, the book encompasses major criticisms of social identity theory on the one hand, and on the other offers new concepts and methods for improving the studies using this approach, in many cases taking it one step further, beyond the confines of the original theory. We hope that the plurality of initiatives within these pages will excite others to go even further outside these boundaries in the search for a new theory on the social identity of women.

Social Identity, or Social Identities, of Women?

One of the most important conclusions to emerge from this volume is that there is not a single social identity of women but many. This book is about some of the different identities which occur within the special roles, relationships and situations which women experience, although the knowledge gained from these areas was designed to be illustrative rather than providing comprehensive coverage of every aspect of women's lives. From these chapters emerges a multiplicity of approaches acknowledging the complex meanings of womanhood, which brings us to the conclusion that we cannot view women as the unified, coherent and homogeneous social cateory, with a single explicit meaning for all members of society, that Williams and Giles implied. On the contrary, research in this book shows that gender usually forms only one of several social identifications for women. In addition, the intensity of identification for women also varies within as well across situations. Several chapters in this book show that women form strong social identifications with those with whom they work; the occupational identities of lawyers (outlined by Marshall and Wetherell) and nurses (Skevington, 1981 and here) provide prime examples.

Women also express different facets of social identity at different stages in their lifespan and these group memberships are exemplified in two papers. Dominic Abrams examines the social identity of schoolgirls and schoolboys at different ages and how this may be bound to their developmental stage of conceptual thought. Deborah Baker shows that motherhood gives rise to a quite distinctive social identity which may be judged in relation to a work-based identity when they first make the transition to motherhood. While memberships associated with age, social class and race are almost certainly important too, we have not explored these in detail here, and investigations to find out how far they are commensurate with gender identity remain interesting territory for future work on social identities. Of course, men may also have social identities which have not yet been investigated in depth within the social identity framework, but seem to be visible in some studies of fatherhood, for example (see Lewis and O'Brien, 1987). For instance, it would be interesting to see if and how men develop identities associated with both work and domestic roles as women increasingly form a greater proportion of the workforce.

These findings about multiple social identities should not be interpreted as implying that other researchers have been unaware that their subjects possessed more than one social identity – Tajfel's definition acknowledges that individuals may identify with more than one group. However, it would be fair to say that social identity researchers working in the laboratory and quasi-experimental settings deliberately simplified the study of this difficult and complex theory in the past to enable them to investigate thoroughly one type of social identification at a time. This strategy arose partly from the need for conceptual clarity in the early stages of the theory's development and to enable the paradigms to be operationalized, but also, more importantly, because the methods that researchers chose were better suited to these purposes than the more recently developed multidimensional approaches used by the authors of the chapters in this book.

So we have found from this book that there is a multiplicity of social identities for women that can be subsumed under the heading of womanhood, and this raises several important issues for social identity theory as it stands today. First, we think that social identity research should continue to unearth in detail what goes on beneath the group labels 'women' and 'men'. The richness of the data from such a strategy should feed back into the theory and help to develop new woman-centred paradigms. In addition, we should also be looking at gender identity as a relative social identification. This means looking at how a person's identification with their gender group is related to the many other group memberships people may hold which have been formed by their being at work, a member of a particular social class and age group, from leisure group activities, and so on. This is not simply a matter of deciding why, and in which social situation, one social identification should be salient rather than another (Oakes, 1987), but is more a matter of understanding how multiple group memberships evolve and coexist at the same time, and more importantly are given meaning by individuals as they live in society.

The Values of Social Identity Theory

Despite the various criticisms levelled at social identity theory, it seems important here to comment on some of the theory's most valuable assets. First, while Susan Condor justly criticizes Tajfel for the way he tackles the issue of social change by focusing too narrowly on strategies of change, it should be noted that social identity theory is a rarity among social psychological theories because it represents one of the very few attempts to analyse and operationalize these strategies in psycho-social terms. It is the success of this attempt which is debatable. So it seems important to retain social change within the theory and to redefine this concept to apply it more directly to what we know about how women and men relate and the resulting social changes created by women working in the Women's Movement. Williams and Giles (1978) were attracted to this aspect of the theory in their analysis of the progress achieved by the Women's Movement of the day, and despite the problems with their analysis (which have been thoroughly elaborated between these covers) their statement provided a vital starting block for most of the research in this volume. Against Williams and Giles' ahistorical account, an integrated historical perspective is called for by several authors here, and when developed this should be particularly useful in retrospectively analysing the considerable changes which have taken place in intergroup relations between the sexes since the inception of the Movement in the 1960s. Any such analysis would also need to embrace the current changes in thinking which accompany the advent of what some writers are now describing as the 'post-feminist' era (Rosenfelt and Stacey, 1987). It would also need to incorporate prevailing political ideologies outside the sex group arena which could be allied to the way gender identity is perceived at any given time.

Secondly, social identity theory was originally developed by examining the three processes of social categorization, social comparisons and social identity (see the Introduction). Much of the work in this book has been concerned with the valuable and intricate links between social categorizations and social identification. Discussions of the social comparison processes have tended to take second place. This is not unique to the study of women but has become part of a general trend to play down the social comparison processes within social identity theory. Turner et al.'s (1987) recent elaboration of a theory of self-categorization is a case in point. However, this gap also reflects researchers' greater concerns not only with how groups categorize the world but also with the content of these categorizations. This book provides some interesting examples of situations where the detailed content of social categorization has been explored with a view to understanding women's social identity. Deborah Baker has adapted the Repertory Grid technique to identify the consensual characteristics of social identity for a group of mothers. Marshall and Wetherell use discourse analysis to illustrate the variable, inconsistent and highly negotiable content of social identity for lawyers, and Chris Griffin uses interview material to show how the content of 'feminism' as a social category varies in relation to the ideological purpose for which it is being employed. We believe that much more could be gained from doing similar types of in-depth contextual analysis. But we also feel that in future studies there is scope for looking at the social comparison processes used by women in intergroup situations – comparisons which women make with men only apply in certain contexts, and it seems important to know more about the types of comparisons women make with other women.

The value of the concept of social categorizations is important in another way. The description, organization and integration of the content of social categorizations dovetail with other areas of thinking in social psychology, so providing concurrent validity. For instance, some of the models which complement social identity theory and are demonstrated in this book include social schemata and social representations. Patricia Gurin and Hazel Markus draw on the gender schema literature to show that social identities derived from membership of a particular social category function as self-schemata. As such they sensitize individuals to events in the social environment and thereby give structure to ambiguous or confusing social situations. The centrality of the social identity within the self-schema is thought to have important implications for that person's attitudes and behaviour.

The link between social identity and social representations is less clearly formulated, partly because as we write, there is a vigorous debate about whether and how to define social representations (Jahoda, 1988; Moscovici, 1988) which prohibits definitive comparisons between the two theories from being drawn. Duveen and Lloyd (1986) have made headway trying to integrate social identity with social representations. Focusing particularly on the categorization process, they see social identity as grounded in social representations. In this volume Lindsay St Claire utilizes the literature of social representations to show how the content of women's identities might be examined by observing and describing natural conversation. Suzanne Skevington looks at the potential use of 'memory work' in recording the cognitive and emotional content of group discussions. So there appears to be some conceptual overlap between the concept of social categorizations in social identity studies and the dimensions of social representations; both are concerned with the nature of collective representations within a social context. The integration of these two theoretical models seems to be a hopeful venture for the future.

A further asset of social identity theory is the intergroup–interpersonal dimension developed by Tajfel and Turner (1979). Dominic Abrams demonstrates ways in which aspects of intergroup behaviour are inextricably intertwined with interpersonal viewpoints, developing

Stephenson's work on bargaining and negotiation. Abrams shows how individuals can simultaneously display both the personal and group aspects of their identity when relating to the opposite sex. Marshall and Wetherell also show that people utilize this distinction in their accounts. In the past the intergroup and interpersonal have been treated as two ends of the same continuum, but these authors show how the two dimensions seem to be orthogonal. They emphasize the need to see these aspects of identification as existing simultaneously; dynamically interacting to transform each other.

Bringing Back the Social Context

Tajfel's emphasis on putting the social back into social psychology has been a powerful influence on the design of new contextual work in social psychological research since the 1970s, but has not always been put into practice by social identity theorists when designing social psychological research. In this book various attempts have been made to locate the meaning of womanhood in some kind of social context. The number of ways of conceptualizing this relationship are many and varied. For some authors, contextualizing the meaning of womanhood means taking apart the ideologies that underpin women's social status; identifying, deconstructing and changing ways in which womanhood is represented in contemporary social settings (for example, Marshall and Wetherell; Griffin; St Claire). Others link the nature and content of social identities to social activity and developmental change (Abrams; Baker), and yet others see the intergroup relations between men and women as relative forms of practice – relative to contemporary and historical contexts (Condor; Skevington). All these forms of investigation are necessary components of any overview of women's social identifications.

But in order to pursue these lines of enquiry, new methodologies needed to be formulated. Some possibilities have been presented in this volume but they do not form a definitive list. They include unstructured and semi-structured interview techniques (Abrams; Griffin), questionnaires (Gurin and Markus), discourse analysis (Marshall and Wetherell), the Repertory Grid technique (Baker) and 'memory work' in groups (Skevington). The sheer variety of different methodological approaches generated by this single theoretical perspective as a result of studying women lays bare the poverty of methods used so far in other areas of social identity research (see the Introduction for further discussion).

As we pointed out in the Introduction, these kind of methods go some way to satisfying the call by feminist researchers for a greater emphasis on qualitative data, which is seen to be more appropriate for tapping into the rich experience of women's lives (Wilkinson, 1986). However, such statements must necessarily be accompanied by a caveat: methodologies are not necessarily more effective or more valid just because they are more qualitative. If these methods are to be used to fully understand social identities, a new accompanying theoretical framework will be needed which not only incorporates the flexible, contradictory and fragmented accounts of people's experience, but also looks beyond the data to the external world to explain why such accounts exist and how they might be formed (Bowers, 1988; Reicher, 1988).

A Positive Social Identity for Women

So what is positive about the social identity of women, and are there optimistic findings arising from these writings which might be absorbed by the Women's Movement in its quest for social change in the intergroup relations between men and women? In reading the social science literature on women it is easy to slip into a negative schema, seeing women as powerless, oppressed, subordinated, lacking in status and short on positive self-esteem, as well as possessing many other so-called undesirable social and personal characteristics, and we hope that this is not the view which predominates in this book. There are some optimistic aspects of women's social identity which arise from the chapters which should be highlighted here.

We have learned that women often develop positive social identifications from group memberships. While St Claire describes the processes whereby women come to be represented as socially handicapped people (using motherhood to illustrate this) in taking this rather pessimistic view, it is clear that the three interesting processes she describes which create women's oppression could also be fruitfully applied to more positive aspects of women's lives. Furthermore, Baker shows how identities that have tended to be ideologically characterized by some writers as negative can be experienced as positive, and her data show that mothers attach little meaning to high- and low-status labels when evaluating their group membership.

There is tremendous variability between women in the way they perceive their group's status. Some women believe that they belong to a high-status group while others support the notion of subordinated women, perceiving themselves and others to be of low status (Stanley and Wise, 1983). This point about a spectrum of very different representations of women is also picked up by Marshall and Wetherell from their discourse data. It is, however, worth noting that this diversity of accounts is to some extent dictated by the qualitative methods used.

The positive atmosphere or climate which women bring to their working environment is drawn out by Skevington. She notes the importance of expressing emotions in intergroup relations, particularly in groups where women are present, and indicates that 'memory work' may provide a suitable method for studies of collective affect. This affective theme is also picked up by Marshall and Wetherell in showing the positive contribution which it is generally acknowledged women lawyers make to specialist areas of the legal system, such as divorce. An extension of this more positive view of women could be to link it with the broader issue of feminist consciousness and ideology.

Feminist Consciousness and Ideology

Several chapters deal with the nature of feminist consciousness. Chris Griffin demonstrates the implicit and explicit way in which women support feminism, and looks at degrees of feminism and the way the concept is under continual negotiation. It seems that the boundaries of feminism are in the eyes of the beholders. She uses the notion of hegemony to show how traditional gender relations come to be seen as natural and inevitable in patriarchies, so concealing and denying women's experiences and resistance. She presents evidence to show how feminism has not been totally secured from patriarchy and that negotiation and struggle over its construction continue. Susan Condor, on the other hand, uses a rhetorical approach to suggest that the category 'woman' is often presented as particular to feminist self-awareness, so undermining flexibility in the meaning and use of this category. She goes on to demonstrate how this view, as epitomized by the work of Williams and Giles (1978) is essentially a historical construction.

Gurin and Markus show how traditional women tend to become more feminist when a sense of common fate is elicited, and this is an exciting departure for those interested in the processes of social change. By encouraging both women who stay at home to care for their children and their working sisters to see that they have many similarities, rather than pointing out the differences, this increased sense of sisterhood might give them not only greater social support but also lead to a greater sense of psychological and physical well-being. This could be tested by a future piece of action research. A belief commonly shared by feminists is that sisterhood is powerful and the data giving support to this central tenet of feminism are available from Gurin and Markus' work. While Griffin also supports this line, coming to it from a different direction, she believes that a powerful sisterhood is not the only answer, and leaves the door open for future research.

A consideration of the relationship between women's group

identifications and ideology is long overdue. The synthesis of this material is an exciting prospect for the future, and requires the flexibility to work with the complex variety of interpretations women offer about themselves without sinking into the mire of ideography. A modified version of social identity theory which allows space for the inclusion of an assessment of different ideologies seems to provide the best way forward, although at present this potential has not been fully exploited. Ideology is an important theme running through several chapters of this book, and the book starts and ends there to reinforce this point (Condor; Griffin). The complex relationship between social identity and ideology has been skilfully developed by these authors. There is clearly scope for more studies of this particularly challenging area – challenging because it is virtually impossible to conceptualize ideology without being truly transdisciplinary, taking on board the literatures of sociology, anthropology and political science.

We hope that this collection will stimulate not only debate but also further research into the social identities of women.

References

Bowers, J. (1988) ' "Discourse and Social Psychology – Beyond Attitudes and Behaviour" by J. Potter and M. Wetherell, review essay', *British Journal of Social Psychology*, 27: 185–92.

Duveen, G. and Lloyd, B. (1986) 'The Significance of Social Identities', *British Journal of Social Psychology*, 25: 219–30.

Jahoda, G. (1988) 'Critical Notes and Reflections on "Social Representations"', *European Journal of Social Psychology*, 18(3): 195–210.

Lewis, C. and O'Brien, M. (eds) (1987) *Reassessing Fatherhood: New Observations on Fathers and the Modern Family*. London: Sage.

Moscovici, S. (1988) 'Notes towards a Description of Social Representations', *European Journal of Social Psychology*, 18(3): 211–50.

Oakes, P. (1987) 'The Salience of Social Categories', in J. C. Turner et al., *Rediscovering the Social Group*. Oxford: Basil Blackwell. pp. 117–41.

Reicher, S. (1988) ' "Arguing and Thinking: A Rhetorical Approach to Social Psychology" by M. Billig, review essay', *British Journal of Social Psychology*, 27: 283–8.

Rosenfelt, D. and Stacey, J. (1987) 'Second Thoughts on the Second Wave', *Feminist Studies*, 13(2): 341–61.

Skevington, S. M. (1981) 'Intergroup Relations in Nursing', *European Journal of Social Psychology*, 11: 43–59.

Stanley, L. and Wise, S. (1983) *Breaking Out: Feminist Consciousness and Feminist Research*. London: Routledge.

Tajfel, H. (ed.) (1978) *Differentiation between Social Groups: Studies in the Social Psychology of Intergroup Relations*. London: Academic Press.

Tajfel, H. and Turner, J. C. (1979) 'An Integrative Theory of Social Conflict', in W. Austin and S. Worchel (eds), *Social Psychology of Intergroup Relations*. Monterey, CA: Brooks-Cole.

Turner, J. C., Hogg, M. A., Oakes, P. J., Reicher, S. and Wetherell, M. (1987) *Rediscovering the Social Group – A Self-Categorization Theory.* Oxford: Basil Blackwell.

Wilkinson, S. (ed.) (1986) *Feminist Social Psychology: Developing Theory and Practice.* Milton Keynes: Open University Press.

Williams, J. and Giles, H. (1978) 'The Changing Status of Women in Society: An Intergroup Perspective', in H. Tajfel (ed.), *Differentiation between Social Groups.* London: Academic Press.

Index

Gurevich, A. 16, 22
Gurin, P. 6, 10, 12, 24, 154, 156, 176–8, 198, 201

handicap 7, 130–49
    definition of 130
    positive 147
    self 146
hegemony 175, 179–80, 185–7, 201
history 16, 17, 19, 29, 30, 34, 54, 98, 174, 179, 187, 197, 201
    historicity 16–17
    historiography 31–4
Hogg, M. A. 2, 3, 24, 62, 73
hostility 40, 41, 46, 55
Hostility and Direction of Hostility Questionnaire 46

identity 107
    career/professional 115–24, 126; *see also* careers; women, and work
    negotiation 197
    personal *see* personal identity
    social *see* Social Identity Theory
ideology 2, 5, 6, 18, 28, 30, 34, 51, 63, 73–4, 88, 98, 109–11, 124, 125, 143, 174, 176, 179–80, 186, 188, 197, 199–202
impairment 131, 132, 134, 135
ingroup 2, 7, 9, 10, 28, 61–2, 75, 86, 87, 89–90, 92, 93–8, 102
    favouritism 9, 62, 154
instability 18, 30, 31
intergroup–interpersonal dimension 198
intergroup relations 3, 16, 40, 44, 59–78, 92, 154, 155, 188, 197, 199
    between the sexes 7, 40, 60–1
internalization 2, 88, 98, 131, 145, 147
interpersonal relations 8, 47, 65, 70, 73
interpretative resource 110
interviews 11, 12, 25, 65–8, 93, 99–101, 107, 110, 111, 112–23, 126, 174–5, 199
intragroup relations 144
    similarities 92
Israel, J. 8, 85
Itzin, C. 140

Jahoda, M. 85, 198

Kalmuss, D. 23, 73

Katz, P. A. 59, 65, 68–9, 71, 72
Kelly, G. A. 91, 92
Kippax, S. 53–4
Klein, R. D., 181
Konecni, V. J. 41

labelling 131, 184, 196
laboratory experiments 8, 12, 43, 91, 154, 158
Landfield, A. W. 94, 95, 96
language 4, 107, 108–11
lawyers 12, 106, 112–24, 195
legitimacy 46, 70, 156, 157, 161, 164, 176
lesbianism 191
liberalism 158
linguistic theory 109
Litton, I. 107
Lloyd, B. 77, 87, 135, 137, 143

McCoy, D. 97
McGuire, C. V. 64–5, 68, 70, 71
McGuire, W. J. 64–5, 68, 70, 71
machismo 174
Mackie, M. 69, 76, 77
McKirnan, D. 29, 61, 188
McPherson, J. M. 76
marginality 6, 86, 124
Markus, H. 7, 12, 153, 166, 198, 201
Marshall, H. 6, 12, 111, 195, 197, 199, 200–1
masculinity 59, 72, 124, 185
matrices 9, 94
media 73, 148, 156, 182; *see also* representations, media
memory work 53–6, 198, 199
men 4, 5, 6, 86, 88, 121, 122, 124, 135, 157, 179, 195–6
    researchers 52
Mercer, J. R. 131, 133–5
merger 3
Merton, R. K. 157, 169
minimal group experiment 8–9, 43
minority group 7, 31–2, 41, 55, 62, 63, 126, 131
Mitchell, J. 31, 34, 180–1
moral development 8
Moscovici, S. 22, 52, 139–40, 198
multidimensional approaches 131, 191

narrative 14, 19, 34

210   *Index*